STUDENT'S SOLUTION

Louis L. Levy • Edward Fritz
Northland Pioneer College

A Problem Solving Approach to
MATHEMATICS
for Elementary School Teachers
FIFTH EDITION

STUDENT'S SOLUTIONS MANUAL

Louis L. Levy • Edward Fritz
Northland Pioneer College

A Problem Solving Approach to

MATHEMATICS
for Elementary School Teachers
FIFTH EDITION

Billstein • Libeskind • Lott

ADDISON-WESLEY PUBLISHING COMPANY
Reading, Massachusetts • Menlo Park, California • New York
Don Mills, Ontario •Wokingham, England • Amsterdam • Bonn • Sydney
Singapore • Tokyo • Madrid • San Juan • Milan • Paris

Cover art: Patchwork Sampler quilt by Margit Echols © 1983. *Photo:* Schecter Lee.

Reproduced by Addison-Wesley from camera-ready copy supplied by the author.

ISBN 0-201-52778-2

Reprinted with corrections, June 1993

Copyright © 1993 by Addison-Wesley Publishing Company, Inc.

3 4 5 6 7 8 9 10-CRS-97 96 95 94

CONTENTS

Chapter 1   Tools for Problem Solving   1

Chapter 2   Sets, Functions, and Logic   10

Chapter 3   Numeration Systems and Whole Numbers   22

Chapter 4   The Integers   38

Chapter 5   Number Theory   49

Chapter 6   Rational Numbers as Fractions   58

Chapter 7   Decimals and Decimal Operations   70

Chapter 8   Probability   84

Chapter 9   Statistics: An Introduction   91

Chapter 10   Introductory Geometry   98

Chapter 11   Constructions, Congruence, and Similarity   110

Chapter 12   Motion Geometry and Tessellations   119

Chapter 13   Concepts of Measurement   128

Chapter 14   Coordinate Geometry   147

STUDENT'S SOLUTIONS MANUAL

Louis L. Levy • Edward Fritz
Northland Pioneer College

A Problem Solving Approach to

MATHEMATICS
for Elementary School Teachers
FIFTH EDITION

CHAPTER 1 - TOOLS FOR PROBLEM SOLVING

<u>Problem Set 1-1</u>

1.   (a)   Each figure in the sequence adds one box each to the top and bottom rows. Next would be:

    (b)   Each figure in the sequence adds one upright and one inverted triangle. Next would be:

    (c)   Each figure in the sequence adds one box to the base and one triangle to each row; adds one row. Next would be:

    (d)   The figures alternate boxes and triangles, while adding one to each succeeding symbol. Next would be:

    (e)   In a clockwise direction, the shaded area moves to a new position separated from the original by one open space, then two open spaces, then by three, etc. The separation in each successive step increases by one unit; next would be:

3.   (a)   Terms that continue a possible pattern are 11, 13, 15, ... This is an arithmetic sequence because we obtain each successive term from the previous term by the addition of the integer 2.

    (b)   Terms that continue a possible pattern are 250, 300, 350, ... This is an arithmetic sequence because we obtain each successive term from the previous term by the addition of the integer 50.

    (c)   Terms that continue a possible pattern are 96, 192, 384, ... This is a geometric sequence because we obtain each successive term from the previous term by multiplying by the integer 2.

    (d)   Terms that continue a possible pattern are 1,000,000, 10,000,000, 100,000,000, ... This is a geometric sequence because we obtain each successive term from the previous term by multiplying by the integer 10.

    (e)   Terms that continue a possible pattern are 5^7, 5^8, 5^9, ... This is a geometric sequence because we obtain each successive term from the previous term by multiplying by the integer 5 ($5^8 = 5 \cdot 5^7$, etc.).

    (f)   Terms that continue a possible pattern are 66, 77, 88, ... This is an arithmetic sequence because we obtain each successive term from the previous term by the addition of the integer 11.

    (g)   Terms that continue a possible pattern are 2^{11}, 2^{13}, 2^{15}, ... This is a geometric sequence because we obtain each successive term from the previous term by multiplying by the integer 2^2.

    (h)   Terms that continue a possible pattern are 33, 37, 41, ... This is an arithmetic sequence because we obtain each successive term from the previous term by the addition of the integer 4.

    (i)   Terms that continue a possible pattern are 216, 343, 512, ... We obtain each successive term by taking the third power of the number of the term in the sequence (i.e., the 6th term in the sequence is $6^3 = 216$). This sequence is neither arithmetic nor geometric.

5.   (a)   In each step, one more row and column of dots is added to the preceeding figure. The next three terms are thus 5 rows by 6 columns = 30 dots, 6 rows by 7 columns = 42 dots, and 7 rows by 8 columns = 56 dots.

5.   (b)   The 100th term would have 100 rows and 101 columns, or $100 \cdot 101 = 10,100$ dots.

       (c)   The nth term has $n \cdot (n + 1)$ dots, or $n^2 + n$.

7.   (a)

Number of Windmill	Number of Squares
1	5
2	9
3	13
4	17
$\vdots$	$\vdots$
9	37
10	41, so 41 squares are required to build the 10th windmill.

       (b)   The number of squares in each windmill form an arithmetic sequence with 1st term 5 and difference between terms 4. We know that the nth term in an arithmetic sequence with first term a and difference d is $a + (n - 1)d$, so the number of squares required for the nth windmill is $5 + (n - 1)4$, or $4n + 1$.

9.   If we make a table:

Day	Amount of Water Remaining
1	$15,360 \cdot \frac{1}{2} = 7680$ liters
2	$7680 \cdot \frac{1}{2} = 3840$ liters
$\vdots$	$\vdots$
9	$60 \cdot \frac{1}{2} = 30$ liters
10	$30 \cdot \frac{1}{2} = 15$ liters, so there will be 15 liters of water left in the tank after 10 days.

Alternatively, note that we have a geometric sequence with 1st term 7680 and ratio of $\frac{1}{2}$. We know that the nth term of a geometric sequence with 1st term a and ratio r is ar^{n-1}. Thus the 10th term would be $7680(\frac{1}{2})^9 = 15$ liters.

11.   (a)   The employee's monthly pay is \$1200 the 1st month, \$1220 the 2nd month, \$1240 the 3rd month, and so on. This is an arithmetic sequence with 1st term 1200 and difference of 20. At the end of 24 months, therefore, the worker's monthly salary will be $1200 + (24 - 1)20 = \$1660$.

       (b)   After 6 months, the employee will have earned $1200 + 1220 + 1240 + 1260 + 1280 + 1300 = \$7500$.

       (c)   Using the general expression for the nth term of an arithmetic sequence, where the nth term is 3240, we have:

$$3240 = 1200 + (n - 1)20$$
$$3240 = 1180 + 20n$$
$$20n = 2060, \text{ or } n = 103.$$ The employee's monthly salary will be \$3240 after 103 months.

13.   Using the general expression for the nth term of an arithmetic sequence with 1st term 24,000 and 9th term 31,680, we have:

$$31,680 = 24,000 + (9 - 1)d$$
$$31,680 = 24,000 + 8d$$
$$7680 = 8d, \text{ or } d = 960,$$ the amount by which Joe's income increased each year. To find the year in which his income was \$45,120, we then have:

$$45,120 = 24,000 + (n - 1)960$$
$$45,120 = 23,040 + 960n$$
$$960n = 22080, \text{ or } n = 23.$$ Joe's income was \$45,120 in his 23rd year.

15. (a)   Looking at the 3rd figure, we have $5 + 3 + 1 = 9$ triangles. The 4th figure would then have $7 + 5 + 3 + 1 = 16$ triangles. An alternative to simply adding 7, 5, 3, and 1 together is to note that $7 + 1 = 8$ and $5 + 3 = 8$. There are $\frac{4}{2} = 2$ of these sums, and $\frac{4}{2}(8) = 16$. Now see that the 100th figure would have $100 + 99 = 199$ triangles in the base, $99 + 98 = 197$ triangles in the second row, and so on until the 100th row where there would be 1 triangle. $199 + 1 = 200$; $197 + 3 = 200$; and so the sum of each pair is 200 and there are $\frac{100}{2} = 50$ of these pairs. $50 \cdot 200 = 10,000$ and so there are 10,000 triangles in the 100th figure.

    (b)   The number of triangles in the nth figure is $\frac{n}{2}$(number of triangles in base $+ 1$). The number of triangles in the base is $n + (n - 1)$, or $2n - 1$. $(2n - 1) + 1 = 2n$. Then $\frac{n}{2}(2n) = n^2$, and there are n^2 triangles in the nth figure.

17. (a)   If the 1st difference of the sequence increases by 2 for each term, then the 5 first differences between the 1st 6 terms of the original sequence are 2, 4, 6, 8, 10. If the 1st term of the original sequence is 3, then the 1st 6 terms are 3, 5, 9, 15, 23, 33.

    (b)   If the 1st term is a, then $a + (a + 2) = 10$, or $a = 4$. Thus the 1st 6 terms of the original sequence are 4, 6, 10, 16, 24, 34.

    (c)   If the 5th term is 35, then:
          The 6th term is $35 + 10 = 45$
          The 4th term is $35 - 8 = 27$
          The 3rd term is $27 - 6 = 21$
          The 2nd term is $21 - 4 = 17$
          The 1st term is $17 - 2 = 15$. Thus the sequence is 15, 17, 21, 27, 35, 45.

19. (a)   Using the general expression for the nth term of an arithmetic sequence with 1st term 51, nth term 151, and difference 1, we have:
          $151 = 51 + (n - 1)1$
          $151 = 50 + n$
          $101 = n$, so there are 101 terms in the sequence.

    (b)   Using the general expression for the nth term of a geometric sequence with 1st term 1, nth term 2^{60}, and ratio 2, we have:
          $2^{60} = 1(2)^{n-1}$
          $2^{60} = 2^{n-1}$
          Since the bases, 2, are the same, then:
          $60 = n - 1$, and $n = 61$. There are 61 terms in the sequence.

    (c)   Using the general expression for the nth term of an arithmetic sequence with 1st term 10, nth term 2000, and difference 10, we have:
          $2000 = 10 + (n - 1)10$
          $2000 = 10n$
          $200 = n$, so there are 200 terms in the sequence.

    (d)   Using the general expression for the nth term of an arithmetic sequence with 1st term 9, nth term 353, and difference 4, we have:
          $353 = 9 + (n - 1)4$
          $353 = 5 + 4n$
          $348 = 4n$
          $87 = n$, so there are 87 terms in the sequence.

    (e)   Using the general expression for the nth term of a geometric sequence with 1st term 1, nth term 1024, and ratio 2, we have:
          $1024 = 1(2)^{n-1}$
          Since $2^{10} = 1024$, then $n - 1 = 10$ and $n = 11$. There are 11 terms in the sequence.

19. (f) This is a geometric expression with 1st term 3, *n*th term $3 \cdot 5^{20}$, and ratio 5. Thus in the general expression for a geometric sequence, ar^{n-1} is $3 \cdot 5^{20}$, and $n - 1 = 20$. $n = 21$ and there are 21 terms in the sequence.

     (g) Note that the number of each term may be obtained by subtracting 3 from the 2nd multiplicand. Then $101 - 3 = 98$ and there are 98 terms in the sequence.

21. (a) No. Each successive term will no longer be obtained from the preceeding one by multiplying by a fixed number.

     (b) Yes. Each successive term will still be obtained from the preceeding one by multiplying by a fixed number.

23. Yes, but only if the ratios of the two sequences are equal. Then the coefficients of the ratio are added to form the coefficients of the ratio of the new sequence.

25. Using the expression for the *n*th term of a geometric sequence with 1st term 32, *n*th term 162, and with 5 terms, we have:
$$162 = 32r^{n-1}$$
$$5.0625 = r^4$$
$r = 1.5$. Thus $a = 32 \cdot 1.5 = 48$; $b = 48 \cdot 1.5 = 72$; and $c = 72 \cdot 1.5 = 108$.

27. (a) 1st term: $(1)^2 + 2 = 3$
          2nd term: $(2)^2 + 2 = 6$
          3rd term: $(3)^2 + 2 = 11$
          4th term: $(4)^2 + 2 = 18$
          5th term: $(5)^2 + 2 = 27$

     (b) 1st term: $5(1) - 1 = 4$
          2nd term: $5(2) - 1 = 9$
          3rd term: $5(3) - 1 = 14$
          4th term: $5(4) - 1 = 19$
          5th term: $5(5) - 1 = 24$

     (c) 1st term: $10^{(1)} - 1 = 9$
          2nd term: $10^{(2)} - 1 = 99$
          3rd term: $10^{(3)} - 1 = 999$
          4th term: $10^{(4)} - 1 = 9999$
          5th term: $10^{(5)} - 1 = 99999$

     (d) 1st term: $3(1) + 2 = 5$
          2nd term: $3(2) + 2 = 8$
          3rd term: $3(3) + 2 = 11$
          4th term: $3(4) + 2 = 14$
          5th term: $3(5) + 2 = 17$

29. (a) 2, 4, 6, 10, 16, 26, 42, 68, 110, 178, 288, 466.

     (b) The sum of the first three terms is 4 less than the fifth; the sum of the first four terms is 4 less than the sixth; the sum of the first five terms is 4 less than the seventh; etc.

     (c) The first two terms are 2 and 4, or $2 + 4 = 6$ followed by a 6. Then there is $10 + 16 = 26$ followed by a 26; $26 + 26 = 52$. Then $42 + 68 = 110$ followed by 110. Thus our sum is about $12 + 52 + 220 + 178 = 462$. The exact sum is 460.

     (d) The sum of the first *n* terms equals the $(n + 2)$th term $- 4$.

31. (a)   1st pentagon has 1 dot
            2nd pentagon has $5 = 1 + 4$ dots
            3rd pentagon has $12 = 1 + 4 + 7$ dots; analyzing the sequence, we have:
            4th pentagon has $22 = 1 + 4 + 7 + 10$ dots
            5th pentagon has $35 = 1 + 4 + 7 + 10 + 13$ dots
            6th pentagon has $51 = 1 + 4 + 7 + 10 + 13 + 16$ dots.

     (b)   The number of additional dots in each pentagon forms an arithmetic sequence with 1st term 1 and difference 3. For the 100th pentagon we would have $1 + (100 - 1)3 = 298$ additional dots. Using the technique of problem 15(a), we would have $\frac{100}{2}(1 + 298) = 50 \cdot 299 = 14{,}950$ dots; i.e., the 100th pentagonal number is 14,950.

33. (a)   We start with 1 peice of paper. Cutting it into five pieces gives us 5. Taking one of the pieces and cutting it into fives pieces again gives us $4 + 5 = 9$ pieces. Continuing this process, we have an arithmetic sequence: $1, 5, 9, 13, \ldots$.

     (b)   The number of pieces after the nth cut would be $1 + (n - 1)4$, or $4n - 3$.

Problem Set 1-2

1.   (a)   Given $1 + 2 + 3 + \cdots + 97 + 98 + 99$, note that $1 + 98 = 99$, $2 + 97 = 99$, $\ldots$. There are $\frac{98}{2}$ pairs, each totalling 99, plus the final 99, or $99 \cdot \frac{98}{2} + 99 = 4950$.

     (b)   Since n is odd, n − 1 is even. Thus $1 + 2 + 3 + \cdots + (n - 2) + (n - 1) + n = \frac{n(n-1)}{2} + n$ (i.e., we are generalizing the approach taken in 1(a)).

     (c)   To use Gauss' approach, we find the number of terms in the sequence. Thus we solve the equation $1 + (n - 1)2 = 1001$ to obtain n = 501. Because 501 is an odd number we add the first 500 terms in pairs, plus the 501st term: $1 + 3 + 5 + \cdots + 997 + 999 + 1001 = (999 + 1) \cdot \frac{500}{2} + 1001 = 251{,}001$.

3.   Each consecutive L has two more squares than the previous L. The general expression for the number of squares in the nth L is then 2n - 1 (from 1, 3, 5, ...) and there are n L's. The series for the number of squares is thus $1 + 3 + 5 + \cdots + (2n - 1)$. The result is always equal to n^2.

5.   The maximum amount is $1.19, composed of:
            1 half-dollar
            1 quarter
            4 dimes
            0 nickels
            4 pennies
     Any other combination would result in less money; e.g., including a nickel would allow only one dime to keep from having change for a quarter.

7.   Start both the 7-minute and 11-minute timers. When the 7-minute timer stops, put the egg on. When the 11-minute timer stops, restart it. When it stops again the egg is done (4 minutes + 11 minutes).

9.   12. There are <u>four</u> choices for the <u>1st digit</u>, then <u>three</u> for the <u>2nd</u> (since one
      has already been used), two for the 3rd digit, and <u>one final digit to finish the number</u>. This gives $4 \cdot 3 \cdot 2 \cdot 1 =$
      24 numbers, but the two nines are indistinguishable so 24 must be divided by 2, giving 12.

11.   Let R be the cost of the ruler and C be the cost of the compass. We can then form the equations:
      R + C = 4.00
      C = R + 0.90
      To solve, we substitute the cost of the compass, R + 0.90, into the first equation:
      R + (R + 0.90) = 4.00
      2R + 0.90 = 4.00
      2R = 3.10
      R = 1.55, so the cost of the ruler is \$1.55, and
      C = 1.55 + 0.90
      C = 2.45, so the cost of the compass is \$2.45.

13.   (a)   42, 55, 68, 81, 94, 107, 120, 133, 146, 159, 172, 185, 198

      (b)   There are 14 "spaces" between the 15 houses and a spread of $211 - 29 = 182$ to be covered.
            Thus each space must be $156 \div 12 = 13$. The difference could also be found by using the general
            expression for an arithmetic sequence, where the nth term is $a + (n - 1)d$. Let $a_{13} = 198$, a = 42,
            and n = 13.

15.   If you are on the middle rung and climb up 3, you are 3 above the middle. If you then go down 5, you are 2
      below the middle. Of the 10 rungs to get onto the roof, it takes 2 to get back to the middle, so there must
      be 8 rungs above the middle. In all, then, there must be 8 above the middle + 8 below the middle + 1
      middle for a total of 17 rungs.

17.   732 marbles. This can best be done by working backward. (A crucial piece of the solution is in
      understanding that if a given number is a fraction of some original number, you must divide by the fraction
      to get the original; e.g., 150 is $\frac{3}{4}$ of some number, so the number is $150 \div \frac{3}{4} = 200$.) Starting with 100, add
      back the 20 Jacobo gave to David. The resulting 120 is $\frac{2}{3}$ of what he had before giving the $\frac{1}{3}$ to another
      friend. Thus he had $120 \div \frac{2}{3} = 180$. Adding back the 2 given to David yields 182, which is half the previous
      quantity of 364. Again adding back 2 given to David gives 366; this is half the original which then must
      have been 732.

19.   (a)   11 coins. He must have 5 pennies to make an even \$1.00. The minimum number of coins would have
            as many quarters as possible, or 3 quarters. The remaining \$0.20 must consist of at least one dime
            and one nickel; the only possibility is one dime and two nickels. Thus the minimum coins are 5
            pennies, 2 nickels, 1 dime, and 3 quarters.

      (b)   63 coins. The maximum number of coins is achieved by having as many pennies as possible. It is a
            requirement to have 1 quarter, 1 dime, and 1 nickel = \$0.40, so there may then be 60 pennies.

21.   Adding the numbers gives 99. This tells you that each row, diagonal, and column must add to $99 \div 3 = 33$.
      Place the center number in a sequence in the center square, then add numbers until achieving the desired
      result. One possible solution is:

17	7	9
3	11	19
13	15	5

23.   (a)   If both numbers were less than or equal to 9, then their product would be less than $9 \times 9 = 81$, which
            is not greater than 82.

      (b)   See (a).

25. Each of the 20 people shook hands with 17 others after dinner. Multiplying, $20 \cdot 17 = 340$. This counts each handshake twice, however (i.e., Mary was one of the 17 Joe shook with and Joe was one of the 17 Mary shook with). Thus there were $340 \div 2 = 170$ handshakes.

27. This problem may be solved in two ways:

   (*i*)   Working backwards, Jose must have had $6000 before buying the house, $12,000 before losing half, and $13,500 before spending $1500 getting married.

   (*ii*)   Algebraically, if we let A be the amount of money Jose started with, then:
   $A - 1500 - \frac{1}{2}(A - 1500) - \frac{1}{2}[\frac{1}{2}(A - 1500)] = 3000$
   (simply translating the wording of the problem into an algebraic statement).
   Solving, $A - 1500 - \frac{1}{2}A + 375 = 3000$, and $A = \$13,500$.

29. (a)   As each line is added, it can cross each of the previous lines. Making a table, we would thus have:

Nr. of Lines	Nr. of Intersections
1	0
2	1
3	$3 = 2 + 1$
4	$6 = 3 + 2 + 1$
5	$10 = 4 + 3 + 2 + 1$
⋮	⋮
20	$19 + 18 + 17 + \cdots + 2 + 1$

   Using Gauss' technique, $19 + 18 + \cdots + 2 + 1 = \frac{19}{2}(19 + 1) = 190$ intersection points.

   (b)   The maximum number of points is $(n - 1) + (n - 2) + (n - 3) + \cdots + 2 + 1 = \frac{n-1}{2}[(n - 1) + 1]$
   $= \frac{n(n-1)}{2}$.

31. (a)   21, 24, 27 (adding 3 to each term to obtain the subsequent term).

   (b)   243, 2, 729 (Multiplying every other term by 3 with 2's in between).

33. See problem 1.(c) above. There are $\frac{83-3}{4} + 1 = 21$ terms. Alternatively, use the expression for the *n*th term of an arithmetic sequence:
   $83 = 3 + (n - 1)4$
   $80 = (n - 1)4$
   $20 = n - 1$
   $21 = n$
Note that we have used the same operations.

Problem Set 1-3

1. (a)   (*i*)   The largest 3- and 2-digit numbers are the 700's and 50's or the 500's and 70's. Using the calculator to try various combinations, we find:
   $\boxed{5}\boxed{4}\boxed{1} \boxed{\times} \boxed{7}\boxed{2} = 38,952$, which is the greatest possible product.

   (*ii*)   For the largest quotient, we want the smallest divisor, or 12, and the largest dividend, or 754. We thus find that $\boxed{7}\boxed{5}\boxed{4} \boxed{\div} \boxed{1}\boxed{2} = 62.8\overline{3}$, which is the greatest possible quotient.

   (b)   (*i*)   The least possible product is: $\boxed{2}\boxed{5}\boxed{7}\boxed{\times}\boxed{1}\boxed{4} = 3598$.

   (*ii*)   The least possible quotient is: $\boxed{1}\boxed{2}\boxed{4}\boxed{\div}\boxed{7}\boxed{5} = 1.65\overline{3}$.

3. Vera bought items costing $3.99 + $5.87 + $6.47 = $16.33.

5. There is a difference of 7 between each term of the sequence. Enter [7][+][K] in your calculator; then enter [1] to place a 1 in the display. Now count the number of times [=] must be depressed to arrive at 113 in the display. You will find that there are 17 terms in the sequence.

7. Try multiplying 5,230,010 by the natural numbers until your result exceeds eight digits (because most calculators have an eight-digit display). You will find that $5{,}230{,}010 \cdot 19$ has eight digits; $5{,}230{,}010 \cdot 20$ has nine digits. $5{,}230{,}010 \cdot 20$ and all larger multipliers must therefore be displayed in scientific notation.

9. Enter [1][0][0][−][2][6][−][1][=] to obtain a display of 73.

11. $\$10 \cdot 60$ minutes$\cdot 24$ hours$\cdot 365$ days $= \$5{,}256{,}000$ per year.

13. Let n be the number for which we are looking. Then $\left(\frac{n}{25} - 18\right)37 = 259$. Solving, we have:

$$\frac{n}{25} - 18 = 7$$

$$\frac{n}{25} = 25, \text{ and } n = 625.$$

15. (a) For example:

$11 \cdot 99 = 1089$
$37 \cdot 99 = 3663$
$54 \cdot 99 = 5346$

The 1st and 3rd digits add to 9; the 2nd and 4th digits also add to 9.

(b) For example:

$11 \cdot 999 = 10989$
$23 \cdot 999 = 22977$
$46 \cdot 999 = 45954$

The middle digit is always 9; the sum of the 1st and 4th digits is 9; the sum of the 2nd and 5th digits is also 9.

17. 40,000 kilometers is 40,000,000 meters. If we assume the distance from fingertip to fingertip of the average person is about 2 meters, then $40{,}000{,}000 \div 2 = 20{,}000{,}000$ people holding hands.

19. Play second and make sure that the sum showing when you hand the calculator to your opponent is a multiple of 3.

21. Play first and press 3. Then make sure that the sum showing when you hand the calculator to your opponent is 3 more than a multiple of 10.

23. Play second and make sure that the sum showing when you hand the calculator to your opponent is a multiple of 4.

25. (a) $1 + 2 + 2^2 + 2^3 + 2^4 + 2^5 = 2^6 - 1$, since:

$$\begin{aligned}(1 + 2 + 2^2 + 2^3 + 2^4) + 2^5 &= 2^5 - 1 + 2^5\\ &= (2^5 + 2^5) - 1\\ &= 2 \cdot 2^5 - 1\\ &= 2^6 - 1\end{aligned}$$

(b) The sum in the nth row of the pattern is $2^n - 1$.

(c) If $n = 15$, then $2^n - 1 = 2^{15} - 1 = 32{,}768 - 1 = 32{,}767$

27. We have an arithmetic sequence with 1st term 12 and difference 20. Thus the nth term is:
$12 + (n - 1)20 = 12 + 20n - 20 = 20n - 8$.

29.   There are nine ways of making change:

Pennies	Nickels	Dimes
1	4	0
1	2	1
1	0	2
6	3	0
6	1	1
11	2	0
11	0	1
16	1	0
21	0	0

CHAPTER 2 - SETS, FUNCTIONS, AND LOGIC

<u>Problem</u> <u>Set</u> <u>2-1</u>

1. (a) "Wealthy" is not defined; thus the set is not well defined.

    (b) "Great" books is not defined; thus the set is not well defined.

    (c) Since we can tell if any given number is or is not in the set, the set is well defined.

    (d) We can tell if any given set is a subset of this set, so the set of subsets is well defined.

3. (a) $B = \{x, y, z, w\}$

    (b) $3 \notin B$

    (c) $\{1, 2\} \subset \{1, 2, 3, 4\}$

    (d) $D \nsubseteq E$

    (e) $A \not\subset B$

    (f) $0 \notin \emptyset$

    (g) $\{0\} \neq \emptyset$

5. (a) Yes, because $\{1, 2, 3, 4, 5\} \sim \{m, n, o, p, q\}$

    (b) No, because $\{m, a, t, h\} \nsim \{f, u, n\}$

    (c) Yes, because $\{a, b, c, d, e, f, \ldots, m\} \sim \{1, 2, 3, 4, 5, 6, \ldots, 13\}$

    (d) No, because $\{x \,|\, x$ is a letter in the word *mathematics*$\} \nsim \{1, 2, 3, 4, \ldots, 13\}$. Note that there are only eight unduplicated letters in the word *mathematics*.

    (e) No, because $\{o, \triangle\} \nsim \{2\}$

7. (a) 24. The 1st element of the 1st set can be paired with any of the four in the 2nd set, leaving three possible pairings for the 2nd element, two for the 3rd, and one for the 4th. There are thus $4 \cdot 3 \cdot 2 \cdot 1 = 24$ possible one-to-one correspondences.

    (b) There are $5 \cdot 4 \cdot 3 \cdot 2 \cdot 1 = 120$ possible one-to-one correspondences.

    (c) There are $n \cdot (n - 1) \cdot (n - 2) \cdot \cdots \cdot 2 \cdot 1 = n!$ possible one-to-one correspondences.

9. A, C, and D are equal; note that the order of the elements is immaterial. E and H are equal; they are both the null set.

11. (a) 7 elements. A proper subset must have at least one less element than the set.

    (b) 1 element. Then B, to be a proper subset, would have no elements; i.e., it would be the null set.

13. No. It is not a proper subset of itself, since it is equal to itself.

15. (a)   ⊄. 3 is not a set and thus cannot be a subset.

     (b)   ⊄. 0 is not a set and thus cannot be a subset of ∅, the null set.

     (c)   ⊆. {1} is actually a proper subset of {1,2}

     (d)   ⊆.

     (e)   ⊆.

17. (a)   True.

     (b)   False. A could equal B; then A would be a subset but not a proper subset of B.

     (c)   True.

     (d)   False. A could be any of the proper subsets of B, thus not equal to B.

19. For natural numbers a and b, a is less than or equal to b if and only if, for sets A and B with $n(A) = a$ and $n(B) = b$, there exists a subset of B equivalent to A. (I.e., simply change from "proper subset" to "subset" to include equality.)

21. If order were important in the subcommittees (i.e., if there were to be a chairman, vice-chairman, and secretary) there would be seven ways of choosing a chairman, six ways of choosing a vice-chairman, and five ways of choosing a secretary, or $7 \cdot 6 \cdot 5 = 210$ different subcommittees. The subcommittee does not have any particular order, though, so we must divide 210 by the number of different possible groupings of three: $3 \cdot 2 \cdot 1 = 6$. $210 \div 6 = 35$, so there are 35 possible subcommittee groupings.

Problem Set 2-2

1.   (a) $A \cap B = \{t, i, e\}$. $B \cap A = \{t, i, e\}$. The sets are therefore equal.   In other words:
            $A \cap B = \{x | x \in A \text{ and } x \in B\} = B \cap A$, so the sets are equal.

     (b) $A \cup B = \{l, i, t, e\} = B \cup A$, so the sets are equal.

     (c) $B \cup C = \{t, i, e, q, u\}$; $A \cup (B \cup C) = \{l, i, t, e, q, u\}$.
            $A \cup B = \{l, i, t, e\}$; $(A \cup B) \cup C = \{l, i, t, e, q, u\}$.
            The sets are therefore equal.

     (d) $A \cup \emptyset = \{l, i, t, e\} = A$. The sets are therefore equal.

     (e) $A \cap A = \{l, i, t, e\}$. $A \cap \emptyset = \emptyset$. The sets are therefore not equal.

     (f) $C = \{q, u, e\}$. $\overline{C} = \{a, l, i, t, y\}$. $\overline{\overline{C}} = \{q, u, e\}$. C and $\overline{\overline{C}}$ are therefore equal.

3.   (a)   If $B \subseteq A$, all elements of B must also be elements of A, so $A \cap B = B$.

     (b) $B \subseteq A$ implies that A is either equal to or larger than B, so $A \cup B = A$.

5.   (a) $\overline{S}$ is the set of all elements in U that are not in S. $S \cup \overline{S}$, therefore, is the set of all elements within the universe, or U.

     (b) $S \cup U = \{x | x \in S \text{ or } x \in U\} = U$; i.e., S can add nothing more to the whole universe.

5.   (c) $\emptyset \cup S = \{x | x \in \emptyset$ or $x \in S\} = S$; i.e., $\emptyset$ has nothing to add to S.

       (d)   If U is the universe, the complement of U can have no elements, thus $\bar{U} = \emptyset$.

       (e) $S \cap U = \{x | x \in S$ and $x \in U\} = S$; i.e., all elements of S must be in U.

       (f)   If the null set has no elements, the complement of the null set must have all elements; thus $\bar{\emptyset} = U$.

       (g)   There are no elements common to S and $\bar{S}$; thus $S \cap \bar{S} = \emptyset$.

       (h)   Since there are no elements common to S and $\bar{S}$, $S - \bar{S} = S$.

       (i) $U \cap \bar{S} = \bar{S}$.

       (j) $\bar{\bar{S}}$ is the complement of $\bar{S}$, or S. Thus, $\bar{\bar{S}} = S$.

       (k)   Since there are no elements in the null set there are none common to it and S; thus $\emptyset \cap S = \emptyset$.

       (l) $U - S = \bar{S}$. Taking the elements of S from U leaves only $\bar{S}$.

7.   (a)   If $A \cap B = \emptyset$, then A and B are disjoint sets; thus anything in A is <u>not</u> in B. Therefore, $A - B = \{x | x \in A$ and $x \notin B\} = A$.

       (b)   Since $B = U$, there can be no elements in A which are not in B. Thus $A - B = \emptyset$.

       (c)   Since A and B are equal, there can be nothing in one set that is not in the other. Thus $A - B = \emptyset$.

       (d)   If A is a subset of B, then all elements of A must be in B; so an element cannot be in A and not be in B at the same time. I.e., $A - B = \{x | x \in A$ and $x \notin B\} = \emptyset$.

9.   (a)   A is shaded except for set B.

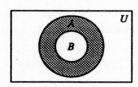

       (b)   The union of A and B is contained within A. Its complement is the universe outside A.

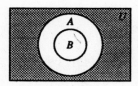

       (c)   The intersection of A and B is contained within B. The complement of A is the total region outside A. Their union is the shaded area.

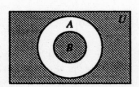

9.   (d)   A - B is the set of all elements in A that are not in B.

11.   (a)   (*i*)   The greatest number of elements in A ∪ B would occur if A and B were disjoint sets. In that case, $n(A \cup B) = 5$

             (*ii*)   The greatest number of elements in A ∩ B would occur if B were a subset of A. In that case , $n(A \cap B) = B = 2.$

      (b)   (*i*)   As in (a), the greatest number of elements in A ∪ B would occur if A and B were disjoint sets. Then $n(A \cup B) = m + n.$

             (*ii*)   The maximum number would occur when either of the sets was a subset of the other. Then $n(A \cap B)$ would be the smaller of *m* or *n*.

13.   (a)   All natural numbers.

      (b)   ∅. Evens and odds have no numbers in common.

      (c)   E. Every even number is not in the set of odds.

      (d)   O. Every odd number is not in the set of evens.

15.   A and B are equal. They have in common everything they both contain, which means they must both contain the same elements.

17.   (a)   Students in band only.   (b)   Students in both band and choir.

      (c)   Students in choir only.   (d)   Students in neither band nor choir.

19.   From the diagram below, there were 4 members who took biology but not mathematics.

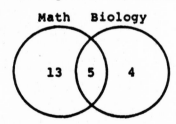

21.   (a)   20 bikes. This occurs if all bikes needing new tires also need gear repairs; symbolically, if TIRES ⊂ GEARS then TIRES ∩ GEARS = 20.

      (b)   10 bikes. Adding the separate repairs gives $20 + 30 = 50$. This indicates that at least 10 bikes were counted twice; i.e., needed both repairs.

      (c)   10 bikes. This occurs if the maximum number of bikes received both repairs, as in (a). All 20 that received tires were among the 30 having gear work, leaving 10 that required no service.

23. Cowboys vs Giants, Vikings vs Packers, Redskins vs Bills, and Jets vs Steelers. All picked the Cowboys to win their game, so the opponent cannot be among any of the choices. The only team not picked was the Giants. Phyllis and Paula both picked the Steelers, so their opponent cannot be among their other choices. This leaves the Jets. Phyllis and Rashid both picked the Vikings which leaves the Packers as the only possible opponent. The Redskins and Bills are left as opponents by elimination.

25. (a)   No. The elements of the ordered pairs are reversed by reversing the order of the sets in the product.

   (b)   No. The parentheses would be oriented differently; e.g., if A = {a}, B = {b}, and C = {c}, then (A × B) × C = {(a, b), c} while A × (B × C) = {a, (b, c)}.

27. (a) $5 \cdot 4 = 20$ elements. Each of the five in A are paired with each of the four in B.

   (b) $m \cdot n$ elements.

   (c) $m \cdot n \cdot p$ elements. A × B has $m \cdot n$ elements, each of which is paired with the p elements in C.

29. If $n[(A \cup B) \times B] = 24$, then $n(A \cup B) = \frac{24}{3} = 8$. If $A \cap B = \emptyset$, then A and B are disjoint sets. Thus if $n(B) = 3$ then $n(A) = 8 - 3 = 5$.

31. 30 games. This is equivalent to the number in the Cartesian product of the two sets of teams; i.e., $6 \cdot 5 = 30$.

33. We are given:
      26 British females
      17 American women
      17 American males
      29 girls
      44 British citizens
      29 women
      24 British adults
   Thus:
      29 women − 17 American women = 12 British women
      26 British females − 12 British women = 14 British girls
      29 girls − 14 British girls = 15 American girls
   And so:

British women=12	American males=17
British men=12	American women=17
British girls=14	American girls=15
British boys=6	
Total British=44	Total American=49

   There were $44 + 49 = 93$ people in the group.

35. Representing the data by a Venn diagram shows: Goldcard   Supercard

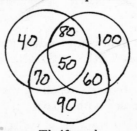

Thriftcard

Totaling all areas gives $40 + 100 + 90 + 80 + 60 + 70 + 50 = 490$ students. Either the editor was right in that an error must have been made because there was not a total of 500 students, or the editor was wrong by not realizing that the "missing" ten students could have had credit cards other than the three shown.

37. Yes. If the numbers are all natural numbers, then 2n is always an even number.

39. (a) {Maine, Maryland, Massachusetts, Michigan, Minnesota, Mississippi, Missouri, Montana}

(b) {x|x is the name of a state in the United States which starts with the letter *M*}.

Problem Set 2-3

1. (a) The second element is the square of the first element. Thus (5, 25) and (6, 36) are two more pairs.

(b) The second element is the husband of the first element. Thus (Hillary, Bill) and (Minnie, Mickey) are two more pairs.

(c) The second element is the capitalization of the first element. Thus (e, E) and (f, F) are two more pairs.

(d) The second element is the cost of the first element. Thus (9 candies, 30 cents) and (12 candies, 40 cents) are two more pairs.

3. Answers may vary. (Fluffy, Sue), (Jinx, Mary), and (Garfield, Jon) are three examples.

5. (a) Not reflexive — a person cannot be a parent to him/herself.
Not symmetric — John can be a parent to Jane, but Jane cannot be a parent to John.
Not transitive — If John is the parent of James and James is the parent of Joseph, John is not the parent of Joseph.
Not an equivalence relation.

(b) Reflexive — Juan is the same age as Juan.
Symmretic — If Juan is the same age as Juanita, then Juanita is the same age as Juan.
Transitive — If Juan is the same age as Jose and Jose is the same age as Victor, Juan is the same age as Victor.
An equivalence relation (because the relation is reflexive, symmetric, and transitive).

(c) Reflexive — Jo Ann has the same last name as herself.
Symmetric — If Jo Ann has the same last name as Cheryl, then Cheryl has the same last name as Jo Ann.
Transitive — If Jo Ann has the same last name as Cheryl and Cheryl has the same last name as Penelope, then Jo Ann has the same last name as Penelope.
An equivalence relation.

(d) Reflexive — Vicky is the same height as herself.
Symmetric — If Barbara is the same height as Margarita, then Margarita is the same height as Barbara.
Transitive — If Willy is the same height as Billy and Billy is the same height as Don, then Willy is the same height as Don.
An equivalence relation.

(e) Not reflexive — Cindy cannot be married to herself.
Symmetric — If Arnold is married to Pam, then Pam is married to Arnold.
Not transitive — If John is married to Clara and Clara is married to James, then John is not married to James.
Not an equivalence relation.

5.   (f)   Reflexive — Peter lives within 10 miles of himself.
             Symmetric — If Jon lives within 10 miles of Evangeline, the Evangeline lives within 10 miles of Jon.
             Not transitive — If Fred lives within 10 miles of Jim and Jim lives within 10 miles of Herb, then Fred
                   does not necessarily live within 10 miles of Herb.
             Not an equivalence relation.

      (g)   Not reflexive — Juan cannot be older than himself.
             Not symmetric — If Jose is older than Mireya then Mireya cannot be older than Jose.
             Transitive — If Jean is older than Mike and Mike is older than Cybil, then Jean is older than Cybil.
             Not an equivalence relation.

7.   (a)   Multiply the given number by 3 and subtract 1 (or 3n - 1).

      (b)   Square the given number and add 1 (or $n^2 + 1$)

      (c)   Square the given number and add the given number to that result (or $n^2 + n$).

9.   (a)   Not a function. The element 1 is paired with both *a* and *d*.

      (b)   Not a function. The element 2 is not paired with any element from the set {a, b, c, d}.

      (c)   A function.

      (d)   Not a function. 1 is paired to more than one element from the set {a, b, c, d}, while 2 and 3 are not
             paired at all.

11.   Yes. Each element of a set is mapped to a single element of a 2nd set (it in fact is a very special function,
      called one-to-one and onto).

13.   (a)   g(0) = 3(0) + 5 = 5.

      (b)   g(2) = 3(2) + 5 = 11.

      (c)   g(10) = 3(10) + 5 = 35.

      (d)   g(a) = 3(a) + 5 = 3a + 5.

15.   (a)

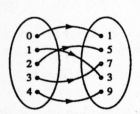

      (b)   {(0, 1), (1, 3), (2, 5), (3, 7), (4, 9)}

      (c)

x	f(x)
0	1
1	3
2	5
3	7
4	9

15. (d)

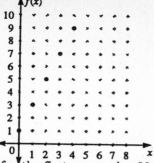

17. Assume 29 cents for the first ounce plus 20 cents for each additional ounce. Then:

(a) $0.29 + 0.20(n - 1)$ is the cost in dollars for an n-ounce letter.

(b) $0.29 + 0.20(3 - 1) = 0.29 + 0.40 = \$0.69$ for a 3-ounce letter.

19. (a)   Two miles is $\frac{1}{2}$ mile plus six $\frac{1}{4}$-mile segments. The fare is thus $2.50 + 6(0.50) = \$5.50$.

(b)   0.50 for each $\frac{1}{4}$ mile gives 2.00 for each mile beyond the first $\frac{1}{2}$ mile. This gives a cost of $2.50 + 2.00(n \text{ miles} - \text{first } \frac{1}{2} \text{ mile}) = 2.50 + 2.00n - 1.00 = \$2.00n + \$1.50$ for an n-mile trip.

21. (a)   The score made most often is 51; its frequency is 7.

(b)   The highest score obtained was 56.

(c)   Two girls scored 54.

23. (a)   Yes. The set of all people has exactly one mother (assuming biological mothers only) each. More or less than one is not possible.

(b)   No. Some elements of the set of all boys do not have a brother.

25. Not a well-defined set; the word "rich" is not defined.

27. (a) $A = \{a, b, c\}$. $\bar{B} = \{a, d\}$. $A \cup \bar{B} = \{a, b, c, d\} = U$.

(b) $A \cap B = \{b, c\}$. $\overline{A \cap B} = \{a, d\}$.

(c)   Since there are no elements in $\emptyset$, $A \cap \emptyset = \emptyset$.

(d)   Since there are no elements common to B and C, $B \cap C = \emptyset$.

(e) $B - A = \{x | x \in B \text{ and } x \notin A\}$. There are no elements in this set, so $B - A = \emptyset$.

29. $\{a, b, c, d\}$ is an equivalent set; the number of elements is the same.

31. We need to show that $(A \cup B) \cup C = A \cup (B \cup C)$:
$A \cup B = \{h, e, l, p, m\}$; $B \cup C = \{m, e, n, o, w\}$
$(A \cup B) \cup C = \{h, e, l, p, m, n, o, w\} \leftrightarrow A \cup (B \cup C) = \{h, l, p, m, e, n, o, w\}$

Problem Set 2-4

1. (a)   False statement (a statement is a sentence that is either true or false, but not both).

(b)   Not a statement.

1. (c) False statement.

   (d) Not a statement (i.e., it can be either true or false).

   (e) Not a statement.

   (f) Not a statement (truth cannot be determined without knowing the value of x).

   (g) True statement.

   (h) Not a statement (could be either true or false depending upon the value of x).

   (i) Not a statement. (This is a paradox. If it is true, it must be false, but then it isn't true ... .)

   (j) Not a statement.

3. (a) For all natural numbers x, x + 8 = 11.

   (b) There is no natural number x such that x + 0 = x.

   (c) For all natural numbers x, $x^2 = 4$.

   (d) There exists a natural number x, such that x + 1 = x + 2.

5. (a)

p	~p	~(~p)
T	F	T
F	T	F

   (b)

p	~p	p∨~p	p∧~p
T	F	T	F
F	T	T	F

   (c) Yes   (d) No

7. (a) False (true if and only if both p and q are true).

   (b) True (false if both p and q are false; true otherwise).

   (c) True (negation of p)

   (d) False.

   (e) False [analgous to -(-x) = x]

   (f) True (both ~p and q are true).

   (g) False (both are false).

   (h) False (p ∨ q is true).

   (i) False (~p ∧ q is true).

   (j) False.

9. (a)

p	q	~p	~q	~p ∨ ~q	~(p ∨ q)
T	T	F	F	F	F
T	F	F	T	T	F
F	T	T	F	T	F
F	F	T	T	T	T

Since the truth table for ~p ∨ ~q is not the same as for ~(p ∨ q), the statements are not logically equivalent.

(b)

p	q	~p	~q	p ∨ q	~(p ∨ q)	~p ∧ ~q
T	T	F	F	T	F	F
T	F	F	T	T	F	F
F	T	T	F	T	F	F
F	F	T	T	F	T	T

Since the truth table for ~(p ∨ q) is the same as for ~p ∧ ~q, the statements are logically equivalent.

(c)

p	q	~p	~q	p ∧ q	~(p ∧ q)	~p ∧ ~q
T	T	F	F	T	F	F
T	F	F	T	F	T	F
F	T	T	F	F	T	F
F	F	T	T	F	T	T

Since the truth table for ~(p ∧ q) is not the same as for ~p ∧ ~q, the statements are not logically equivalent.

(d)

p	q	~p	~q	p ∧ q	~(p ∧ q)	~p ∨ ~q
T	T	F	F	T	F	F
T	F	F	T	F	T	T
F	T	T	F	F	T	T
F	F	T	T	F	T	T

Since the truth table for ~(p ∧ q) is the same as for ~p ∨ ~q, the statements are logically equivalent.

11.

p	q	~p	~q	~p ∨ q
T	T	F	F	T
T	F	F	T	F
F	T	T	F	T
F	F	T	T	T

Problem Set 2-5

1. (a)   p → q.

    (b)   ~p → q.

1.   (c) $p \to \sim q$.

    (d) $p \to q$.

    (e) $\sim q \to \sim p$.

    (f) $p \leftrightarrow q$.

3.   (a)

p	q	$p \vee q$	$p \to (p \vee q)$
T	T	T	T
T	F	T	T
F	T	T	T
F	F	F	T

    (b)

p	q	$p \wedge q$	$(p \wedge q) \to q$
T	T	T	T
T	F	F	T
F	T	F	T
F	F	F	T

    (c)

p	$\sim p$	$\sim(\sim p)$	$p \leftrightarrow \sim(\sim p)$
T	F	T	T
F	T	F	T

    (d)

p	q	$p \to q$	$\sim(p \to q)$
T	T	T	F
T	F	F	T
F	T	T	F
F	F	T	F

5.   (a) $\sim p$ is T; $\sim q$ is T; so $\sim p \to \sim q$ is T.

    (b) $(p \to q)$ is T; so $\sim(p \to q)$ is F.

    (c) $(p \vee q)$ is F; $(p \wedge q)$ is F; so $(p \vee q) \to (p \wedge q)$ is T.

    (d) p is F; $\sim p$ is T; so $p \to \sim p$ is T.

    (e) $(p \vee \sim p)$ is T; p is F; so $(p \vee \sim p) \to p$ is F.

    (f) $(p \vee q)$ is F; $(p \wedge q)$ is F; so $(p \vee q) \leftrightarrow (p \wedge q)$ is T.

7.   No. If it does not rain, then Iris can either go to the movies or not without making her statement false.

9.   The contrapositive is logically equivalent: "If a number is not a multiple of 4, then it is not a multiple of 8."

11.   (a) $p \to q$ is analgous to $\{p | p \in P \text{ and } p \in Q\}$. $q \not\to p$ is analgous to $\{q | q \in Q \text{ and } q \notin P\}$.
           Therefore they are analgous to the relationship $P \subset Q$.

    (b) $p \to q$ is analgous to $\{p | p \in P \text{ and } p \in Q\}$. $q \to p$ is analgous to $\{q | q \in Q \text{ and } q \in P\}$.
           Therefore they are analgous to the relationship $P = Q$.

    (c) $A \subseteq B$ is analgous to $p \to q$. $\overline{A} \subseteq \overline{B}$ is analgous to $\sim p \to \sim q$.
           $A \subseteq B = \{x | x \in A \text{ and } x \in B\}$. $\overline{A} \subseteq \overline{B} = \{x | x \notin A \text{ and } x \notin B\}$.
           Which is true only if $A = B$.

13. (a)   Let p = Mary's little lamb follows her to school.
          q = It will break the rules.
          r = Mary will be sent home.
    Then $p \rightarrow (q \wedge r)$.

   (b)   Let p = Jack is nimble.
          q = Jack is quick.
          r = Jack makes it over the candlestick.
    Then $\sim(p \wedge q) \rightarrow \sim r$.

   (c)   Let p = The apple hit Newton on the head.
          q = The laws of gravity were discovered.
    Then $\sim p \rightarrow \sim q$.

15. (a)   Let p = Helen is a college student.
          q = All college students are poor.
    Then we have $p \rightarrow q$, or if Helen is a college student she is poor.
               p is true, she is a college student.
    So q is true, Helen is poor.

   (b)   Let p = Some freshmen like math.
          q = All who like math are intelligent.
    Then $p \rightarrow q$, or some freshmen are intelligent.

   (c)   Let p = I study for the final.
          q = I pass the course.
          r = I look for a teaching job.
    Then $p \rightarrow q$, if I study for the final I pass the course.
          $q \rightarrow r$, if I pass the course I look for a teaching job.
          $p \rightarrow r$, if I study for the final I will look for a teaching job.

   (d)   Let p = Equilateral triangle.
          q = Isosceles triangle.
    Then $p \rightarrow q$
        $\sim p \rightarrow \sim q$, or, there may exist triangles that are not equilateral.

CHAPTER 3 - NUMERATION SYSTEMS AND WHOLE NUMBERS

Problem Set 3-1

1. (a) $\overline{\overline{M}}$CDXXIV. The double bar over the M represents $1000 \cdot 1000 \cdot 1000$, while a single bar over the M represents only $1000 \cdot 1000$.

   (b) 46,032. The 46 in 46,032 means $4 \cdot 10^4 + 6 \cdot 10^3$, while 46 in 4632 represents $4 \cdot 10^3 + 6 \cdot 10^2$.

   (c) ⟨ ▼▼. The space between ⟨ and ▼▼ represents $10 \cdot 60$ rather than 10.

   (d) ⵊ∩ι . ⵊ has a place value of 1000, while ⟩ has a place value of only 100.

   (e) ⏝ . ⏝ represents three groups of 20 plus zero 1's; ⚏ means three 5's and three 1's, or 15.

3. MCMXXII is $1000 + 900 + 22$, or the year 1922.

5. Group by symbol. Then borrow one heel bone and add ten vertical staffs; subtract 5 vertical staffs from 13 vertical staffs to record 8 vertical staffs. Borrow one scroll and add ten heel bones; subtract 4 heel bones from 11 heel bones to record 7 heel bones. The difference is thus ∩∩∩∩∩∩∩|||||||||

7. (a) ∩∩∩∩∩∩|| (b) ⟩|||

   (c) ⬭||| (d) ∩∩∩|||||||||

9. Answers may vary. Three examples are in dates, paragraph numbering, and super bowl names.

11. (a) With no place values, listing the symbols can become cumbersome.

    (b) Place values of 60 are awkward; numbers can be ambiguously written.

    (c) Arithmetic operations are difficult.

13. (a) Hundreds (from the decimal point left: units → tens → hundreds)

    (b) Tens (units → tens)

    (c) Thousands (units → tens → hundreds → thousands)

    (d) Hundred thousands (units → tens → hundreds → thousands → ten thousands → hundred thousands)

15. To separate groupings of hundreds, thousands, millions, billions, etc.

17. The number could be either 811 or 910. They satisfy the conditions that the hundreds digit must be 8 or 9, the tens digit must be odd, and the sum of the digits must equal 10.

19. After setting 9 as the constant in your calculator's memory, enter 9 and then depress the ⊟ key six times. Your result should be 4,782,969.

21. (a) We need to subtract a number with a 2 in the thousands place and a 2 in the tens place, or 2020. Thus $32,420 - 2020 = 30,400$.

    (b) $67,357 - 50 = 67,307$.

1.   (a)   5 is less than 7 if and only if there exists a natural number k such that $5 + k = 7$. In this case, $k = 2$ (a natural number).

    (b)   6 is greater than 3 if and only if there exists a natural number k such that $3 + k = 6$. $k = 3$.

3.   Suppose A and B were not disjoint; let $A = \{1, 2, 3\}$ and $B = \{3, 4, 5\}$. Then $A \cup B = \{1, 2, 3, 4, 5\}$ and $n(A \cup B) = 5$. But $n(A) + n(B) = 3 + 3 = 6$; thus sets must be disjoint to define addition.

5.   (a)   Using the missing-addend model, $(7 - 2) + 2 = 7$. Thus $\boxed{5} + 2 = 7$.

    (b) $(6 - 4) + 4 = 6$; thus $\boxed{2} + 4 = 6$.

    (c)   Whole numbers which can make this statement true are $\boxed{0}$, $\boxed{1}$, and $\boxed{2}$.

    (d)   Any whole number larger than or equal to $\boxed{3}$ will make this statement true.

7.   (a)   Closed.   (b)   Closed.

    (c)   Closed.   (d)   Not closed. $3 + 7 \notin \{3, 5, 7\}$.

    (e)   Closed.

9.   (a)   Commutative property of addition of whole numbers.

    (b)   Associative property of addition of whole numbers.

    (c)   Commutative property of addition [i.e., $(6 + 3) = (3 + 6)$].

11.   (a)   Each term is found by adding 5 to the previous term, so the next three are $28 + 5 = \underline{33}$, $33 + 5 = \underline{38}$, and $38 + 5 = \underline{43}$.

    (b)   Each term is found by subtracting 7 from the previous term, so the next three are $63 - 7 = \underline{56}$, $56 - 7 = \underline{49}$, and $49 - 7 = \underline{42}$.

13.   Let $A = \{1, 2, 3\}$ and $B = \{1, 2, 3, 4, 5\}$; so $n(A) = 3$ and $n(B) = 5$. Then $B - A = \{4, 5\}$ and $n(B - A) = 2$, corresponding to $n(B) - n(A) = 5 - 3 = 2$.

15.   (a)   9. A number greater than 9 would have two digits.

    (b)   8. If A were larger, C must be larger than 9.

    (c)   3. A and B must be 1 and 2; no smaller single digit numbers are available.

    (d)   6 or 8. A and B must be 2 and 4 or 2 and 6.

    (e)   5. If $B + A = A + 5 = C$, then B must be 5 for the equation to be true.

    (f)   4 or 8. B could be 1 and A then must be 3; or B could be 2 and then A must be 6.

    (g)   9. B must be 2 and A must be 7.

17.   Note that even rows sum to 0, while odd rows sum to 1. Since row 50 is even, its sum is 0.

19. Assign letters to each of the blanks, as below:

a	b
c	d

We can then write equations: $a + b = 11$; $a + c = 12$; and $b + c = 7$.
Solving this system of equations, we find: $a = 8$, $b = 3$, and $c = 4$. Substituting these values for a, b, and c, then d must equal 12, and so our squares are:

8	3
4	12

21. First decide on three combinations that total 13 as a sum. Then arrange them so that the middle numbers fit the "across" boxes:

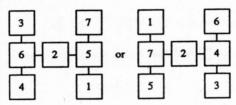

23. (a)   Answers may vary.

1	2
3	5
4	6

1	3
2	5
4	6

(b)   Yes, for example:

1	4
2	5
3	6

25. If Millie and Samantha both start with $0, then Millie's savings will be $3, $6, $9, ... and Samantha's will be $5, $10, $15, ... After five months Millie will have $15 and Samantha will have $25.

27. We can treat this problem as an arithmetic sequence: $1 + 3 + 5 + 7 + \ldots$. Using the methods of Chapter 1, to find the number of guests arriving on the 20th ring we would have:

$$\text{20th term} = 1 + (20 - 1) \cdot 2 = 39.$$

The sum of all 20 arrival groups would be:

$$\text{Sum} = \frac{20}{2} \cdot (1 + 39) = 400 \text{ guests.}$$

29. Answers may vary. One reason is that no one strategy best fits all addition/subtraction problems.

31. Change the problem to $9 + 3$ and then use the "counting on" strategy.

33. Calculators may vary; some systems are shown below:

(a)   Enter ①⊞ as the constant. Enter ① and then depress ▱ 100 times.

(b)   Enter ②⊞ as the constant. Enter ② and then depress ▱ 50 times.

(c)   Enter ⑤⊞ as the constant. Enter ⑤ and then depress ▱ 20 times.

35. Start with ②⊞②, or two 2's. Keep adding by 2, counting each time. After the 13th operation, the calculator will display 26.

37. There are fewer symbols to remember and place value is used.

Problem Set 3-3

1.

3. (a) Closed. $0 \cdot 0 = 0$, $0 \cdot 1 = 0$, $1 \cdot 0 = 0$, and $1 \cdot 1 = 1$ are all products contained in $\{0, 1\}$.

(b) Closed. $0 \cdot 0 = 0$, and $0 \in \{0\}$.

(c) Closed. The product of any two even numbers is also an even number.

(d) Closed. The product of any two odd numbers is also an odd number.

(e) Closed. If we multiply any two terms in the sequence, we will still have an arithmetic sequence with 1st term 1 and difference 3.

(f) No. $2 \cdot 2 = 4 \notin \{0, 1, 2\}$.

5. This is false; consider the set $A = \{1\}$.

7. (a) Commutative property of multiplication of whole numbers.

(b) Associative property of multiplication of whole numbers.

(c) Commutative property of addition of whole numbers. Note that the order of multiplication is unchanged.

(d) Zero multiplication property.

(e) Identity property of multiplication of whole numbers.

(f) Commutative property of multiplication of whole numbers.

(g) Distributive property of multiplication over addition.

(h) Distributive property of multiplication over addition.

9. (a) Given $(a + b)(c + d)$ and applying the distributive property twice, we have:
$$a(c + d) + b(c + d)$$
$$= ac + ad + bc + bd$$

(b) $3 \cdot x + 3 \cdot y + 3 \cdot 5 = 3x + 3y + 15$

(c) $\square \cdot \triangle + \square \cdot \circ$

(d) $x(x + y + z) + y(x + y + z)$
$$= xx + xy + xz + yx + yy + yz$$
$$= xx + xy + xy + xz + yy + yz$$
$$= x^2 + 2xy + xz + y^2 + yz$$

11. (a) $4 + (3 \times 2) = 14$ (Parentheses are unneeded if the order of operations is observed.)

   (b) $(9 \div 3) + 1 = 4$ (Parentheses unneeded)

   (c) $(5 + 4 + 9) \div 3 = 6$

   (d) $(3 + 6 - 2) \div 1 = 7$ (Parentheses unneeded)

13. (a)   True (associative property of multiplication).

   (b)   False; a misstatement of the distributive property.

   (c)   False; a misstatement of the distributive property.

   (d)   False; a misstatement of the distributive property.

15. (a) $18 \div 3 = \boxed{6}$ (b) $\boxed{0} \div 76 = 0$

   (c) $28 \div \boxed{4} = 7$

17. (a) $40 = 8 \cdot 5$ (b) $326 = 2 \cdot x$

   (c) $48 = 16 \cdot x$ (d) $x = 5 \cdot 17$

19. (a) $(5 \otimes 2) \oplus 6 = 16$ (b) $(5 \oplus 3) \otimes 5 = 40$

   (c) $(15 \oslash 3) \ominus 4 = 1$ (where $\oslash$ is $\div$ in the circle)   (d) $(6 \oslash 3) \otimes (5 \ominus 3) = 4$

21. $\$160 \div 5$ months $= \$32$ per month.

23. A log (of any length) cut into ten pieces means nine cuts. Nine cuts at 1 minute per cut $= 9$ minutes.

25. Sequentially divide 36 by all whole factors: We find 1 and 36, 2 and 18, 3 and 12, 4 and 9, and 6 and 6.

27. Since Tony has 6 ways to continue after each of the 5 ways to the park, his total choices are $5 \cdot 6 = 30$.

29. Division is multiplication by the reciprocal of the divisor.

31. (a)   Yes. The system is closed because the result of any operation is in the set S.

   (b)   Yes. It is commutative because a $\odot$ b $=$ b $\odot$ a, a $\odot$ c $=$ c $\odot$ a, and b $\odot$ c $=$ c $\odot$ b.

   (c)   Yes. The identity is *a* because a $\odot$ a $=$ a, a $\odot$ b $=$ b, and a $\odot$ c $=$ c.

   (d)   Yes. For example, (a $\odot$ b) $\odot$ c $=$ a $\odot$ (b $\odot$ c)

33. (a) $3 = 1 + 9 - 7$; $4 = 1^7 + \sqrt{9}$; $5 = 7 - \sqrt{9} + 1$; $6 = 7 - 1^9$; $7 = 7 \cdot 1^9$; $8 = 7 + 1^9$; $9 = 1^7 \cdot 9$; $10 = 1^7 + 9$; $11 = 7 + 1 + \sqrt{9}$; $12 = 19 - 7$; $13 = 91 \div 7$; $14 = 7(\sqrt{9} - 1)$; $15 = 7 + 9 - 1$; $16 = (7 + 9) \cdot 1$; $17 = 7 + 9 + 1$; $18 = \sqrt{9}(7 - 1)$; $20 = 7 \cdot \sqrt{9} - 1$.

   (b)   Answers may vary. One solution is $(4 \cdot 4 \cdot 4 - 4 - 4 - 4) \div 4$.

   (c) $22 + 2$.

   (d) $111 - 11$.

35. $35,206 = 3 \cdot 10^4 + 5 \cdot 10^3 + 2 \cdot 10^2 + 0 \cdot 10^1 + 6 \cdot 1.$

37.   Subtraction is not commutative. For example, $3 - 2 \neq 2 - 3.$

Problem Set 3-4

1.   (a)   Scratch
        $^{1}3 \quad ^{2}7 \quad ^{1}8 \quad 9$
        $\cancel{9}_3 \quad \cancel{2}_1 \quad \cancel{9}_8 \quad \cancel{6}_5$
        $+ \; 6 \quad 8 \quad \cancel{4}_2 \quad 3$
        $\overline{1 \quad 9 \quad 9 \quad 2 \quad 8}$

              Conventional
              $\begin{array}{cccc} 1 & 2 & 1 & \\ 3 & 7 & 8 & 9 \\ 9 & 2 & 9 & 6 \\ + \; 6 & 8 & 4 & 3 \\ \hline 1 \; 9 & 9 & 2 & 8 \end{array}$

        Estimating, by rounding to the nearest thousand, $4000 + 9000 + 7000 = 20,000$, so the answers are reasonable.

     (b)   Scratch
        $^{1}5 \quad ^{2}2 \quad 4$
        $3 \quad 2 \quad \cancel{8}_2$
        $\cancel{5}_4 \quad \cancel{6}_2 \quad 7$
        $+ \; 1 \quad 3 \quad \cancel{5}_4$
        $\overline{1 \quad 5 \quad 5 \quad 4}$

              Conventional
              $\begin{array}{ccc} 1 & 2 & \\ 5 & 2 & 4 \\ 3 & 2 & 8 \\ 5 & 6 & 7 \\ + \; 1 & 3 & 5 \\ \hline 1 \; 5 & 5 & 4 \end{array}$

        Estimating, by rounding to the nearest hundred, $500 + 300 + 600 + 100 = 1500$, so the answers are reasonable.

3.   The columns separate place value and show that $7 + 8 = 15$ and $20 + 60 = 80$. Finally, $15 + 80 = 95.$

5.   (a) $\begin{array}{ccccc} 8 & 7 & 6 & 9 & 3 \\ - \; 4 & 6 & 4 & 1 & 4 \\ \hline 4 & 1 & 2 & 7 & 9 \end{array}$

     (b) $\begin{array}{cccc} 8 & 1 & 3 & 5 \\ - \; 4 & 6 & 8 & 2 \\ \hline 3 & 4 & 5 & 3 \end{array}$

     (c) $\begin{array}{ccc} 3 & 8 & 3 \\ - \; 1 & 5 & 9 \\ \hline 2 & 2 & 4 \end{array}$

     (d) $\begin{array}{ccccc} 1 & 3 & 2 & 9 & 6 \\ - \; & 8 & 3 & 0 & 9 \\ \hline & 4 & 9 & 8 & 7 \end{array}$

7.   (a) $\begin{array}{ccc} \boxed{8} & \boxed{7} & \boxed{6} \\ - \; \boxed{2} & \boxed{3} & \boxed{5} \\ \hline 6 & 4 & 1 \end{array}$

     (b) $\begin{array}{ccc} \boxed{6} & \boxed{2} & \boxed{3} \\ - \; \boxed{5} & \boxed{8} & \boxed{7} \\ \hline & 3 & 6 \end{array}$

9.   (a)   Each term of the sequence is found by adding 5 to the preceding term; thus the next three are:
             $29 + 5 = \underline{34}; \; 34 + 5 = \underline{39}; \; 39 + 5 = \underline{44}.$

     (b)   Each term of the sequence is found by subtracting 3 from the preceding term; thus the next three are:
             $85 - 3 = \underline{82}; \; 82 - 3 = \underline{79};$ and $79 - 3 = \underline{76}.$

11.   By dinner time Tom had consumed $90 + 120 + 119 + 185 + 110 + 570 = 1194$ calories. Subtracting from 1500: $1500 - 1194 = 306$. Tom may have steak or salad, but not both.

13.   Wally's income was $150 + 54 + 260 = \$464$. His expenses were $22 + 60 + 15 + 58 + 185 = \$340$.
      Wally's savings were $464 - 340 = \$124.$

15.   (a)   (i)   Clustering can be used when a group of numbers cluster around a common value. In case (i), the numbers are at wide variance, so clustering would not be a good strategy.

15. (a) (*ii*) These numbers cluster around 500, so the strategy would be a good one.

(b) (*i*) Case (*i*): Total value of lead digits is $1000 + 3000 = 3000$. $64 + 445$ is about 500. $474 + 467$ is about 900. The estimate is about $3000 + 500 + 900 = 4400$. (The exact sum is 4450.)

Case (*ii*): Total value of lead digits is $400 + 400 + 500 + 500 + 500 = 2300$. $83 + 28$ is about 100. $75 + 30$ is about 100. 3 may be disregarded. The estimate is about $2300 + 100 + 100 = 2500$. (The exact sum is 2519.)

(*ii*) Case (*i*): $64 + 2445$ is about 2500. $1467 + 474$ is about 1900. The estimate is about $2500 + 1900 = 4400$.

Case (*ii*): 503 is about 500. $528 + 475$ is about 1000. $530 + 483$ is about 1000. The estimate is about $500 + 1000 + 1000 = 2500$.

(*iii*) Case (*i*): 474 rounds to 500; 1467 rounds to 1500; 64 rounds to 100; 2445 rounds to 2400. The estimate is $500 + 1500 + 100 + 2400 = 4500$.

Case (*ii*): 483 rounds to 500; 475 rounds to 500; 530 rounds to 500; 503 rounds to 500; 528 rounds to 500. The estimate is $5 \cdot 500 = 2500$.

17. (a) 2 years is 104 weeks; 4 months is about 16 weeks; 9 days is about 1 week. Lewis and Clark spent about $104 + 16 + 1 = 121$ weeks in the Northwest.

(b) $1126 \div 365$ is slightly over 3 years.

(c) There are 365 days per year $\cdot$ 24 hours per day $\cdot$ 60 minutes per hour $\cdot$ 60 seconds per minute $= 31,536,000$ seconds per year.

(d) There are $365 \cdot 24 \cdot 60 = 525,600$ minutes per year. If your average pulse is 72, your heart will beat $72 \cdot 525,600 = 37,843,200$ times per year.

19. Algorithms are step-by-step systematic procedures for performing operations. They are taught to give students the tools necessary for solving problems in their disciplines.

21. Answers may vary. One situation might lie in estimating your time of arrival from an automobile trip.

23. Answers may vary. Easier to keep partial sums in proper order; time-consuming.

25. (a) (*i*) $93 + 39 = 132$; $132 + 231 = 363$, which is a palindrome.

(*ii*) $588 + 885 = 1473$; $1473 + 3741 = 5214$; $5214 + 4125 = 9339$, which is a palindrome.

(*iii*) $2003 + 3002 = 5005$, which is a palindrome.

(b) 569,327

27. Trial and error (preferably with a calculator) will yield $8 + 8 + 8 + 88 + 888 = 1000$. The starting point would be 888, since that is close to but not over 1000; the other values come with the remaining five 8's.

29. It appears that the second number was being entered twice: $8 + 6 + 6 = 20$; $5 + 4 + 4 = 13$; $15 - 3 - 3 = 9$.

31. $5 \cdot 10^3 + 2 \cdot 10^2 + 8 \cdot 10^1 + 0 \cdot 1$.

33.

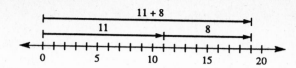

35. (a)   ax + a = a(x + 1)

(b)   3(x + y) + a(x + y) = (3 + a)(x + y)

Problem Set 3-5

1. (a)   (*i*)   Conventional

```
        7 2 8
      ×   9 4
      ─────────
      2 9 1 2
    6 5 5 2
    ─────────
    6 8 4 3 2
```

(*ii*)   Lattice

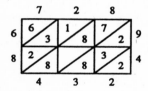

(b)   (*i*)   Conventional

```
        3 0 6
      ×   2 4
      ─────────
      1 2 2 4
    6 1 2
    ─────────
    7 3 4 4
```

(*ii*)   Lattice

3. (a)   Start with multiplication of 4 _ 6 by 3. The _ must be 2, since we have carried 1 from 3·6, and only 3·2 + 1 = 7. Similar reasoning gives:

```
        4 2 6
      ×   7 8 3
      ─────────
      1 2 7 8
    3 4 0 8
  2 9 8 2
  ─────────
  3 3 3 5 5 8
```

. (b)

$$
\begin{array}{r}
3\ 2\ 7 \\
\times\ \ 9\ 4\ 1 \\
\hline
3\ 2\ 7 \\
1\ 3\ 0\ 8 \\
2\ 9\ 4\ 3 \\
\hline
3\ 0\ 7\ 7\ 0\ 7
\end{array}
$$

5. (a) There are $7 + 12 = 19$ factors of 5, so $5^7 \cdot 5^{12} = 5^{7+12} = 5^{19}$.

   (b) $6^{10} \cdot 6^2 \cdot 6^3 = 6^{10+2+3} = 6^{15}$

   (c) $10^{296} \cdot 10^{17} = 10^{296+17} = 10^{313}$

   (d) $2^7 \cdot 10^5 \cdot 5^7 = 2^7 \cdot 5^7 \cdot 10^5 = (2 \cdot 5)^7 \cdot 10^5 = 10^7 \cdot 10^5 = 10^{7+5} = 10^{12}$

7. (a)

$6 \cdot 23 = 6 \cdot (20 + 3) = 6 \cdot 20 + 6 \cdot 3$

7. (b)

$18 \cdot 25 = (20 + 5) \cdot (10 + 8) = 20 \cdot 10 + 20 \cdot 8 + 5 \cdot 10 + 5 \cdot 8$

9.

$$
\begin{array}{rl}
\rightarrow\ 1\ 7\ \times & 6\ 3 \\
8 & 1\ 2\ 6 \\
4 & 2\ 5\ 2 \\
2 & 5\ 0\ 4 \\
\rightarrow\ \ \ 1 & 1\ 0\ 0\ 8
\end{array}
$$

and $63 + 1008 = 1071$

11. (a) $300 \div 14 = 21$ plus a remainder. To find the least number greater than 300 we round up; $n = 22$.

   (b) $4369 \div 23 = 189$ plus a remainder; $n = 190$.

   (c) $782 \div 183 = 6$ plus a remainder; $n = 7$.

   (d) $8654 \div 222 = 38$ plus a remainder; $n = 39$.

13. Use division to reverse multiplication and subtraction to reverse addition. We thus find:

a	b	a·b	a + b
6 7	5 6	3 7 5 2	1 2 3
3 2	7 8	2 4 9 6	1 1 0
1 5	1 8	2 7 0	3 3

15. $2 \cdot 666 = 1332$ calories per day expended in swimming.
$1500 - 1332 = 168$ calories per day increased intake.
$168 \cdot 14 = 2352$ excess calories consumed in the 14 days. Since $2352 < 3500$, he gained less than 1 pound.

17. (a) (i) Repeated Subtraction

```
8 ⌐ 6 2 3
    5 6 0      7 0  eights
    ─────
      6 3
      5 6        7  eights
    ─────      ─────
        7      7 7  remainder 7
```

(ii) Familiar

```
      7 7      remainder 7
  8⌐6 2 3
    5 6
    ───
    6 3
    5 6
    ───
      7
```

(b) (i) Repeated Subtraction

```
3 6 ⌐ 2 9 8
      2 8 8      8  36's
      ─────    ───
        1 0      8  remainder 10
```

(ii) Familiar

```
          8      remainder 10
  3 6 ⌐ 2 9 8
        2 8 8
        ─────
          1 0
```

(c) (i) Repeated Subtraction

```
3 9 1 ⌐ 4 0 0 1
        3 9 1 0      10   391's
        ───────    ────
          9 1      10   remainder 91
```

(ii) Familiar

```
            1 0      remainder 91
  3 9 1 ⌐ 4 0 0 1
          3 9 1
          ─────
            9 1
```

19. (a) $450 \cdot 24$ months $= \$10,800$; $10,800 + 1500 = \$12,300$ total price if paid monthly. Thus the monthly payment option is the more expensive.

(b) $12,300 - 8600 = \$3700$ more expensive if paid monthly.

21. Reversing the operation, $300 \div 10 = 30$. Then $30 \div 10 = 3$, the correct answer.

23. $2 \rightarrow 11$; $4 \rightarrow 15$; $0 \rightarrow 7$; $6 \leftarrow 19$; $12 \leftarrow 31$. (Reverse operations when given an output.)

25. (a) Examples may vary. One such is: $36 \cdot 84 = 3024$; $63 \cdot 48 = 3024$.

    (b) Let the digits of the two numbers be *a*, *b*, *c*, and *d*. Then if ab·cd = ba·dc, a·c must equal b·d. Thus in the example above, $3 \cdot 8 = 24$ and $6 \cdot 4 = 24$.

27. (a) Numbers may vary; pick 7. $2 \cdot 7 = 14$; $14 \cdot 3 = 42$; $42 + 24 = 66$; $66 \div 6 = 11$; $11 - 7 = 4$.

    (b) Let *n* be the chosen number. Then the operations result in: $[3(2n) + 24] \div 6 - n$ $= (6n + 24) \div 6 - n = n + 4 - n = 4$. Thus, regardless of the value of *n*, the result will always be 4.

29. Sami's exact collections are $12 \cdot 38 = \$456$, so her estimate is high; she probably multiplied $15 \cdot 40$ for her \$600 guess. She would have had a closer estimate if she'd rounded 12 to 10 and 38 to 40, or $10 \cdot 40 = \$400$.

31. The cat must make up 100 feet with a speed differential of $30 - 20 = 10$ ft/sec. 100 ft $\div 10$ ft/sec $= 10$ seconds to catch the dog.

33. 1672 students $\div 29$ students per bus $= 57.7$ buses. 58 buses will be needed, but not all will be full.

35. The two digits of the number are repeated in the product; i.e., $25 \cdot 101 = 2525$. If we let the two digits be designated by *a* and *b*, then:

```
    1 0 1
×     a b
  ---------
    b 0 b
  a 0 a
  ---------
  a b a b
```

Note that no partial products are greater than 9, so no carrying is involved.

37. (a) (*i*) $27 \times 198 = 5346$; all digits are used.

       (*ii*) $48 \times 159 = 7632$; all digits are used.

       (*iii*) $39 \times 186 = 7254$; all digits are used.

    (b) Use trial and error with digits not in the given product:

       (*i*) $1963 \times 4 = 7852$; all digits are used.

       (*ii*) $483 \times 12 = 5796$; all digits are used.

       (*iii*) $297 \times 18 = 5346$; all digits are used.

    (c) 1. Any factor times 1 would give that factor in return; it would thus be used more than once.

39. (a) For the greatest product, we need the largest multiplicands which can be formed using the five
    ⑦⑥②   numbers. 83×762 is greater than 82×763 because $80 \times 700 = 70 \times 800$, but 3×62 is
    × ⑧③   greater than 2×63.

    (b) For the least product, we need the smallest multiplicands which can be formed using the five
    ③⑦⑧   numbers. 26×378 is smaller than 36×278 because $20 \times 300 = 30 \times 200$, but 26×78 is
    × ②⑥   smaller than 36×78.

41. (a) $3 \cdot 37 = 111$, the first partial product. $40 \cdot 37 = 1480$, the second partial product. We have:

$$
\begin{array}{r}
3\ 7 \\
\times\ \ 4\ 3 \\
\hline
1\ 1\ 1 \\
1\ 4\ 8\ 0 \\
\hline
1\ 5\ 9\ 1
\end{array}
$$

(b) $558 \div 6 = 93$, so the missing multiplicand is 93. $30 \times 93 = 2790$, the 2nd partial product. We have:

$$
\begin{array}{r}
9\ 3 \\
\times\ \ 3\ 6 \\
\hline
5\ 5\ 8 \\
2\ 7\ 9\ 0 \\
\hline
3\ 3\ 4\ 8
\end{array}
$$

(c)   The only quotient of 12 which could leave a remainder of 3 is 9; $9 \times 1 = 9$. Thus:

$$
\begin{array}{r}
1\ 3 \\
9\overline{)\ 1\ 2\ 3} \\
9 \\
\hline
3\ 3 \\
2\ 7 \\
\hline
6
\end{array}
$$

43.   \$1 per second·60 seconds = \$60 per minute.
\$60 per minute·60 minutes = \$3600 per hour.
\$3600 per hour·24 hours = \$86,400 per day.
\$86,400 per day·7 days = \$604,800 per week.
\$86,400 per day·30 days = \$2,595,000 per month (assuming a 30-day month).
\$86,400 per day·365 days = \$31,536,000 per year (assuming a non-leap year).
\$31,536,000·20 = \$630,720,000 in 20 years.

45.   𝟫𝟫𝟫𝟫 𝟫𝟫 ΛΛΛΛΛ ΛΛΛIIII

47.   Numbers may vary. One example is: $5 + 0 = 5 = 0 + 5$.

49. $59,260 - 52,281 = 6,979$ miles traveled.

1.   (a)   Remember that place values represent powers of 2; i.e.,

$$1 = 1 \cdot 2^0$$
$$10 = 1 \cdot 2^1 + 0 \cdot 2^0$$
$$100 = 1 \cdot 2^2 + 0 \cdot 2^1 + 0 \cdot 2^0, \text{ etc.}$$ Thus the first 15 counting numbers are:
$(1, 10, 11, 100, 101, 110, 111, 1000, 1001, 1010, 1011, 1100, 1101, 1110, \text{ and } 1111)_{two}$.

(b) $(1, 2, 10, 11, 12, 20, 21, 22, 100, 101, 102, 110, 111, 112, 120)_{three}$.

(c) $(1, 2, 3, 10, 11, 12, 13, 20, 21, 22, 23, 30, 31, 32, 33)_{four}$.

(d) $(1, 2, 3, 4, 5, 6, 7, 10, 11, 12, 13, 14, 15, 16, 17)_{eight}$.

3. $2032_{four} = (2 \cdot 10^3 + 0 \cdot 10^2 + 3 \cdot 10 + 2)_{four}$

5.   (a) $EE0_{twelve} = (11 \cdot 10^2 + 11 \cdot 10 + 0)_{twelve}.$
Thus $EE0_{twelve} - 1 = (11 \cdot 10^2 + 10 \cdot 10 + 11)_{twelve} = ETE_{twelve}$, and
$EE0_{twelve} + 1 = (11 \cdot 10^2 + 11 \cdot 10 + 1)_{twelve} = EE1.$

  (b) $100000_{two} - 1 = 11111_{two}$, and $100000_{two} + 1 = 100001_{two}$

  (c) $555_{six} - 1 = 554_{six}$, and $555_{six} + 1 = 1000_{six}$

  (d) $100_{seven} - 1 = 66_{seven}$, and $100_{seven} + 1 = 101_{seven}$

  (e) $1000_{five} - 1 = 444_{five}$, and $1000_{five} + 1 = 1001_{five}$

  (f) $110_{two} - 1 = 101_{two}$, and $110_{two} + 1 = 111_{two}$

7.   (a)   There are 3 groups of 125 in 432, with remainder 57.
There are 2 groups of 25 in 57, with remainder 7.
There is 1 group of 5 in 7, with remainder 2.
Thus $432_{ten} = 3212_{five}$

  (b)   There is 1 group of 1728 in 1963, with remainder 235.
There is 1 grouup of 144 in 235, with remainder 91.
There are 7 groups of 12 in 91, with remainder 7.
Thus $1963_{ten} = 1177_{twelve}$

  (c)   There is 1 group of 256 in 404, with remainder 148.
There are 2 groups of 64 in 148, with remainder 20.
There is 1 group of 16 in 20, with remainder 4.
There is 1 group of 4 in 4, with remainder 0.
Thus $404_{ten} = 12110_{four}$

  (d)   There is 1 group of 32 in 37, with remainder 5.
There are 0 groups of 16 in 5, with remainder 5.
There are 0 groups of 8 in 5, with remainder 5.
There is 1 group of 4 in 5, with remainder 1.
There are 0 groups of 2 in 1, with remainder 1.
Thus $32_{ten} = 100101_{two}$

  (e) $(4 \cdot 10^4 + 3 \cdot 10^2)_{ten} = 40300_{ten}$
There is 1 group of 20736 in 40300, with remainder 19564.
There are 11 groups of 1728 in 19564, with remainder 556.
There are 3 groups of 144 in 556, with remainder 124.
There are 10 groups of 12 in 124, with remainder 4.
Thus $40300_{ten} = 1E3T4_{twelve}$

9.   (a) $432_{five} = 4 \cdot 5^2 + 3 \cdot 5 + 2 = 100 + 15 + 2 = 117_{ten}$

  (b) $101101_{two} = 1 \cdot 2^5 + 1 \cdot 2^3 + 1 \cdot 2^2 + 1 = 32 + 8 + 4 + 1 = 45_{ten}$

  (c) $92E_{twelve} = 9 \cdot 12^2 + 2 \cdot 12 + 11 = 1296 + 24 + 11 = 1331_{ten}$

  (d) $T0E_{twelve} = 10 \cdot 12^2 + 11 = 1440 + 11 = 1451_{ten}$

  (e) $111_{twelve} = 1 \cdot 12^2 + 1 \cdot 12 + 1 = 144 + 12 + 1 = 157_{ten}$

  (f) $346_{seven} = 3 \cdot 7^2 + 4 \cdot 7 + 6 = 147 + 28 + 6 = 181_{ten}$

11. To give the fewest number of prizes, the dollar amount of each must be maximized. Thus $900 =$:
    1 prize at $625 with $275 left over.
    2 prizes at $125 with $25 left over.
    1 prize at $25 with nothing left over; thus no $5 or $1 prizes awarded.

13. (a) There are 8 groups of 7 days (1 week), with 2 days left over, so 58 days = 8 weeks and 2 days.

    (b) There are 4 groups of 12 months (1 year), with 6 months left over, so 54 months = 4 years and 6 months.

    (c) There is 1 group of 24 hours (1 day), with 5 hours left over, so 29 hours = 1 day and 5 hours.

    (d) There are 5 groups of 12 (5 feet), with 8 inches left over, so 68 inches = 5 feet 8 inches.

15. (a) There are 6 groups of 7 in 44, so b = 6.

    (b) There are 5 groups of 144 in 734, with remainder 14. There is 1 group of 12 in 14, so b = 1.

    (c) There must be 2 groups of b in 23, with remainder 5; thus $2b + 5 = 23 \Rightarrow 2b = 18 \Rightarrow b = 9$. Thus $23_{ten} = 25_{nine}$.

17. A minimum of four weights are needed to check from 1 through 15 ounces: one each of 8, 4, 2, and 1 ounce. For 32 ounces, the inspector would need one each of 16, 8 4, 2, and 1 ounce.

19. (a)
$$\begin{array}{r} 1 \\ 4\ 3 \\ +\ 2\ 3 \\ \hline 1\ 2\ 1_{five} \end{array}$$
Note that in the units column, $(3 + 3)_{five} = 11_{five}$; in the fives column, $(1 + 4 + 2)_{five} = 12_{five}$.

    (b)
$$\begin{array}{r} 4\ 3 \\ -\ 2\ 3 \\ \hline 2\ 0_{five} \end{array}$$
We need no borrowing, since we are not subtracting any number from one smaller than itself.

    (c)
$$\begin{array}{r} 1\ \ 1 \\ 4\ 3\ 2 \\ +\ \ \ 2\ 3 \\ \hline 1\ 0\ 1\ 0_{five} \end{array}$$
In the units column, $(2 + 3)_{five} = 10_{five}$; in the fives column $(1 + 3 + 2)_{five} = 11_{five}$; and in the 25's column $(1 + 4)_{five} = 10_{five}$.

    (d)
$$\begin{array}{r} 3\ \ 12 \\ \cancel{4}\ \cancel{2} \\ -\ 2\ 3 \\ \hline 1\ 4_{five} \end{array}$$
10_{five} was borrowed from the fives column to make $(10 + 2)_{five} = 12_{five}$ in the units column; $(12 - 3)_{five} = 4_{five}$.

    (e)
$$\begin{array}{r} 1 \\ 1\ 1\ 0 \\ +\ \ 1\ 1 \\ \hline 1\ 0\ 0\ 1_{two} \end{array}$$
In the twos (i.e., 10_{two}) column, $(1 + 1)_{two} = 10_{two}$. In the fours column, $(1 + 1)_{two} = 10_{two}$.

19. (f)

$$
\begin{array}{cccccc}
 & \overset{1}{} & \overset{1}{} & & \\
 & \overset{1}{\cancel{1\phi}} & \overset{1}{\cancel{1\phi}} & \overset{10}{} & \\
\cancel{1} & \cancel{\phi} & \cancel{\phi} & \cancel{\phi} & 1 \\
- & & 1 & 1 & 1 \\
\hline
1 & 0 & 1 & 0_{two}
\end{array}
$$

We had to borrow 10_{two} from the 16's, eights, and fours columns in order to subtract $(10 - 1)_{two}$. Further subtraction required no more borrowing.

21. (a) Note that in performing these calculations we are working with base 60. Thus if we carry forward we carry forward in sixties rather than in tens.

$$
\begin{array}{ccc}
\overset{1}{} & \overset{1}{} & \\
3 \text{ hours} & 36 \text{ minutes} & 58 \text{ seconds} \\
+\ 5 \text{ hours} & 56 \text{ minutes} & 27 \text{ seconds} \\
\hline
9 \text{ hours} & 33 \text{ minutes} & 25 \text{ seconds}
\end{array}
$$

(In each operation, we carry forward; e.g., 58 seconds + 27 seconds = 85 seconds; we put down 25 seconds and carry 60 seconds = 1 minute

(b) Note that in performing these calculations we are working with base 60. Thus if we must borrow, we borrow 60 rather than 10 as we would in base 10.

$$
\begin{array}{ccc}
 & \overset{95}{} & \\
\overset{4}{} & \overset{\cancel{\cancel{5}}}{} & \overset{98}{} \\
\cancel{5} \text{ hours} & \cancel{3\phi} \text{ minutes} & \cancel{3\phi} \text{ seconds} \\
-\ 3 \text{ hours} & 56 \text{ minutes} & 58 \text{ seconds} \\
\hline
1 \text{ hour} & 39 \text{ minutes} & 40 \text{ seconds}
\end{array}
$$

(We first borrowed 60 seconds from 36 minutes, then borrowed 60 minutes from 5 hours)

23. 20 friends·2 cups each = 40 cups needed. There are 2 cups per pint·2 pints per quart·4 quarts per gallon, or 16 cups per gallon. 40 cups needed ÷ 16 cups per gallon = 2.5 gallons; she would have to buy 3 gallons to have enough.

25. In these operations, we are borrowing and carrying, respectively, in 12's:

(a)
$$
\begin{array}{ccc}
\overset{3}{} & \overset{15}{\cancel{5}} & \\
\cancel{4} \text{ gross} & \cancel{4} \text{ dozen} & \overset{18}{\cancel{\phi}} \text{ ones} \\
- & 5 \text{ dozen} & 9 \text{ ones} \\
\hline
3 \text{ gross} & 10 \text{ dozen} & 9 \text{ ones}
\end{array}
$$

(b)
$$
\begin{array}{ccc}
\overset{1}{} & \overset{1}{} & \\
2 \text{ gross} & 9 \text{ dozen} & 7 \text{ ones} \\
+\ 3 \text{ gross} & 5 \text{ dozen} & 9 \text{ ones} \\
\hline
6 \text{ gross} & 3 \text{ dozen} & 4 \text{ ones}
\end{array}
$$

27. (a) $3 \cdot 20 + 10 = 70$ (b) $4 \cdot 20 + 7 = 87$

29. (a) Work backwards to fill in the blanks. For example, in the units column, $(10 - 2)_{five} = 3_{five}$. Remember to borrow when working backward in the $(10)_{five}$ column. Thus:

$$
\begin{array}{ccc}
2 & 3 & \underline{0} \\
- & 2 & 2 \\
\hline
\underline{2} & 0 & 3_{five}
\end{array}
$$

(b) In the units column (working backward), $(1 + 2)_{three} = 10_{three}$. We would have had to borrow in the $(10)_{three}$ column; now $(1 + 2)_{three} = (10)_{three}$. Continuing to work backward:

$$
\begin{array}{ccccc}
2 & 0 & 0 & 1 & 0 \\
- & & 2 & 0 & 2 & 2 \\
\hline
1 & \underline{0} & 2 & \underline{1} & 1_{three}
\end{array}
$$

31. (a)   The base must be nine, since in the units column $(3 + 8)_{nine} = 12_{nine}$.

(b)   The base must be four, since in the units column $(3 + 3)_{four} = 12_{four}$.

(c)   The base must be six, since in the units column $(2 \cdot 3)_{six} = 10_{six}$.

(d)   Any base greater than or equal to 2.

33.   If we let a be the base a and let b be the base b, then:

$$3a + 2 = 2b + 3$$
$$3a - 2b = 1$$

and the smallest numbers a and b for which this is true are $a = 3$ and $b = 4$. Thus $32_{three} = 23_{four}$.

CHAPTER 4 - THE INTEGERS

<u>Problem</u> <u>Set</u> <u>4-1</u>

1.   (a)   If 2 is an integer, then the unique integer ⁻2 is called the opposite of 2. The opposite of an integer is the integer of the opposite sign.

    (b)   5. The opposite of a negative number is a positive number.

    (c)   ⁻m. The opposite of a variable is the variable with the opposite sign, just as with integers (or any real number).

    (d)   0. Since zero is neither positive nor negative, it is its own opposite.

    (e)   m.

    (f)   ⁻a + ⁻b

3.   (a)   Absolute value is the distance on a number line between 0 and a specified number. The distance between 0 and ⁻5 is 5 units, or $|{}^{-}5| = 5$.

    (b)   10. Remember that absolute value does not mean opposite sign; rather, the distance from 0 on a number line.

    (c)   ⁻|⁻5| means the opposite of the absolute value of ⁻5. Since $|{}^{-}5| = 5$, its opposite is ⁻5.

5.   Black chips represent positive numbers; white chips represent negative numbers. Thus:

    (a)

Net result: 2 positive chips

    (b)

Net result: 1 positive chip

    (c)

Net result: 1 negative chip

    (d)

Net result: 5 negative chips

7.   To add integers with unlike signs, subtract the lesser of the two absolute values (e.g., $|10| = 10$, $|{}^{-}3| = 3$) from the greater. The sum of the two integers will be that difference with the same sign as the integer with the greater absolute value.

    (a) $10 + {}^{-}3 = |10| - |{}^{-}3| = 10 - 3 = 7$. The sign is positive because the integer 10 has the greater absolute value.

    (b)   ⁻2. $|{}^{-}12| - |10| = 2$; the sign is negative because 12 has the larger absolute value and it is negative.

7. (c) If two integers with unlike signs have equal absolute value, their sum is 0. Thus,
$10 + {}^-10 = |{}^-10| - |{}^-10| = 10 - 10 = 0.$

(d) 0

To add integers with like signs, add the absolute values of the integers. The sum will have the same sign as the integers.

(e) ${}^-10.\ {}^-2 + {}^-8 = |{}^-2| + |{}^-8| = 2 + 8$; the sign will be negative because the integers are both negative.

(f) $({}^-2 + {}^-3) + 7 = {}^-5 + 7 = 2.$

(g) ${}^-2 + ({}^-3 + 7) = {}^-2 + 4 = 2.$

9. (a) ${}^-45 + {}^-55 + {}^-165 + {}^-35 + {}^-100 + 75 + 25 + 400 = {}^-400 + 500 = 100.$

(b) $400. 300 (beginning) + $100 (net result of transactions from a)

11. (a) The car starts at 0 and backs up 4 units. It then turns around and faces in the negative direction (to indicate subtraction) and backs up 1 unit (for ${}^-1$). Thus:

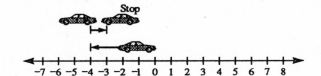

(b)

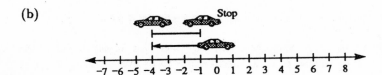

13. (a) ${}^-1$ (b) 1

(c) 3

15. (a) ${}^-2 + (3 - 10) = {}^-2 + ({}^-7) = {}^-2 + {}^-7 = {}^-9.$

(b) $[8 - ({}^-5)] - 10 = [8 + {}^-({}^-5)] - 10 = [8 + 5] - 10 = 13 - 10 = 3.$

(c) $({}^-2 - 7) + 10 = ({}^-2 + {}^-7) + 10 = {}^-9 + 10 = 1.$

(d) ${}^-2 - (7 + 10) = {}^-2 - (17) = {}^-2 + {}^-17 = {}^-19.$

(e) $8 - 11 - 10 = 8 + {}^-11 + {}^-10 = {}^-3 + {}^-10 = {}^-13.$

(f) ${}^-2 - 7 + 3 = {}^-2 + {}^-7 + 3 = {}^-9 + 3 = {}^-6.$

17. (a) We make use of the distributive property of multiplication over addition (Chapter 3); thus:
$3 - (2 - 4x) = 3 + {}^-(2 + {}^-4x) = 3 + {}^-2 - {}^-4x = 3 + {}^-2 + 4x = 1 + 4x.$

(b) $x - ({}^-x - y) = x + {}^-({}^-x - y) = x + x - {}^-y = x + x + y = 2x + y.$

(c) $4x - 2 - 3x = (4x - 3x) - 2 = x - 2.$

19. 784 BC. $1492 - 2275 = {}^-785$, but since there is no year "0", the date is one year after 785 BC.

21. Adding all numbers gives ${}^-9$. Dividing by 3 tells us each row, column, and diagonal must add to ${}^-3$. One possible solution is:

8	${}^-7$	${}^-4$
${}^-13$	${}^-1$	11
2	5	${}^-10$

23. 33 points. Subtract to find out how far off she was: $12 - {}^-21 = 33$. (21 is negative since they lost by 21.)

25. $5 + {}^-10 + 8 + {}^-2 + 3 + {}^-1 + {}^-1 = (5 + 8 + 3) + ({}^-10 + {}^-2 + {}^-1 + {}^-1) = 16 + {}^-14 = 2$. Her stock went up by 2 points.

27. (a)   10W-30 or 10W-40.

    (b)   5W-30.

    (c)   10W-30, or 10W-40.

    (d)   None of the oils shown.

    (e)   10W-30 or 10W-40

29. (a) $f(10) = |1 - 10| = |1 + {}^-10| = |{}^-9| = 9$.

    (b) $f({}^-1) = |1 - {}^-1| = |1 + 1| = |2| = 2$.

    (c)   The result inside the absolute value symbol can be either 1 or ${}^-1$, so x can be 0 or 2.

    (d)   The range is all the values f(x) can assume. In this case, since we have an absolute value, f(x) can only be positive or zero. Thus the range is the set of all integers equal to or greater than 0.

31. For problems such as this, subtract the smaller from the larger, then:
    (*i*)   Add 1 if the ends are to be counted (so as to include the last as well as the first, or vice-versa); or
    (*ii*)   Subtract 1 if neither end is to be counted; e.g., $3 - 2 = 1$, but there are no integers in between, so $1 - 1 = 0$.

    (a)   89. $100 - 10 - 1 = 89$.   (b)   19. ${}^-10 - {}^-30 - 1 = 19$.

    (c)   19. $10 - {}^-10 - 1 = 19$.   (d) $y - x - 1$

33. (a)   Subtract 3 from each preceding term; ${}^-12, {}^-15$.

    (b)   Subtract 4 from each preceding term; ${}^-9, {}^-13$.

    (c)   Subtract y from each preceding term; $x - 2y, x - 3y$.

    (d)   Add 2x to each preceding term; $1 + 3x, 1 + 5x$.

35. (a) ${}^-14$ (b) ${}^-24$

    (c)   2   (d)   5

37. (a)   Estimate: $343 + {}^-42 - 402 \doteq 300 - 400 = {}^-100$. Actual: ${}^-101$.

    (b)   Estimate: ${}^-1992 + 3005 - 497 \doteq {}^-2000 + 3000 - 500 = 500$. Actual: 516.

37. (c)   Estimate: $992 - ^-1003 - 101 \doteq 1000 + 10{,}000 - 100 = 10{,}900.$ Actual: 10,894.

     (d)   Estimate: $^-301 - ^-1303 + 4993 \doteq ^-300 + 1300 + 5000 = 6000.$ Actual: 5995.

39. (a) $(^-a + ^-b) + (a + b) = (^-a + a) + (^-b + b) = 0 + 0 = 0.$

     (b) $^-a + ^-b$ added to $(a + b)$ gives a sum of zero, so $^-a + ^-b$ is the additive inverse, or opposite, of $(a + b)$; i.e., $^-(a + b)$.

41. (a)   True   (b)   True

     (c)   True   (d)   True

     (e)   False, if x is negative; e.g., let $x = ^-2.$ Then $\left|(^-2)^3\right| = |^-8| = 8 \neq ^-8 = (^-2^3).$

     (f)   True

Problem Set 4-2

1. $(3)(^-1) = ^-1 + ^-1 + ^-1 = ^-3$
     $(2)(^-1) = ^-1 + ^-1 = ^-2$
     $(1)(^-1) = ^-1$
     $(0)(^-1) = 0,$ so continuing the pattern of an answer increasing by 1 each time, we have:
     $(^-1)(^-1) = 1.$

3.   The car goes back 4 twice, leaving it back 8.

     If you are now at 0 moving west at 4 km/h, you will be at 8 km
     west of 0 two hours from now.

     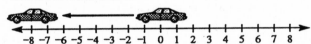

5.   (a)   For any whole numbers a and b, $(^-a)(^-b) = ab.$ Thus $^-3(^-4) = 12.$

     (b)   For any whole numbers a and b, $(^-a)b = b(^-a) = ^-(ab).$ Thus $3(^-5) = ^-15.$

     (c) $(^-5){\cdot}3 = ^-15.$

     (d)   For any number n, $n{\cdot}0 = 0.$ Thus $^-5{\cdot}0 = 0.$

     (e) $^-2(^-3{\cdot}5) = ^-2(^-15) = 30.$

     (f) $[2(^-5)](^-3) = [^-10](^-3) = ^-30.$

     (g) $(^-4 + 4)(^-3) = (0)(^-3) = 0.$

     (h) $(^-5 - ^-3)(^-5 - 3) = (^-5 + 3)(^-5 + ^-3) = (^-2)(^-8) = 16.$

7.   (a) $(^-10 \div ^-2)(^-2) = (5)(^-2) = ^-10.$

     (b) $(^-40 \div 8)8 = (^-5)8 = ^-40.$

     (c)   See (b) above. $(a \div b)b = a$ for any integers a and b $(b \neq 0).$

     (d) $(^-10{\cdot}5) \div 5 = (^-50) \div 5 = ^-10.$

7.   (e)   See (d) above. $(a \cdot b) \div b = a$ for any integrs *a* and *b* (b ≠ 0).

     (f) $(^-8 \div ^-2)(^-8) = (4)(^-8) = ^-32.$

     (g) $(^-6 + ^-14) \div 4 = (^-20) \div 4 = ^-5.$

     (h) $(^-8 + 8) \div 8 = (0) \div 8 = 0.$

     (i) $^-8 \div (^-8 + 8) = ^-8 \div (0) \Rightarrow$ the quotient is undefined.

     (j) $(^-23 - ^-7) \div 4 = (^-23 + 7) \div 4 = (^-16) \div 4 = ^-4.$

     (k) $(^-6 + 6) \div (^-2 + 2) = (0) \div (0) \Rightarrow$ the quotient is undefined.

     (l) $^-13 \div (^-1) = 13$

     (m) $(^-36 \div 12) \div 3 = (^-3) \div 3 = ^-1.$

     (n) $|^-24| \div (3 - 15) = 24 \div (^-12) = ^-2.$

9.   (a) $4(^-11) = ^-44$, or 44 yards lost.

     (b) $^-66 \div 11 = ^-6$, or 66 yards lost over 11 plays means an average of 6 yards lost per play.

11.   The distributive property is that $a(b + c) = ab + ac.$

     (a) $^-1(^-5 + ^-2) = ^-1(^-7) = 7 \Leftrightarrow (^-1)(^-5) + (^-1)(^-2) = 5 + 2 = 7.$

     (b) $^-3(^-3 + 2) = ^-3(^-1) = 3 \Leftrightarrow (^-3)(^-3) + (^-3)(2) = 9 + ^-6 = 3.$

     (c) $^-5(2 + ^-6) = ^-5(^-4) = 20 \Leftrightarrow (^-5)(2) + (^-5)(^-6) = ^-10 + 30 = 20.$

13.   (a) $^-2 + 3 \cdot 5 - 1 = ^-2 + 15 + ^-1 = 13 + ^-1 = 12.$

     (b) $10 - 3 \cdot 7 - 4(^-2) + 3 = 10 - 21 - (^-8) + 3 = 10 + ^-21 + 8 + 3 = ^-11 + 8 + 3 = 0.$

     (c) $10 - 3 - 12 = 10 + ^-3 + ^-12 = 7 + ^-12 = ^-5.$

     (d) $10 - (3 - 12) = 10 - (^-9) = 10 + 9 = 19.$

     (e) $(^-3)^2 = (^-3)(^-3) = 9.$

     (f) $^-3^2 = ^-(3)(3) = ^-9.$

     (g) $^-5^2 + 3(^-2)^2 = ^-(5)(5) + 3(^-2)(^-2) = ^-25 + 3(4) = ^-25 + 12 = ^-13.$

     (h) $^-2^3 = ^-(2)(2)(2) = ^-8.$

     (i) $(^-2)^5 = (^-2)(^-2)(^-2)(^-2)(^-2) = ^-32.$

     (j) $^-2^4 = ^-(2)(2)(2)(2) = ^-16.$

15.   (b) and (c); (d) and (e); (g) and (h).

17.   (a)   Distributive property of multiplication over addition.

17. (b)   Subtraction is the inverse of addition; i.e., $a - b = a +$ ‾b.

    (c)   Commutative property of multiplication.

    (d)   Commutative property of addition.

    (e)   Addition as the inverse of subtraction.

19. Use the definition of division backward for problems (a) to (d); forward on (e) to (h).

    (a)   ‾$3x = 6 \Rightarrow x = 6 \div ($‾$3) = $‾$2$.

    (b)   ‾$3x = $‾$6 \Rightarrow x = $‾$6 \div ($‾$3) = 2$.

    (c)   ‾$2x = 0 \Rightarrow x = 0 \div ($‾$2) = 0$.

    (d) $5x = $‾$30 \Rightarrow x = $‾$30 \div 5 = $‾$6$.

    (e) $x \div 3 = $‾$12 \Rightarrow x = 3 \cdot ($‾$12) = $‾$36$.

    (f) $x \div ($‾$3) = $‾$2 \Rightarrow x = ($‾$3) \cdot ($‾$2) = 6$.

    (g) $x \div ($‾$x) = $‾$1$ if and only if $($‾$1)($‾$x) = x$ and $x \neq 0$ (because division by 0 is undefined). Because the second statement is true for all x such that $x \neq 0$, the original statement is true for all $x \neq 0$.

    (h) $0 \div x = 0 \Rightarrow 0 = (x)(0) = 0$. As in (g), x may represent any number except 0.

    (i)   Since division by 0 is undefined, no value of x will make this true.

    (j) $x^2 = 9 \Rightarrow ($‾$3)^2 = 9$ or $(3)^2 = 9$. x may equal ‾3 or 3.

    (k)   Any number to the second power will give a positive result. No value of x will then yield ‾9.

    (l)   This is similar to (g). Again, x may be any number except 0.

    (m) x^2 is always positive, so ‾x^2 is always negative ($x \neq 0$, since 0 is neither positive nor negative). Another way of stating this result is that x may be any non-zero number.

    (n)   All numbers, by the distributive property; i.e., ‾$(1 - x) = $‾$1 - $‾$x = $‾$1 + x = x - 1$.

    (o)   All integers. $x - 3x = x + $‾$3x = $‾$2x$.

21. The difference-of-squares formula is: $(a + b)(a - b) = a^2 - b^2$.

    (a) $(50 + 2)(50 - 2) = 50^2 - 2^2 = 2500 - 4 = 2496$.

    (b) $(5 - 100)(5 + 100) = 5^2 - 100^2 = 25 - 10{,}000 = $‾$9975$.

    (c) $($‾$x - y)($‾$x + y) = ($‾$x)^2 - y^2 = x^2 - y^2$.

    (d) $(2 + 3x)(2 - 3x) = 2^2 - (3x)^2 = 4 - 9x^2$.

    (e) $(x - 1)(1 + x) = (x - 1)(x + 1) = x^2 - 1^2 = x^2 - 1$.

    (f) $213^2 - 13^2 = (213 + 13)(213 - 13) = (226)(200) = 45{,}200$.

23. (a) $3x + 5x = (3)x + (5)x = x(3 + 5) = 8x.$

(b) $ax + 2x = x(a + 2).$

(c) $xy + x = (y)x + (1)x = x(y + 1).$

(d) $ax - 2x = (a)x - (2)x = x(a - 2).$

(e) $x^2 + xy = (x)x + (y)x = x(x + y).$

(f) $3x - 4x + 7x = (3 - 4 + 7)x = 6x.$

(g) $3xy + 2x - xz = (3y)x + (2)x - (z)x = x(3y + 2 - z).$

(h) $3x^2 + xy - x = (3x)x + (y)x - (1)x = x(3x + y - 1).$

(i) $abc + ab - a = (bc)a + (b)a - (1)a = a(bc + b - 1) = a[b(c + 1) - 1].$

(j) $(a + b)(c + 1) - (a + b) = (a + b)[(c + 1) - 1] = (a + b)[c] = c(a + b).$

(k) $16 - a^2 = 4^2 - a^2 = (4 + a)(4 - a).$

(l) $x^2 - 9y^2 = x^2 - (3y)^2 = (x + 3y)(x - 3y).$

(m) $4x^2 - 25y^2 = (2x)^2 - (5y)^2 = (2x + 5y)(2x - 5y).$

(n) $(x^2 - y^2) + x + y = (x + y)(x - y) + (x + y) = (x + y)[(x - y) + 1] = (x + y)(x - y + 1).$

25. The argument is correct. $a^2 + 2a(^-b) + (^-b)^2 = a^2 + (^-2ab) + (^-b)^2 = a^2 - 2ab + (^-b)^2 = a^2 - 2ab + b^2.$

27. (a)   The sums are always 9 times the middle number.

(b)   The dates in rows 1 and 3 are 7 less than and 7 more than, respectively, their counterparts in row 2. The dates in rows 1 and 2 will then average to the values in row 2. Similarly, the values in columns 1 and 3 average to the values in column 2. Averaging in both directions forces the average to be the middle number. Thus, 9 numbers with an average equal to the middle number m will have a sum of $9 m$.

29. Use the expression for sums of arithmetic sequences with n terms, first term a_1, and nth term a_n: $\frac{n}{2}(a_1 + a_n)$

(a) $a_n = 3n - 13 \Rightarrow a_{100} = 3(100) - 13 = 287.$
The sum is $\frac{100}{2}(^-10 + 287) = 50(277) = 13{,}850.$

(b)   Since all corresponding terms are the additive inverses of the terms in (a), the sum will be the additive inverse of the sum in (a); i.e., $^-13{,}850.$

31. To solve, we must find the common difference and then work back from $^-8$. Treat $^-8$ as a "first" term, which makes $^-493$ the "98th" term. Using the expression for the nth term $[= a + (n - 1)d]$ gives: $^-493 = ^-8 + (98 - 1)d$, so $^-493 = 97d$ and $d = ^-5$. To obtain a succeeding term, then, we would add $^-5$; and to obtain a preceding term we would subtract $^-5$, or, equivalently, add $^+5$. Thus if $^-8$ is the 3rd term, $^-8 + 5 = ^-3$ is the 2nd term, and $^-3 + 5 = 2$ is the 1st term.

33. The argument is valid, but lacks proof that $(^-1)a + a = 0$. $(^-1)a + 1 \cdot a = (^-1 + 1)a = 0 \cdot a = 0$, which implies that $(^-1)a$ is the additive inverse of a. Thus $(^-1)a = ^-a$, so $(^-1)ab = ^-(ab).$

35. (a)   Enter $\boxed{2}\boxed{7}\boxed{+/-}\boxed{\times}\boxed{3}\boxed{=}$ to obtain $^-81.$

Problem Set 4-2

35. (b)   Enter $\boxed{4}\boxed{6}\boxed{+/-}\boxed{\times}\boxed{4}\boxed{+/-}\boxed{=}$ to obtain 184.

    (c)   Enter $\boxed{2}\boxed{6}\boxed{+/-}\boxed{\div}\boxed{1}\boxed{3}\boxed{=}$ to obtain ¯2.

    (d)   Enter $\boxed{2}\boxed{6}\boxed{+/-}\boxed{\div}\boxed{1}\boxed{3}\boxed{+/-}\boxed{=}$ to obtain 2.

37.   Go back 8, then back 5 more, for a total of 13 back, or ¯13.

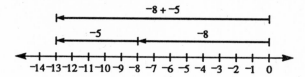

39. (a)   14   (b) $|{}^{-}14| + 7 = 14 + 7 = 21$

    (c) $8 - |{}^{-}12| = 8 - 12 = 8 + {}^{-}12 = {}^{-}4$ (d) $|11| + |{}^{-}11| = 11 + 11 = 22$

Problem Set 4-3

1. (a)   ¯20, ¯13, ¯5, ¯3, 0, 4   (b)   ¯6, ¯5, 0 5, 6

    (c)   ¯100, ¯20, ¯15, ¯13, 0   (d)   ¯3, ¯2, 5, 13

3. (a) $x + 3 = {}^{-}15 \Rightarrow x + 3 - 3 = {}^{-}15 - 3 \Rightarrow x = {}^{-}15 + {}^{-}3 \Rightarrow x = {}^{-}18.$

    (b) $x + 3 > {}^{-}15 \Rightarrow x + 3 - 3 > {}^{-}15 - 3 \Rightarrow x > {}^{-}15 + {}^{-}3 \Rightarrow x > {}^{-}18$ and x is an integer.

    (c) $3 - x = {}^{-}15 \Rightarrow 3 - 3 - x = {}^{-}15 - 3 \Rightarrow {}^{-}x = {}^{-}18 \Rightarrow x = 18.$

    (d) ${}^{-}x + 3 > {}^{-}15 \Rightarrow {}^{-}x + 3 - 3 > {}^{-}15 - 3 \Rightarrow {}^{-}x > {}^{-}18 \Rightarrow x < 18$ and x is an integer. (Remember that when both sides of an inequality are multiplied by a negative integer, the direction of inequality is reversed.)

    (e) ${}^{-}x - 3 = 15 \Rightarrow {}^{-}x - 3 + 3 = 15 + 3 \Rightarrow {}^{-}x = 18 \Rightarrow x = {}^{-}18.$

    (f) ${}^{-}x - 3 \geq 15 \Rightarrow {}^{-}x - 3 + 3 \geq 15 + 3 \Rightarrow {}^{-}x \geq 18 \Rightarrow x \leq {}^{-}18$ and x is an integer.

    (g) $3x + 5 = {}^{-}16 \Rightarrow 3x + 5 - 5 = {}^{-}16 - 5 \Rightarrow 3x = {}^{-}21 \Rightarrow \frac{3}{3}x = \frac{{}^{-}21}{3} \Rightarrow x = {}^{-}7.$

    (h) $3x + 5 < {}^{-}16 \Rightarrow 3x + 5 - 5 < {}^{-}16 - 5 \Rightarrow 3x < {}^{-}21 \Rightarrow \frac{3}{3}x < \frac{{}^{-}21}{3} \Rightarrow x < {}^{-}7$ and x is an integer.

    (i) ${}^{-}3x + 5 = 11 \Rightarrow {}^{-}3x = 6 \Rightarrow x = {}^{-}2.$

    (j) ${}^{-}3x + 5 \leq 11 \Rightarrow {}^{-}3x \leq 6 \Rightarrow x \geq {}^{-}2$ and x is an integer.

    (k) $5x - 3 = 7x - 1 \Rightarrow 5x - 7x - 3 = 7x - 7x - 1 \Rightarrow {}^{-}2x - 3 = {}^{-}1 \Rightarrow {}^{-}2x - 3 + 3 = {}^{-}1 + 3 \Rightarrow {}^{-}2x = 2 \Rightarrow x = {}^{-}1.$

    (l) $5x - 3 > 7x - 1 \Rightarrow {}^{-}2x > 2 \Rightarrow x < {}^{-}1$ and x is an integer.

    (m) $3(x + 5) = {}^{-}4(x + 5) + 21 \Rightarrow 3x + 15 = {}^{-}4x + {}^{-}20 + 21 \Rightarrow 3x + 15 = {}^{-}4x + 1 \Rightarrow 7x = {}^{-}14 \Rightarrow x = {}^{-}2.$

    (n) ${}^{-}5(x + 3) > 0 \Rightarrow {}^{-}5x + {}^{-}15 > 0 \Rightarrow {}^{-}5x > 15 \Rightarrow x < {}^{-}3$ and x is an integer.

5.   (a) $\{1, \bar{2}, 0\}$
     (*i*)   Let x = 1 $\Rightarrow$ Does $(1)^3 + (1)^2 = 2(1)$? $\Rightarrow$ $1 + 1 = 2$ $\Rightarrow$ True.
     (*ii*)   Let x = $\bar{1}$ $\Rightarrow$ Does $(\bar{1})^3 + (\bar{1})^2 = 2(\bar{1})$? $\Rightarrow$ $\bar{1} + 1 \neq \bar{2}$ $\Rightarrow$ False.
     (*iii*) Let x = $\bar{2}$ $\Rightarrow$ Does $(\bar{2})^3 + (\bar{2})^2 = 2(\bar{2})$? $\Rightarrow$ $\bar{8} + 4 = \bar{4}$ $\Rightarrow$ True.
     (*iv*)   Let x = 0 $\Rightarrow$ Does $(0)^3 + (0)^2 = 2(0)$? $\Rightarrow$ $0 + 0 = 0$ $\Rightarrow$ True.

     (b) $\{9\}$
     (*i*)   Let x = $\bar{9}$ $\Rightarrow$ Does $3(\bar{9}) - 3 = 24$? $\Rightarrow$ $\bar{21} - 3 \neq 24$ $\Rightarrow$ False.
     (*ii*)   Let x = 9 $\Rightarrow$ Does $3(9) - 3 = 24$? $\Rightarrow$ $24 = 24$ $\Rightarrow$ True.

     (c) $\{\bar{6}, \bar{7}\}$
     (*i*)   Let x = 6 $\Rightarrow$ Is $\bar{}(6) \geq 5$? $\Rightarrow$ $\bar{6} \not\geq 5$ $\Rightarrow$ False.
     (*ii*)   Let x = $\bar{6}$ $\Rightarrow$ Is $\bar{}(\bar{6}) \geq 5$? $\Rightarrow$ $6 \geq 5$ $\Rightarrow$ True.
     (*iii*) Let x = 7 $\Rightarrow$ Is $\bar{}(7) \geq 5$? $\Rightarrow$ $\bar{7} \not\geq 5$ $\Rightarrow$ False.
     (*iv*)   Let x = $\bar{7}$ $\Rightarrow$ Is $\bar{}(\bar{7}) \geq 5$? $\Rightarrow$ $7 \geq 5$ $\Rightarrow$ True.

     (d) $\{$All except $\bar{4}, 4\}$
     (*i*)   Let x = $\bar{4}$ $\Rightarrow$ Is $(\bar{4})^2 < 16$? $\Rightarrow$ $16 \not< 16$ $\Rightarrow$ False.
     (*ii*)   Let x = $\bar{3}$ $\Rightarrow$ Is $(\bar{3})^2 < 16$? $\Rightarrow$ $9 < 16$ $\Rightarrow$ True.
     $\vdots$ $\vdots$
     (*viii*) Let x = 3 $\Rightarrow$ Is $(3)^2 < 16$? $\Rightarrow$ $9 < 16$ $\Rightarrow$ True.
     (*ix*)   Let x = 4 $\Rightarrow$ Is $(4)^2 < 16$? $\Rightarrow$ $16 \not< 16$ $\Rightarrow$ False.

7.   (a)   "Difference" means to subtract, so the difference of 6 and another number is n $-$ 6 or 6 $-$ n (the order was not specified).

     (b)   n + 14 or 14 + n. "Sum" means addition; the order makes no difference.

     (c)   4n $-$ 7. Four times n is 4n. "Seven less than" a number means that we subtract 7 from that number.

     (d)   3n + 8. "Eight greater than" implies adding 8; three times n is 3n.

     (e)   n + 10. "Increased by" means to add.

     (f)   4n.

     (g)   13 $-$ n. "Decreased by" means to subtract. Note the order $-$ thirteen decreased by the number means that we subtract the number from 13, while n $-$ 13 would be "the number decreased by 13."

     (h)   n $-$ 4. "Less four" indicates subtracting 4 from the number.

9.   The following relationships are stated: (*i*) A = 2N + 982,800; (*ii*) N = S + 1,186,000 $\Rightarrow$ S = N $-$ 1,186,000; (*iii*) N = E + 4,383,000 $\Rightarrow$ E = N $-$ 4,383,000. Now, N is common to all the relationships. Thus: A + N + S + E = 35,692,000
     (2N + 982,000) + N + (N $-$ 1,186,000) + (N $-$ 4,383,000) = 35,692,000
     (2N + N + N + N) + (982,000 $-$ 1,186,000 $-$ 4,483,000) = 35,692,000
     5N $-$ 4,587,000 = 35,692,000
     5N = 40,279,000 $\Rightarrow$ N = 8,055,800 square miles, and:
     A = 2(8,055,800) + 982,000 = 17,093,600 square miles;
     S = 8,055,800 $-$ 1,186,000 = 6,869,800 square miles;
     E = 8,055,800 $-$ 4,383,000 = 3,672,800 square miles.

11. Translating: $\bar{6}$n + 20 = 50 $\Rightarrow$ $\bar{6}$n = 30 $\Rightarrow$ n = $\bar{5}$.

13. Assume that B is between A and C. Then if we let *d* be the distance from A to B, 2d is the distance from A to C (from the given relationship). B to C is 5 inches, so $AB + BC = AC \Rightarrow d + 5 = 2d \Rightarrow d = 5$ (i.e., AB = 5), so AC = 5 + 5 = 10 inches. If A is between B and C, then $d + 2d = 5 \Rightarrow d = \frac{5}{3}$ and $AC = 3\frac{1}{3}$ inches.

15. Let x = the number of pounds of 60¢ tea; then 100 − x = the number of pounds of 45¢ tea. The value of the tea is the price per pound times the number of pounds, and adding the values of the two teas gives the value of the blend:

$$60x + 45(100 - x) = 51(100)$$
$$60x + 4500 - 45x = 5100 \Rightarrow 15x = 600, \text{ and } x = 40.$$

Thus there are 40 pounds of 60¢ tea and (100 − 40) = 60 pounds of 45¢ tea in the 100-pound blend.

17. The three consecutive integers may be represented by n, n + 1, and n + 2. Then:
$$n + (n + 1) + (n + 2) = 237$$
$$3n + 3 = 237 \Rightarrow 3n = 234 \Rightarrow n = 78.$$
The three integers are thus 78, 78 + 1, and 78 + 2, or 78, 79, and 80.

19. If the two integers are represented by x and y: x + y = 21 and x = 2y. The first equation may be rewritten as: y = 21 − x, so, substituting, x = 2y = 2(21 − x). Solving:
$$x = 42 - 2x \Rightarrow 3x = 42 \Rightarrow x = 14.$$
The two integers are thus 14 and 21 − 14 = 7.

21. Three consecutive even integers may be represented by n, n + 2, and n + 4. Then:
$$7n = 5(n + 4)$$
$$7n = 5n + 20 \Rightarrow 2n = 20 \Rightarrow n = 10. \text{ The three integers are thus 10, 12, and 14.}$$

23. Ron will overtake Pete when they are the same distance from Albuquerque. First, find how many hours this will take by equating distances (i.e., rates·times). Let P be Pete's time from Albuquerque; then P − 2 will be Ron's time (because he leaves two hours later). Thus, equating:
$$40P = 45(P - 2)$$
$$40P = 45P - 90 \Rightarrow P = 18 \text{ hours from Albuquerque (Ron will have ridden } 18 - 2 = 16 \text{ hours).}$$
The distance from Albuquerque will be 40 kph·18 hours = 720 km.

25. Total travel time is 7 hours (not counting the stay at the Grandparent's). Let the time going to Zenith be z; then the time going back to Aurora = 7 − z. The distance (rate·time) is the same each way, so:
$$16z = 12(7 - z)$$
$$16z = 84 - 12z \Rightarrow z = 3 \text{ hours to ride to Zenith.}$$
The distance is then 16 mph·3 hours = 48 miles.

27. (a)   Yes. $x^2 + y^2 \geq 2xy$ if and only if $x^2 - 2xy + y^2 \geq 0$ if and only if $(x - y)^2 \geq 0$. Any number squared must be nonnegative (i.e., not less than 0); consequently $(x - y)^2 \geq 0$ is true for all x and y, and so is the original statement.

   (b) $x^2 + y^2 = 2xy$ when $x^2 - 2xy + y^2 = 0$, or when $(x - y)^2 = 0$. Only $0^2 = 0$, so x − y must be equal to 0, which occurs when x = y.

29. No. This is false for any negative integer *a* with a greater absolute value than *b*; for example, let a = ⁻5 and b = 3. Then $(^{-}5)^2 > 3^2$.

31. (a)   x + 1 < 3   and   ⁻x + 1 < 5
           x < 2   and   ⁻x < 4
           x < 2   and   x > ⁻4
       For these to be true, values of x must be greater than ⁻4 and less than 2, or {⁻3, ⁻2, ⁻1, 0, 1}.

31. (b) $2x < {}^-6$ or $1 + x < 0$
          $x < {}^-3$ or $x < {}^-1$
          For these to be true for one or both inequalities, x must be less than ${}^-1$, or $\{\ldots, {}^-4, {}^-3, {}^-2\}$.
          (Integers satisfying $x < {}^-3$ are a subset of those satisfying $x < {}^-1$)

33. (a) ${}^-3 + {}^-7 = {}^-10$ (b) ${}^-3 - {}^-7 = {}^-3 + 7 = 4$

    (c) $3 + {}^-7 = {}^-4$ (d) $3 - {}^-7 = 3 + 7 = 10$

    (e) ${}^-3 \cdot 7 = {}^-21$ (f) ${}^-3 \cdot {}^-7 = 21$

    (g) $3 - 7 = 3 + {}^-7 = {}^-4$ (h) ${}^-21 \div 7 = {}^-3$

    (i) ${}^-21 \div {}^-7 = 3$ (j) $7 - 3 - 8 = 7 + {}^-3 + {}^-8 = {}^-4$

    (k) $8 + 2 \cdot 3 - 7 = 8 + 6 + {}^-7 = 7$ (l) ${}^-8 - 7 - 2 \cdot 3 = {}^-8 + {}^-7 + {}^-6 = {}^-21$

    (m) $|{}^-7| \cdot |{}^-3| = 7 \cdot 3 = 21$ (n) $|{}^-7| \cdot |{}^-8| = 7 \cdot 8 = 56$

    (o) $|{}^-7| + 8 = 7 + 8 = 15$

    (p) $|{}^-7| - |{}^-8| = 7 - 8 = 7 + {}^-8 = {}^-1$

CHAPTER 5 - NUMBER THEORY

Problem Set 5-1

1. (a) True. $30 = 5 \cdot 6$.   (b) True. $30 \div 6 = 5$.

   (c) True. $2|30$ and $3|30$, so $6|30$.   (d) True. $30 \div 6 = 5$.

   (e) True. $6 \cdot 5 = 30$.   (f) False. No integer times 30 equals 6.

3. Yes. The question is really, "Does $9|1379$?" Using the divisibility test for 9, $9\nmid(1+3+7+9)$, so $9\nmid1379$. Thus there will be a remainder; i.e., a group of less than 9 players.

5. (a) Theorem 5-1 with $k = 113$.

   (b) Theorem 5-2(b) with $a = 100$ and $b = 13$.

   (c) None. In fact, $4|1300$.

   (d) Theorem 5-2(b), if $(a + b)$ is thought of as a single integer.

   (e) Theorem 5-1 with $k = a$.

7. (a) 1, 2, 4, 5, 8, 11.

   (b) 1 touchdown and 11 field goals or 4 touchdowns and 4 field goals. (Consider 0 touchdowns - $3\nmid40$, impossible; 2 touchdowns - $3\nmid(40 - 14)$, impossible; etc.)

   (c) An impossible score if an extra point was scored with each touchdown. If not, then there were 5 field goals.

9. (a) (*i*) 4   (*ii*) 4   (*iii*) 4

   (b) (*i*) 8   (*ii*) 8   (*iii*) 8

   (c) (*i*) 3   (*ii*) 12   (*iii*) 3

   (d) (*i*) 8   (*ii*) 26   (*iii*) 8

   (e) (*i*) 2   (*ii*) 20   (*iii*) 2

   (f) The remainder in the quotient of a given number divided by 9 is the same as the remainder when the sum of the number's digits is divided by 9.

11. (a) False. Consider $d = 7$, $a = 10$, $b = 4$; $7|(10 + 4)$ but $7\nmid10$ and $7\nmid4$.

    (b) False. See above; substitute "or" for "and".

    (c) True .

    (d) False. $4|60$ but $4\nmid6$ and $4\nmid10$.

    (e) True.   (f) True.

    (g) True.

    (h) False. If $a = 5$ and $b = {}^{-}5$, then $a|b$ and $b|a$ but $a \neq b$.

11. (i)   True.   (j)   False. $3\not|5$ and $3\not|7$ but $3|(5 + 7)$.

     (k)   False. $4|10^2$ but $4\not|10$.

     (l)   False. $4\not|6$ but $4|6^2$.   (m)   True.

13. (a)   Always.   (b)   Sometimes. E.g., 360.

     (c)   Never   (d)   Always.

     (e)   Always.   (f)   Sometimes. E.g., 24.

     (g)   Always.

15. Yes; equal \$651 installments. The real question is, "Does $12|7812$?"
     Checking: $4|7812$ (since $4|12$)
                    $3|7812$ [since $3|(7+8+1+2)$]
     So $12|7812$ (this is true only because 4 and 3 have no factors in common).

17. 85,041. The number must be divisible by 9 and 11. If we write it as 85ab1, then $9|(8+5+a+b+1)$ and
     $11|[(8+a+1) - (5+b)]$, or $9|(14+a+b)$ and $11|(4+a-b)$. So $a + b = 4$ or 13 and $a - b = {}^-4$ or 7.

     Solving, and using trial and error, we find 0 and 4 to be the solutions.

19. (a)   No. If $5\not|n$, then n cannot end in 0, so $10\not|n$.

     (b)   Yes. Any number ending in 5 is divisible by 5, but not by 10.

21. The sum of the digits will be of the form $k + k + k + m + m + m + q + q + q = 3k + 3m + 3q$
     $= 3(k + m + q)$, which is divisible by 3.

23. (a)   Yes. $4|76$.   (b)   No. $4\not|86$

     (c)   Yes. $4|100$ and $400|2000$.   (d)   Yes. $4|24$.

25. (a)   The two numbers with reversed digits will differ by 9.

     (b)   The numbers will always differ by 18.

     (c)   Any two-digit number's value may be represented as $10t + u$ (10 times the tens digit plus the units
            digit). With digits reversed, the value becomes $10u + t$. Taking the difference gives
            $10t + u - (10u + t) = 9t - 9u = 9(t - u)$, a multiple of 9.

     (d)   The difference of the two numbers is 9 times the difference of their tens digits.

27. For an equation of the form $ax + by = c$ to have integer solutions, the greatest number which divides a and
     b must divide c.

     (a)   No solutions. The greatest number to divide both 18 and 27 is 9, and $9\not|3111$.

     (b)   No solutions.   (c)   No solutions.

     (d)   Infinite number of solutions.   (e)   No solutions.

     (f)   Infinite number of solutions.

29. Prove: If d|a and d∤ab, then d∤(a + b).

d|a implies a = md; d∤b implies b = nd + r, 0 < r < d. Then a + b = md + nd + r = (m + n)d + r; so (a + b)÷d = [(m + n)d + r]÷d = m + n + $\frac{r}{d}$. Since 0 < r < d, $\frac{r}{d}$ is not an integer ⇒ m + n + $\frac{r}{d}$ is not an integer ⇒ d∤(a + b).

31. Note that 7·11·13 = 1001. Multiplying any three-digit number by 1001 gives a product with that three-digit number repeated twice. Going the other way, if any "repeated" number of the form *abcabc* is divided by 1001, the quotient is *abc*.

Problem Set 5-2

1. (a)

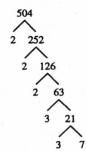

$$504 = 2^3 \cdot 3^2 \cdot 7$$

(b)

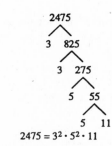

$$2475 = 3^2 \cdot 5^2 \cdot 11$$

(c)

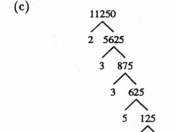

$$11250 = 2 \cdot 3^2 \cdot 5^4$$

3. 73. $73^2 < 5669$, but $79^2 > 5669$. (73 is prime and 79 is the next largest prime.)

5. Use the following procedure:
   (*i*) Write the natural numbers from 1 to 200.
   (*ii*) Circle 2 because 2 is prime.
   (*iii*) Cross out multiples of 2; they are not prime.
   (*iv*) Circle 3 because 3 is prime.
   (*v*) Cross out multiples of 3 that have not already been crossed out.
   (*vi*) Circle 5, 7, 11, and 13; cross out their multiples that have not already been crossed out. (We can stop after 13 because 13 is the largest prime whose square is less than 200.)
   (*vii*) All the numbers remaining in the list and not crossed out are prime. You should end with the following:
   2, 3, 5, 7, 11, 13, 17, 19, 23, 29, 31, 37, 41, 43, 47, 53, 59, 61, 67, 71, 73, 79, 83, 89, 97, 101, 103, 107, 109, 113, 127, 131, 137, 139, 149, 151, 157, 163, 167, 173, 179, 181, 191, 193, 197, 199.

7. (a) All pairs of factors of 48 would be possible arrays: 1 × 48, 2 × 24, 3 × 16, or 4 × 12.

   (b) Since 47 is prime, the only possibility would be 1 × 47.

9. (a) Find the prime factorization of 435: $3 \cdot 5 \cdot 29$. Committees can have these numbers of members or products thereof. Thus the possibilities are 3, 5, 15, or 29 members.

(b) 145 three-member committees ($435 \div 3$)
87 five-member committees
29 fifteen-member committees
15 twenty nine-member committees.

11. 64. Take the smallest prime (2) to one less than the desired number of factors; i.e., $2^6 = 64$. The seven factors are 2^0, 2^1, 2^2, 2^3, 2^4, 2^5, and 2^6 (1, 2, 4, 8, 16, 32, and 64).

13. (a) Any natural number that is a multiple of 41 (41, 82, 123, ...) will yield a composite number divisible by 41 when substituted into $n^2 - n + 41$. One such number is 6683, where n = 82.

(b) Consider a natural number that is a multiple of 41; e.g., 41k. Substituting gives $(41k)^2 - (41k) + 41 = 41(41k^2 - k + 1)$. For each natural number k (an infinite set), there exists such a number divisible by 41.

15. No. Since all pairs of consecutive integers contains one even number, which is divisible by 2 thus making it composite, 2 is the only even prime.

17. (a) 6 can be written as a product of primes in only one way; i.e., $2 \cdot 3$. Since $2|n$ and $3|n$ and both are prime, they must be included in the unique factorization. Thus $(2 \cdot 3)(p_1 \cdot p_2 \cdot \cdots \cdot p_m) = n$, and $6|n$.

(b) $a|n$ implies $n = ra$. $b|n$ implies $n = sb$. Then $n^2 = (ra)(sb) = (rs)(ab) \Rightarrow ab|(rs)(ab)$ so $ab|n^2$.

19. Every number would have its "usual" factorization $1 \cdot (p_1 \cdot p_2 \cdot \cdots \cdot p_n)$, along with infinitely many other such factorizations because $1^n = 1$; *n* may be any natural number.

21. No. 5^2 has no factors of either 2 or 3.

23. (a) 49, 121, and 169. They are the squares of numbers in the 2 column.

(b) 81, 625, and 2401. They are the 4th powers of numbers in the 2 column.

(c) 38, 39, and 46. Numbers in the 4 column (i.e., numbers with four divisors including 1 and themselves) can be either the cubes of numbers in the 2 column (e.g., divisors of 8 are 2^0, 2^1, 2^2, or 2^3) or products of two primes from the 2 column (e.g., 38 has divisors 1, 2, 19, and 38).

25. 9409. Any number with an odd number of factors must be a perfect square. For exactly three factors, the factors must be of the form 1, p, p^2, where p is a prime. Find the largest two-digit prime and square it; i.e., $97^2 = 9409$.

27. In any set of three consecutive integers, exactly one is divisible by (i.e., has a factor of) 3 and either one or two are divisible by 2 (even). The product of these numbers will then contain 2 and 3 as factors, making it divisible by 6.

29. Any number with 3, 6, 9, ... 1's will be divisible by 3 and thus will be composite.

31. Using n = 1, 2, ... , 15 gives primes; 16 and 17 yield composite numbers.

33. (a) Divisors are 2, 3, 6.   (b) Divisors are 2, 3, 5, 6, 9, 10.

35. Only among eight people; each would get $422. $8|3376$ but $7 \nmid 3376$.

1. (a) (i) $D_{18} = \{1, 2, 3, 6, 9, 18\}$ and $D_{10} = \{1, 2, 5, 10\}$.
             Thus GCD(18, 10) = 2.

         (ii) $M_{18} = \{18, 36, 54, 72, 90, \dots\}$ and $M_{10} = \{10, 20, 30, \dots, 90, \dots\}$.
              Thus LCM(18, 10) = 90.

    (b) (i) $D_{24} = \{1, 2, 4, 6, 8, 12, 24\}$ and $D_{36} = \{1, 2, 3, 4, 6, 9, 12, 18, 36\}$.
             Thus GCD(24, 36) = 12.

         (ii) $M_{24} = \{24, 48, 72, 96, \dots\}$ and $M_{36} = \{36, 72, 108, \dots\}$
              Thus LCM(24, 36) = 72.

    (c) (i) $D_8 = \{1, 2, 4, 8\}$, $D_{24} = \{1, 2, 3, 4, 6, 8, 12, 24\}$, and $D_{52} = \{1, 2, 4, 13, 26, 52\}$
             Thus GCD(8, 24, 52) = 4.

         (ii) $M_8 = \{8, 16, 24, \dots, 312, \dots\}$, $M_{24} = \{24, 48, 72, \dots, 312, \dots\}$,
              and $M_{52} = \{52, 104, 156, \dots, 312, \dots\}$.
              Thus LCM(8, 24, 52) = 312.

3. (a) GCD(2904, 220) = GCD(220,64) because $2924 \div 220 \to$ R64
                        = GCD(64, 28) because $220 \div 64 \to$ R28
                        = GCD(28,8) because $64 \div 28 \to$ R8
                        = GCD(8,4) because $28 \div 8 \to$ R4
                        = GCD(4,0) because $8 \div 4 \to 0$
                        = 4

    (b) GCD(14595, 10856) = GCD(10856, 3739) because $14595 \div 10856 \to$ R3739
                          = GCD(3739, 3378) because $10856 \div 3739 \to$ R3378
                          = GCD(3378, 361) because $3739 \div 3378 \to$ R361
                          = GCD(361, 129) because $3378 \div 361 \to$ R129
                          = GCD(129, 103) because $361 \div 129 \to$ R103
                          = GCD(103, 26) because $129 \div 103 \to$ R26
                          = GCD(26, 25) because $103 \div 26 \to$ R25
                          = GCD(25, 1) because $26 \div 25 \to$ R1
                          = GCD(1, 0) because $25 \div 1 \to$ R0
                          = 1

    (c) GCD(123152, 122368) = GCD(122368, 784) because $123152 \div 122368 \to$ R784
                           = GCD(784, 64) because $122368 \div 784 \to$ R64
                           = GCD(64, 16) because $784 \div 64 \to$ R16
                           = GCD(16, 0) because $64 \div 16 \to$ R0
                           = 16

5. (a) GCD(2924, 220)·LCM(2924, 220) = 2924·220
         4·LCM(2924, 220) = 643,280
         LCM(2924, 220) = $643,280 \div 4 = 160,820$

    (b) GCD(14595, 10856)·LCM(14595, 10856) = 14595·10856
         1·LCM(14595, 10856) = 158,443,320
         LCM(14595, 10856) = 158,443,320

    (c) GCD(123152, 122368)·LCM(123152, 122368) = 123,152·122,368
         16·LCM(123152, 122368) = 123,152·122,368
         LCM(123152, 122368) = $123,152 \cdot 122,368 \div 16 = 941,866,496$

7. (a)   The real question is "What is LCM(15, 40, 60)?", since this is when the alarms will coincide. LCM(15, 40, 60) = 120, or 120 minutes = 2 hours later, at 8:00 AM.

    (b)   No. This would be equivalent to changing locations of clocks A and B in the room.

9. (a) $60. The smallest number divisible by 1 through 6 is needed; i.e., LCM(1, 2, 3, 4, 5, 6) = 60.

    (b) $60 \div 5 = \$12$.

    (c)   If winners can make change among themselves, 30 bills are needed. If payouts must come exactly from the chest, 60 bills ($120) must be in the chest, since four winners of a total of $60 would get $15 each - not payable in $2 bills.

11. 24 nights. The question is really "What is the LCM(8, 6)?" LCM(8, 6) = $2^3 \cdot 3$ = 24.

13. 2:30 A.M. LCM(90, 75) = 450 minutes = $7\frac{1}{2}$ hours. $7\frac{1}{2}$ hours later than 7:00 P.M. is 2:30 A.M.

15. (a)   LCM(a, b) = ab, since *a* and *b* have no common factors.

    (b)   GCD(a, a) = a and LCM(a, a) = a. *a* has all factors in common with *a*.

    (c)   GCD(a^2, a) = a and LCM(a^2, a) = a^2.

    (d)   GCD(a, b) = a and LCM(a, b) = b.

    (e)   GCD(a, b) = 1 and LCM(a, b) = ab since *a* and *b* have no factors in common.

    (f)   a|b. If GCD(a, b) = a, then *a* must divide both *a* and *b*.

    (g)   b|a. If LCM(a, b) = a, then b·n = a (where *n* can be any integer). Thus $a \div b$ = n, or b|a.

17. GCD(120, 75) = GCD(75, 45) = GCD(45, 30) = GCD(30, 15) = GCD(15, 0), so GCD(120, 75) = 15.
    Now GCD(105, 15) = GCD(15, 0), so GCD(105, 15) = 15.
    Thus GCD(120, 75, 105) = 15.

19. (a)   2 is the only prime factor of 4, and 2∤97,219,988,751.

    (b)   11 is its own only prime factor and 11∤181,345,913 since 11∤(1+1+4+9+3) − (8+3+5+1).

    (c)   3 and 11 are the only prime factors of 33; 11 was ruled out in (b) and 3∤181,345,913 since 3∤(1+8+1+3+4+5+9+1+3).

21. (a)   28. (1 + 2 + 4 + 7 + 14 = 28)

    (b)   Proper divisors of 220 are 1, 2, 4, 5, 10, 11, 20, 22, 44, 55, and 110. Their sum is 284.
           Proper divisors of 284 are 1, 2, 4, 71, and 142. Their sum is 220.

23. Let x = 64 and y = 15,625. 1,000,000 = 10^6 = $2^6 \cdot 5^6$; if a 2 is paired with a 5 in any factor a 0 results. The only way to keep them separate, and thus have no 0's, is to let x = 2^6 = 64 and let y = 5^6 = 15,625.

25. No. 3|(3+1+1+1) so 3|3111.

27. The question is really "What is LCM(1, 2, ... , 11, 12)?"
    Their factors are 1, 2, 3, 2^2, 5, 2·3, 7, 2^3, 3^2, 2·5, 11, and $2^2 \cdot 3$; thus LCM = $2^3 \cdot 3^2 \cdot 5 \cdot 7 \cdot 11$ = 27,720.

29. The various requirements eliminate numbers one by one:

"between 62 and 72" eliminates 61;

"composite" eliminates 67;

"sum of digits prime" eliminates 63;

"has more than four factors" eliminates 65 (which has <u>exactly</u> four factors);

leaves 70 (which has eight factors - 1, 2, 5, 7, 10, 14, 35, 70).

Problem Set 5-4

1. (a)   3. $(7 + 8 - 12)$ (b)   2. $(4 + 10 - 12)$

(c)   6. $(3 - 9 + 12)$ (d)   8. $(4 - 8 + 12)$

(e)   3. $(3 \cdot 9 - 2 \cdot 12)$ (f)   4. $(4 \cdot 4 - 12)$

(g)   Not possible. $1 \oslash 3 = y$ (where $\oslash$ represents division) implies $1 = 3 \otimes y$. But $3 \otimes n$ is always $\equiv$ either 0, 3, 6, or 9; so $3 \otimes y \neq 1$.

(h)   10. $2 \oslash 5 = y$ implies $2 = 5 \otimes y$. Checking numbers 1, 2, 3, ... , 11, 12 finds $y = 10$.

3. (a)

$\oplus$	1	2	3	4	5	6	7
1	2	3	4	5	6	7	1
2	3	4	5	6	7	1	2
3	4	5	6	7	1	2	3
4	5	6	7	1	2	3	4
5	6	7	1	2	3	4	5
6	7	1	2	3	4	5	6
7	1	2	3	4	5	6	7

(b)   (*i*)   Defining subtraction in terms of addition, $5 \ominus 6 = x$ if $5 = 6 \oplus x$. Thus we can follow down the 6 column to find 5 as the answer. This occurs in row 6, so $5 \ominus 6 = 6$.

(*ii*) $2 \ominus 5 = x$ if $2 = 5 \oplus x$. Follow down the 5 column to 2, which is on row 4. Thus $2 \ominus 5 = 4$.

(c)   See (b)(*i*) above.

5. (a)   (*i*)

$\otimes$	1	2	3
1	1	2	3
2	2	1	3
3	3	3	3

(*ii*)

$\otimes$	1	2	3	4
1	1	2	3	4
2	2	4	2	4
3	3	2	1	4
4	4	4	4	4

(*iii*)

$\otimes$	1	2	3	4	5	6
1	1	2	3	4	5	6
2	2	4	6	2	4	6
3	3	6	3	6	3	6
4	4	2	6	4	2	6
5	5	4	3	2	1	6
6	6	6	6	6	6	6

5. (a) (iv)

⊗	1	2	3	4	5	6	7	8	9	10	11
1	1	2	3	4	5	6	7	8	9	10	11
2	2	4	6	8	10	1	3	5	7	9	11
3	3	6	9	1	4	7	10	2	5	8	11
4	4	8	1	5	9	2	6	10	3	7	11
5	5	10	4	9	3	8	2	7	1	6	11
6	6	1	7	2	8	3	9	4	10	5	11
7	7	3	10	6	2	9	5	1	8	4	11
8	8	5	2	10	7	4	1	9	6	3	11
9	9	7	5	3	1	10	8	6	4	2	11
10	10	9	8	7	6	5	4	3	2	1	11
11	11	11	11	11	11	11	11	11	11	11	11

(b) Division can always be performed by numbers other than the additive identity in the 3 and 11 tables since all numbers occur in each row except the additive identity (i.e., 3 and 11). This is true for all prime number hour clocks.

(c) In those clocks where division cannot always be performed, some rows (and columns) do not contain all numbers (e.g., in the 4-hour clock table in (a), division by 2 is not always possible since 1 and 3 are not in the 2nd row or column. As such, it is not possible to work backwards to find $3 \oslash 2 = x$ (where $\oslash$ represents division) by changing to $3 = 2 \otimes x$.

7. Adding or subtracting multiples of 7 will give dates which fall on the same day of the week.

(a) 2, 9, 16, 30. $(23 - 21, 23 - 14, 23 - 7, 23 + 7)$

(b) 3, 10, 17, 24, 31. (Tuesday the 2nd implies Wednesday the 3rd; then add 7's).

(c) Wednesday. Since next year is a leap year, it has 366 days. Converting to mod 7, $366 \equiv 52 \cdot 7 + 2 \equiv 2 \pmod 7$. Thus September 3 will be 52 weeks and 2 days later.

9. (a) $81 - 1 = 10 \cdot 8$ (a multiple of 8), so $81 \equiv 1 \pmod 8$. Alternatively: $81 = 10 \cdot 8 + 1 = 1 \pmod 8$.

(b) $81 - 1 = 8 \cdot 10$ (a multiple of 10), so $81 \equiv 1 \pmod{10}$.

(c) $1000 - {}^{-}1 = 1001 = 77 \cdot 13$ (a multiple of 13), so $1000 \equiv {}^{-}1 \pmod{13}$.

(d) Just as $10^2 = 99 + 1$, $10^{84} = 9999...99$ (84 nines) $+ 1$. 10^{84} is thus 1 greater than a multiple of 9, so $10^{84} \equiv 1 \pmod 9$.

(e) Looking for a pattern, $10^1 \equiv 10 \pmod{11}$, $10^2 \equiv 1 \pmod{11}$, $10^3 \equiv 10 \pmod{11}$, $10^4 \equiv 1 \pmod{11}$, etc. Odd powers of $10 \equiv 10 \pmod{11}$ and even powers of $10 \equiv 1 \pmod{11}$, so $10^{100} = 1 \pmod{11}$.

(f) $937 - 37 = 900$ (a multiple of 100), so $937 \equiv 37 \pmod{100}$.

11. (a) Since $8|24$, the remainder of $24 \div 8$ is 0. Thus $24 \equiv 0 \pmod 8$.

(b) ${}^{-}90 \equiv 0 \pmod 3$.

(c) $n|n$ so $n \div n \rightarrow$ remainder of 0, or $n \equiv 0 \pmod n$.

13. (a) $5^2 = 100 \equiv 1 \pmod 6$
Then $5^{100} = (5^2)^{50} \equiv (1)^{50} \pmod 6 \equiv 1 \pmod 6$
So 5^{100} has remainder 1 when divided by 6.

13.   (b) $5^2 \div 6 \equiv 1 \pmod 6$. Thus $5^{101} = 5^1 \cdot (5^2)^{50} \equiv 5^1 \cdot (1)^{50} \pmod 6 \equiv 5 \pmod 6$.
               The remainder is 5.

      (c) $10^2 = 100 \equiv 1 \pmod{11}$. Thus $10^{99} = 10 \cdot (10^{98}) = 10 \cdot (10^2)^{49} \equiv 10 \cdot (1)^{49} \pmod{11} \equiv 10 \pmod{11}$.
               So the remainder is 10.

      (d)   Since $10^2 \equiv 1 \pmod{11}$, then $10^{100} = (10^2)^{50} \equiv (1)^{50} \pmod{11} \equiv 1 \pmod{11}$.
               The remainder is 1.

15.   (a) $^-1$. $10^3 = 76 \cdot 13 + 12 \equiv 12 \pmod{13}$. $12 \pmod{13} \equiv {}^-1 \pmod{13}$ since $12 - 13 = {}^-1$.

      (b) $10^{99} = (10^3)^{33} \equiv ({}^-1)^{33} \pmod{13} \equiv {}^-1 \pmod{13} \equiv 12 \pmod{13}$. The remainder is 12.

17.   In particular, this fails when $ac \equiv 0 \pmod m$; e.g., $3 \cdot 4 \pmod{12} \equiv 9 \cdot 4 \pmod{12}$ but $3 \neq 9 \pmod{12}$.

CHAPTER 6 - RATIONAL NUMBERS AS FRACTIONS

<u>Problem Set 6-1</u>

1. (a) The solution to $8x = 7$ is $\frac{7}{8}$.

   (b) Joe ate 7 of the 8 slices of the apple.

   (c) The ratio of boys to girls in this math class is 7 to 8 (also written 7:8).

3. The diagrams illustrate the fundamental law of fractions; i.e., the value of a fraction does not change if its numerator and denominator are multiplied by the same nonzero number.

   (a) Two of the three parts are shaded $\rightarrow$ $\frac{2}{3}$.

   (b) Four of the six parts are shaded $\rightarrow$ $\frac{4}{6} = \frac{2}{3}$.

   (c) Six of the nine parts are shaded $\rightarrow$ $\frac{6}{9} = \frac{2}{3}$.

   (d) Eight of the twelve parts are shaded $\rightarrow$ $\frac{8}{12} = \frac{2}{3}$.

5. (a) $\dfrac{\text{Dots in circle}}{\text{Total dots}} = \dfrac{9}{24} = \dfrac{3}{8}$

   (b) $\dfrac{\text{Dots in rectangle}}{\text{Total dots}} = \dfrac{12}{24} = \dfrac{1}{2}$

   (c) $\dfrac{\text{Dots in intersection}}{\text{Total dots}} = \dfrac{4}{24} = \dfrac{1}{6}$

   (d) $\dfrac{\text{Dots in rectangle} - \text{circle}}{\text{Total dots}} = \dfrac{8}{24} = \dfrac{1}{3}$

7. (a) $\frac{156}{93} = \frac{3 \cdot 52}{3 \cdot 31} = \frac{52}{31}$ (b) $\frac{27}{45} = \frac{9 \cdot 3}{9 \cdot 5} = \frac{3}{5}$

   (c) $\frac{{}^-65}{91} = \frac{{}^-5 \cdot 13}{7 \cdot 13} = \frac{{}^-5}{7}$ (d) $\frac{0}{68} = \frac{0}{1}$

   (e) $\dfrac{84^2}{91^2} = \dfrac{(7 \cdot 12)^2}{(7 \cdot 13)^2} = \dfrac{7^2 \cdot 12^2}{7^2 \cdot 13^2} = \dfrac{12^2}{13^2} = \dfrac{144}{169}$

   (f) $\frac{662}{703}$ is already in its simplest form because there are no factors common to both the numerator and denominator.

9. (a) Undefined. Division by 0 is undefined.

   (b) Undefined. Division by 0 is undefined.

   (c) 0. $\frac{0}{5} = 0$ because $0 \cdot 5 = 0$.

   (d) Cannot be simplified. Since 2 and a have no common factors other than 1, $\frac{2+a}{4}$ cannot be simplified.

   (e) Cannot be simplified. Note that $\frac{15+x}{3x}$ is not the same as $\frac{15 \cdot x}{3x} = \frac{15x}{3x} = 5$.

   (f) $\frac{2}{3}$. $\dfrac{2^6 + 2^5}{2^4 + 2^7} = \dfrac{2^5(2^1 + 1)}{2^4(1 + 2^3)} = \dfrac{2^5(3)}{2^4(9)} = \dfrac{32 \cdot 3}{16 \cdot 9} = \dfrac{2 \cdot 16 \cdot 3}{16 \cdot 3 \cdot 3} = \dfrac{2}{3}$.

   (g) $\frac{5}{3}$. $\dfrac{2^{100} + 2^{98}}{2^{100} - 2^{98}} = \dfrac{2^{98}(2^2 + 1)}{2^{98}(2^2 - 1)} = \dfrac{2^{98} \cdot 5}{2^{98} \cdot 3} = \dfrac{5}{3}$.

11. (a) $\frac{375}{1000} = \frac{125 \cdot 3}{125 \cdot 8} = \frac{3}{8}$. The pairs are equal.

(b) $\frac{18}{54} = \frac{18}{3 \cdot 18} = \frac{1}{3}$. $\frac{23}{69} = \frac{23}{3 \cdot 23} = \frac{1}{3}$. The pairs are equal.

(c) $\frac{600}{1000} = \frac{6 \cdot 100}{10 \cdot 100} = \frac{6}{10}$. The pairs are equal.

(d) $\frac{17}{27}$ is in its simplest form. $\frac{25}{45} = \frac{5 \cdot 5}{5 \cdot 9} = \frac{5}{9}$. The pairs are not equal.

13. Yes. $\frac{3}{8} = \frac{3 \cdot 4}{8 \cdot 4} = \frac{12}{32}$, so the board is thick enough. Shaving off $\frac{1}{32}$ will bring it to the required thickness.

15. To obtain equivalent fractions, multiply numerator and denominator by the same number. All fractions equivalent to $\frac{3}{4}$ will then be of the form $\frac{3x}{4x}$. To satisfy the given requirement, $3x + 4x = 84$, or $x = 12$. The desired fraction is $\frac{3 \cdot 12}{4 \cdot 12} = \frac{36}{48}$.

17. Mr. Gomez had $16 - 6 = 10$ gallons left. $\frac{10}{16} = \frac{5}{8}$ tank remained; the needle points to the 5th division of 8, as shown to the right.

19. The product is smaller than either. A fraction less than one is multiplied by another fraction less than one; i.e., a part of a part is taken.

21. Depending on the application, it may be desireable to leave a fraction unreduced. For example, most will grasp $\frac{65}{100}$ of a dollar (65¢) better than $\frac{13}{20}$ of a dollar.

23. (a) For equal fractions $\frac{a}{b} = \frac{c}{d}$, $ad = bc$. With $\frac{2}{3} = \frac{x}{16}$, $2 \cdot 16 = 3 \cdot x \Rightarrow 32 = 3x \Rightarrow x = \frac{32}{3}$.

(b) $3 \cdot x = 4 \cdot (^-27) \Rightarrow 3x = ^-108 \Rightarrow x = ^-36$.

(c) $3 \cdot x^2 = x \cdot 3x \Rightarrow 3x^2 = 3x^2$. All nonzero rational numbers are solutions.

25. (a) True. Integers may be made rational with a denominator of 1.

(b) True. $I \cup W = I$ is a proper subset of Q because there exist elements of Q that are not in I; e.g., $\frac{1}{2}$.

(c) False. The elements of Q that are not in I are not in W.

(d) False. $Q \cap I = I$.

(e) True. The intersection of rational numbers with whole numbers (i.e., numbers that are common to both sets) is the set of whole numbers, since all whole numbers are rational.

Problem Set 6-2

1. Since the LCD $= 15$, we need increments of $\frac{1}{15}$ on the number line. $\frac{1}{5} = \frac{3}{15}$ and $\frac{2}{3} = \frac{10}{15}$, so we have:

$$\frac{1}{5} + \frac{2}{3} = \frac{13}{15}$$

$$\frac{1}{5} = \frac{3}{15} \qquad \frac{2}{3} = \frac{10}{15}$$

0      $\frac{3}{15}$ $\frac{13}{15}$ 1

3. If $\frac{a}{b}$ and $\frac{c}{d}$ are any two rational numbers, then $\frac{a}{b} + \frac{c}{d} = \frac{ad + bc}{bd}$.

(a) $\frac{6}{5} + \frac{^-11}{4} = \frac{6}{5} - \frac{11}{4} = \frac{6 \cdot 4 - 5 \cdot 11}{5 \cdot 4} = \frac{24 - 55}{20} = \frac{^-31}{20}$

3.   (b) $\frac{4}{5} + \frac{6}{7} = \frac{4\cdot 7 + 5\cdot 6}{5\cdot 7} = \frac{28 + 30}{35} = \frac{58}{35}$

    (c) $\frac{^-7}{8} + \frac{2}{5} = \frac{^-7\cdot 5 + 8\cdot 2}{8\cdot 5} = \frac{^-35 + 16}{40} = \frac{^-19}{40}$

    (d) $\frac{5}{x} + \frac{^-3}{y} = \frac{5\cdot y - x\cdot 3}{x\cdot y} = \frac{5y - 3x}{xy}$

5.   Two methods are shown; either is acceptable.

    (a) $\frac{56}{3} = \frac{3\cdot 18 + 2}{3} = \frac{3\cdot 18}{3} + \frac{2}{3} = 18 + \frac{2}{3} = 18\frac{2}{3}$

    (b) $14 \div 5 = 2$, remainder $4 \Rightarrow 2\frac{4}{5}$

    (c) $-\frac{293}{100} = -\left(\frac{2\cdot 100 + 93}{100}\right) = -2\frac{93}{100}$

    (d) $47 \div 8 = 5$, remainder $7 \Rightarrow -5\frac{7}{8}$

7.   (a) $\frac{5}{6} + 2\frac{1}{8} = \frac{5}{6} + \frac{17}{8} = \frac{5\cdot 8 + 6\cdot 17}{6\cdot 8} = \frac{40 + 102}{48} = \frac{142}{48} = \frac{71}{24} = 2\frac{23}{24}$

    (b) $^-4\frac{1}{2} - 3\frac{1}{6} = ^-4\frac{3}{6} - 3\frac{1}{6} = ^-7\frac{4}{6} = ^-7\frac{2}{3} \left(\text{or } \frac{^-23}{3}\right)$

    (c) $LCD = 2^4\cdot 3^4.$ $\frac{5}{2^4\,3^2} - \frac{1}{2^3\,3^4} = \frac{5\cdot 3^2}{2^4\cdot 3^2\cdot 3^2} - \frac{1\cdot 2}{2^3\cdot 3^4\cdot 2} = \frac{45 - 2}{2^4\cdot 3^4} = \frac{43}{2^4\cdot 3^4}$

    (d) $LCD = 45.$ $11 - \left(\frac{3}{5} + \frac{^-4}{45}\right) = \frac{11\cdot 45}{1\cdot 45} - \frac{3\cdot 9}{5\cdot 9} + \frac{4}{45} = \frac{495 - 27 + 4}{45} = \frac{472}{45} = 10\frac{22}{45}$

9.   (a)   Round 46 to 45 for ease of computation. $\frac{15}{45} = \frac{1}{3}$. This estimate is too high because the denominator is smaller than actual.

    (b)   Change the denominator to 42. $\frac{7}{42} = \frac{1}{6}$. This estimate is too low because the denominator is larger than actual.

    (c)   Round 62 to 60. $\frac{60}{80} = \frac{3}{4}$. This estimate is too low because the numerator is smaller than actual.

    (d)   Round the numerator to 10 and the denominator to 20. $\frac{10}{20} = \frac{1}{2}$. This estimate is too low because the numerator was increased by a greater percentage than the denominator.

11.   (a) $\frac{1}{2}$; too high. $\frac{19}{38} = \frac{1}{2}$ so $\frac{19}{39} < \frac{1}{2}$.   (b)   0; too low.

    (c) $\frac{3}{4}$; too high. $\frac{150}{200} = \frac{3}{4}$ so $\frac{150}{201} < \frac{3}{4}$.   (d)   1; too high.

    (e)   1; too low.   (f)   0; too high. $\frac{^-2}{117} < 0$.

    (g) $\frac{3}{4}$; too low. $\frac{150}{200} = \frac{3}{4}$ so $\frac{150}{198} > \frac{3}{4}$.   (h) $\frac{1}{2}$; too high. $\frac{1000}{2000} = \frac{1}{2}$ so $\frac{999}{2000} < \frac{1}{2}$.

13.   (a) $5 + 2 + 3 = 10$ (b) $3 + 5 + 4\frac{1}{2} - 12\frac{1}{2} = 0$

    (c) $5\frac{1}{2} + 3\frac{1}{2} + 4 = 13$ (d) $149 + 2 = 151$

15.   Possible thought processes could be:

    (a) $\frac{4}{4} - \frac{3}{4} = \frac{1}{4}$ (b) $(5 + 1) - \frac{7}{8} = 5 + \left(\frac{8}{8} - \frac{7}{8}\right) = 5\frac{1}{8}$

    (c) $\left(3 + 2 + \frac{3}{8} + \frac{2}{8}\right) - 5\frac{5}{8} = 5\frac{5}{8} - 5\frac{5}{8} = 0$

    (d) $\left(2 + 4 + 3 + \frac{6}{10} + \frac{1}{10} + \frac{3}{10}\right) = 9 + \frac{10}{10} = 10$

17.   (a) $\frac{d}{b} + \frac{a}{bc} = \frac{d\cdot c}{b\cdot c} + \frac{a}{bc} = \frac{dc + a}{bc}$

17. (b) $\dfrac{a}{a-b} + \dfrac{b}{a+b} = \dfrac{a(a+b)+b(a-b)}{(a-b)(a+b)} = \dfrac{a^2+ab+ab-b^2}{a^2-b^2} = \dfrac{a^2+2ab-b^2}{a^2-b^2}$

   (c) $LCD = (a^2-b^2) = (a+b)(a-b)$.

       $\dfrac{a}{a^2-b^2} - \dfrac{b}{a-b} = \dfrac{a}{a^2-b^2} - \dfrac{b(a+b)}{(a-b)(a+b)} = \dfrac{a-ab-b^2}{a^2-b^2}$

19. The whole student population is represented by 1. We then subtract to obtain the senior's fraction; i.e., seniors make up $1 - \frac{2}{5} - \frac{1}{4} - \frac{1}{10}$ of the class. Using a LCD of 20: $\frac{20}{20} - \frac{8}{20} - \frac{5}{20} - \frac{2}{20} = \frac{5}{20} = \frac{1}{4}$. Thus seniors make up $\frac{1}{4}$ of the class.

21. Using the completed diagonal, all rows, columns, and diagonals must add to $1 + \frac{11}{12} + \frac{5}{6} = \frac{12}{12} + \frac{11}{12} + \frac{10}{12} = \frac{33}{12}$. Then subtracting to obtain the missing values, we have:

5/3	1/12	1
1/4	11/12	19/12
5/6	7/4	1/6

23. It might be easier, but she'd not have a correct solution. Think of the numerator as the number of pieces of pie cut into the denominator's value of slices. Then to add the pieces of pie, we'd add the numerators and have that number of pieces.

25. He should put in $3\frac{1}{2} - \frac{3}{4} - 1 = 3\frac{2}{4} - \frac{3}{4} - \frac{4}{4} = \frac{14}{4} - \frac{3}{4} - \frac{4}{4} = \frac{7}{4}$, or $1\frac{3}{4}$ cups more.

27. The amount of fabric to be used is $1\frac{7}{8} + 2\frac{3}{8} + 1\frac{2}{3} = 1\frac{21}{24} + 2\frac{9}{24} + 1\frac{16}{24} = 4\frac{46}{24} = 5\frac{22}{24}$ yards. She bought $8\frac{3}{4}$ yards, so there will be $8\frac{18}{24} - 5\frac{22}{24} = 7\frac{42}{24} - 5\frac{22}{24} = 2\frac{20}{24} = 2\frac{5}{6}$ yards left over.

29. (a)   Team 4; they collected $35\frac{3}{16} + 41\frac{1}{2} = 76\frac{11}{16}$ pounds.

    (b)   Collections in April were $28\frac{3}{4} + 32\frac{7}{8} + 28\frac{1}{2} + 35\frac{3}{16} = 125\frac{5}{16}$ pounds.

        Collections in May were $33\frac{1}{3} + 28\frac{5}{12} + 25\frac{3}{4} + 41\frac{1}{2} = 129$ pounds.

        The difference is $129 - 125\frac{5}{16} = 3\frac{11}{16}$ pounds.

31. (a)   According to this property, if two rational numbers are added, the sum should also be rational; e.g., $\frac{1}{2} + \frac{3}{4} = \frac{5}{4}$, which is a rational number.

    (b) $\frac{a}{b} + \frac{c}{d}$ should equal $\frac{c}{d} + \frac{a}{b}$; e.g., $\frac{1}{4} + \frac{2}{3} = \frac{11}{12} = \frac{2}{3} + \frac{1}{4}$.

    (c)   The associative property states that $\frac{a}{b} + \left(\frac{c}{d} + \frac{e}{f}\right) = \left(\frac{a}{b} + \frac{c}{d}\right) + \frac{e}{f}$. E.g., $\frac{1}{2} + \left(\frac{2}{3} + \frac{3}{4}\right) = \frac{23}{12} = \left(\frac{1}{2} + \frac{2}{3}\right) + \frac{3}{4}$.

33. (a) $\frac{3}{2}, \frac{7}{4}, 2$. Arithmetic; difference is $\frac{1}{4}$.

    (b) $\frac{6}{7}, \frac{7}{8}, \frac{8}{9}$. Each term is $\frac{n}{n+1}$; it is not arithmetic because there is no constant difference.

    (c) $\frac{17}{3}, \frac{20}{3}, \frac{23}{3}$. Arithmetic; difference is $\frac{3}{3}$.

    (d) $\frac{^-5}{4}, \frac{^-7}{4}, \frac{^-9}{4}$. Arithmetic; difference is $\frac{^-1}{2}$.

35. Use the methodology for arithmetic sequences from Chapter 1 [i.e., $a_n = a_1 + (n-1)d$]. Our sequence is: $1, a_2, a_3, a_4, a_5, a_6, 2$. Thus $a_1 = 1$ and $a_7 = 2$, so $2 = 1 + (7-1)d$. Solving for d, we have $d = \frac{1}{6}$. Then $a_2 = 1 + \frac{1}{6} = \frac{7}{6}$; $a_3 = \frac{7}{6} + \frac{1}{6} = \frac{8}{6}$; etc.

    Our sequence is $1, \frac{7}{6}, \frac{8}{6}, \frac{9}{6}, \frac{10}{6}, 2$.

37. (a) $f(0) = \frac{0+2}{0-1} = \frac{2}{-1} = {}^-2$

   (b) $f({}^-2) = \frac{{}^-2+2}{{}^-2-1} = \frac{0}{-3} = 0$

   (c) $f({}^-5) = \frac{{}^-5+2}{{}^-5-1} = \frac{{}^-3}{{}^-6} = \frac{1}{2}$

   (d) $f(5) = \frac{5+2}{5-1} = \frac{7}{4}$

39. (a) $\frac{14}{21} = \frac{2 \cdot 7}{3 \cdot 7} = \frac{2}{3}$

   (b) $\frac{117}{153} = \frac{3 \cdot 3 \cdot 13}{3 \cdot 3 \cdot 17} = \frac{13}{17}$

   (c) $\frac{5^2}{7^2} = \frac{25}{49}$

   (d) $\frac{a^2 + a}{1 + a} = \frac{a(a + 1)}{a + 1} = \frac{a}{1}$

   (e) $\frac{a^2 + 1}{a + 1}$ is already in simplest form.

Problem Set 6-3

1. (a) The shaded vertical region represents $\frac{1}{3}$ of the total area. The shaded horizontal region represents $\frac{1}{4}$ of the total area. The cross-hatched region represents $\frac{1}{4}$ of $\frac{1}{3}$, or the product of the two fractions. Since one of the twelve blocks is cross-hatched, then, the product of $\frac{1}{4}$ and $\frac{1}{3}$ is $\frac{1}{12}$.

   (b) The shaded vertical region represents $\frac{3}{5}$ of the total area. The shaded horizontal region represents $\frac{2}{4}$ of the total area. The cross-hatched region represents $\frac{2}{4}$ of $\frac{3}{5}$, or the product of the two fractions. Since six of the twenty blocks are cross-hatched, then, the product of $\frac{2}{4}$ and $\frac{3}{5}$ is $\frac{6}{20}$.

3. B. The product of C and D can be neither greater than C or D nor negative.

5. (a) $4\frac{1}{2} \cdot 2\frac{1}{3} = (4 + \frac{1}{2}) \cdot (2 + \frac{1}{3}) = 4(2 + \frac{1}{3}) + \frac{1}{2}(2 + \frac{1}{3}) = 8 + \frac{4}{3} + 1 + \frac{1}{6} = 9 + \frac{8}{6} + \frac{1}{6} = 10\frac{1}{2}$

   (b) $3\frac{1}{3} \cdot 2\frac{1}{2} = (3 + \frac{1}{3}) \cdot (2 + \frac{1}{2}) = 3(2 + \frac{1}{2}) + \frac{1}{3}(2 + \frac{1}{2}) = 6 + \frac{3}{2} + \frac{2}{3} + \frac{1}{6} = 6 + \frac{9}{6} + \frac{4}{6} + \frac{1}{6} = 8\frac{1}{3}$

   (c) $248\frac{2}{5} \cdot 100\frac{1}{8} = 248(100 + \frac{1}{8}) + \frac{2}{5}(100 + \frac{1}{8}) = 24,800 + 31 + 40 + \frac{1}{20} = 24,871\frac{1}{20}$

7. The plumber needs $5 \cdot 2\frac{1}{8} = 10\frac{5}{8}$ feet of pipe. Assuming no waste in cutting, there will be $12 - 10\frac{5}{8} = 1\frac{3}{8}$ feet of pipe left over.

9. (a) 20. $3\frac{11}{12} \cdot 5\frac{3}{100}$ is approximately $4 \cdot 5$.

   (b) 16. $2\frac{1}{10} \cdot 7\frac{7}{8}$ is approximately $2 \cdot 8$.

   (c) 2. $20\frac{2}{3} \div 9\frac{7}{8}$ is approximately $20 \div 10$.

   (d) 1. $\frac{1}{101}$ and $\frac{1}{103}$ are approximately equal.

11. (a) Less than 1. $\frac{13}{14} \cdot \frac{17}{19}$ is the product of two proper fractions, thus each less than 1. Their product is therefore less than 1, or a fraction of a fraction is less than 1.

   (b) Less than 1. $3\frac{2}{7} \div 5\frac{1}{9}$ is a number divided by a larger number, so the quotient would be less than 1.

   (c) Greater than 2. $4\frac{1}{3} \div 2\frac{3}{100}$ is a number larger than 4 divided by a number <u>very</u> slightly more than 2.

   (d) Less than 4. $16 \div 4\frac{3}{18}$ is 16 divided by more than 4.

   (e) Greater than 4. $16 \div 3\frac{8}{9}$ is 16 divided by less than 4.

13. Possible thought processes are described.

   (a) $3 \cdot 8 = 24$, $\frac{1}{4} \cdot 8 = 2$, and $24 + 2 = 26$.

13. (b) $7 \cdot 4 = 28$, $\frac{1}{4} \cdot 4 = 1$, and $28 + 1 = 29$.

(c) $9 \cdot 10 = 90$, $\frac{1}{5} \cdot 10 = 2$, and $90 + 2 = 92$.

(d) $8 \cdot 2 = 16$, $8 \cdot \frac{1}{4} = 2$, and $16 + 2 = 18$.

(e) $3 \div \frac{1}{2} = 3 \cdot \frac{2}{1} = 6$.

(f) $3\frac{1}{2} \div \frac{1}{2} = 3\frac{1}{2} \cdot 2 = 7$.

(g) $3 \div \frac{1}{3} = 3 \cdot 3 = 9$.

(h) $4\frac{1}{2} \div 2 = 4\frac{1}{2} \cdot \frac{1}{2}$. Then $4 \cdot \frac{1}{2} = 2$, $\frac{1}{2} \cdot \frac{1}{2} = \frac{1}{4}$, and $2 + \frac{1}{4} = 2\frac{1}{4}$.

15. (a) Use the multiplicative indenty property:
$\frac{1}{3}x = \frac{7}{8} \Rightarrow \frac{3}{1} \cdot \frac{1}{3}x = \frac{3}{1} \cdot \frac{7}{8} \Rightarrow x = \frac{21}{8}$.

(b) $\frac{1}{5} = \frac{7}{3}x \Rightarrow \frac{3}{7} \cdot \frac{1}{5} = \frac{3}{7} \cdot \frac{7}{3}x \Rightarrow \frac{3}{35} = x$.

(c) $\frac{1}{2}x - 7 = \frac{3}{4}x \Rightarrow \frac{1}{2}x - \frac{1}{2}x - 7 = \frac{3}{4}x - \frac{1}{2}x \Rightarrow {}^{-}7 = \frac{1}{4}x \Rightarrow \frac{4}{1}({}^{-}7) = \frac{4}{1} \cdot \frac{1}{4}x \Rightarrow {}^{-}28 = x$.

(d) $\frac{2}{3}(\frac{1}{2}x - 7) = \frac{3}{4}x \Rightarrow \frac{1}{3}x - \frac{14}{3} = \frac{3}{4}x \Rightarrow \frac{1}{3}x - \frac{1}{3}x - \frac{14}{3} = \frac{3}{4}x - \frac{1}{3}x \Rightarrow \frac{{}^{-}14}{3} = \frac{5}{12}x$

$\Rightarrow \frac{12}{5} \cdot (\frac{{}^{-}14}{3}) = \frac{12}{5} \cdot \frac{5}{12}x \Rightarrow \frac{{}^{-}56}{5} = x$.

(e) $\frac{2}{5} \cdot \frac{3}{6} = x \Rightarrow \frac{1}{5} = x$.

(f) $x \div \frac{3}{4} = \frac{5}{8} \Rightarrow x \cdot \frac{4}{3} = \frac{5}{8} \Rightarrow \frac{3}{4} \cdot \frac{4}{3}x = \frac{3}{4} \cdot \frac{5}{8} \Rightarrow x = \frac{15}{32}$.

(g) $2\frac{1}{3}x + 7 = 3\frac{1}{4} \Rightarrow \frac{7}{3}x + 7 - 7 = \frac{13}{4} - 7 \Rightarrow \frac{7}{3}x = \frac{{}^{-}15}{4} \Rightarrow \frac{3}{7} \cdot \frac{7}{3}x = \frac{3}{7} \cdot (\frac{{}^{-}15}{4}) \Rightarrow x = \frac{{}^{-}45}{28}$.

(h) $\frac{{}^{-}2}{5}(10x + 1) = 1 - x \Rightarrow {}^{-}4x + \frac{{}^{-}2}{5} = 1 - x \Rightarrow {}^{-}4x + x - \frac{2}{5} + \frac{2}{5} = 1 + \frac{2}{5} - x + x$

$\Rightarrow {}^{-}3x = \frac{7}{5} \Rightarrow (\frac{{}^{-}1}{3}) \cdot ({}^{-}3)x = (\frac{{}^{-}1}{3}) \cdot \frac{7}{5} \Rightarrow x = \frac{{}^{-}7}{15}$.

17. If F is the number of faculty members originally, then $F - \frac{1}{5}F = 320 \Rightarrow \frac{4}{5}F = 320 \Rightarrow F = \frac{5}{4} \cdot 320$ $\Rightarrow F = 400$ members originally.

19. (a) If U is the number of uniforms to be made, then (assuming no waste) $U = 29\frac{1}{2} \div \frac{3}{4} \Rightarrow U = \frac{59}{2} \cdot \frac{4}{3}$ $\Rightarrow U = \frac{118}{3} = 39\frac{1}{3}$. Thus 39 uniforms can be made.

(b) Enough material for $\frac{1}{3}$ of a uniform will be left over. Each uniform requires $\frac{3}{4}$ yard of material; there will be $\frac{1}{3} \cdot \frac{3}{4} = \frac{1}{4}$ yard of material remaining.

21. (a) $\frac{1}{2} \div \frac{2}{3} \neq \frac{2}{3} \div \frac{1}{2}$. $\frac{1}{2} \div \frac{2}{3} = \frac{3}{4}$; $\frac{2}{3} \div \frac{1}{2} = \frac{4}{3}$.

(b) $(\frac{1}{2} \div \frac{2}{3}) \div \frac{3}{4} = 1$, but $\frac{1}{2} \div (\frac{2}{3} \div \frac{3}{4}) = \frac{9}{16}$.

(c) The identity property for division would require that for the identity I, $\frac{a}{b} \div I = \frac{a}{b} = I \div \frac{a}{b}$. The left half of this relationship is true, but the right half fails because of non-commutivity.

(d) The inverse of $\frac{a}{b}$ would be the number which would divide $\frac{a}{b}$ to give the identity as a quotient. Since there is no identity, this is impossible.

23. The 6000 students living in dorms are $\frac{5}{8}$ of the student population, P; i.e., $6000 = \frac{5}{8}P$. Then $\frac{8}{5} \cdot 6000 = \frac{8}{5} \cdot \frac{5}{8}P \Rightarrow 9600 = P$.

25. (a) Increasing a salary by $\frac{1}{10}$ means the salary will be $1\frac{1}{10}$, or $\frac{11}{10}$, of its previous value. With two such raises, Martha will make $(100,000\cdot\frac{11}{10})\cdot\frac{11}{10} = \$121,000$.

(b) $99,000 is $\frac{11}{10}$ of what Aaron made last year; i.e., $99,000 = \frac{11}{10}S$ (where S is Aaron's salary one year ago). Then, solving for S, $\frac{10}{11}\cdot99,000 = \frac{10}{11}\cdot\frac{11}{10}S \Rightarrow S = \$90,000$.

(c) Let S be Juanita's salary two years ago. Then $363,000 = \frac{11}{10}(\frac{11}{10}S)$, since two raises brought her to that value. Solving, $\frac{100}{121}\cdot363,000 = \frac{100}{121}\cdot\frac{121}{100}S \Rightarrow S = \$300,000$.

27. Jasmine has read $\frac{3}{4}$ of the book so she has $1 - \frac{3}{4} = \frac{1}{4}$ yet to read; i.e., 82 pages $= \frac{1}{4}$. Then $\frac{3}{4} = 3\cdot82 = 246$ pages read so far.

29. (a) Peter: $\frac{1}{2}\cdot60$ min. $= 30$ min. Paul: $\frac{5}{12}\cdot60$ min. $= 25$ min. Mary: $\frac{1}{3}\cdot60$ min. $= 20$ min.

(b) Each will be back at the starting line in multiples of the time it takes for one lap; i.e., the LCM of 30, 25, and $20 = 300$ minutes, or 5 hours. Thus: Peter, 10 times; Paul, 12 times; Mary, 15 times.

31. (a) $F = \frac{9}{5}\cdot32 + 32 = \frac{288}{5} + \frac{32\cdot5}{5} = \frac{448}{5} = 89\frac{3}{5}°$ F.

(b) $^{-}40 = \frac{9}{5}C + 32 \Rightarrow {^{-}72} = \frac{9}{5}C \Rightarrow \frac{5}{9}(^{-}72) = \frac{5}{9}\cdot\frac{9}{5}C \Rightarrow C = {^{-}40}°$ C. (This is the only temperature where Celsius and Fahrenheit are numerically the same.

33. Al's marbles are halved three times in the process of Dani receiving 4 marbles; i.e., $\frac{1}{2}\cdot\frac{1}{2}\cdot\frac{1}{2}\cdot A = 4$, or $\frac{1}{8}A = 4$. Solving, $A = 32$ marbles (where A is the number of marbles Al had originally).

35. Use commutivity and associativity. $\frac{1}{4}\cdot15\cdot12 = (\frac{1}{4}\cdot12)\cdot15 = 3\cdot15 = 45$.

37. (i) Multiply by $\frac{1}{2}$. $\frac{1}{32}, \frac{1}{64}$. Geometric (common ratio).

(ii) Multiply by $\frac{^{-}1}{2}$. $\frac{^{-}1}{32}, \frac{1}{64}$. Geometric.

(iii) Multiply by $\frac{3}{4}$. $\frac{81}{256}, \frac{243}{1024}$. Geometric.

(iv) $\frac{n}{3^n}$. $\frac{5}{3^5}, \frac{6}{3^6}$. Not geometric (no common ratio).

39. (a) (i) $f(0) = \frac{3\cdot0 + 4}{3\cdot0 - 5} = \frac{^{-}4}{5}$

(ii) $f(\frac{2}{5}) = \frac{3\cdot\frac{2}{5} + 4}{4\cdot\frac{2}{5} - 5} = \frac{\frac{6}{5} + \frac{20}{5}}{\frac{8}{5} - \frac{25}{5}} = \frac{26}{5}\cdot(\frac{^{-}5}{17}) = \frac{^{-}26}{17}$

(iii) $f(\frac{^{-}2}{5}) = \frac{3\cdot\frac{^{-}2}{5} + 4}{2\cdot\frac{^{-}2}{5} - 5} = \frac{\frac{^{-}6}{5} + \frac{20}{5}}{\frac{^{-}8}{5} - \frac{25}{5}} = \frac{14}{5}\cdot(\frac{^{-}5}{33}) = \frac{^{-}14}{33}$

(b) (i) $\frac{3x + 4}{4x - 5} = 0$ only if $3x + 4 = 0 \Rightarrow 3x = {^{-}4} \Rightarrow x = \frac{^{-}4}{3}$

(ii) $\frac{3x + 4}{4x - 5} = \frac{2}{5} \Rightarrow 5(3x + 4) = 2(4x - 5) \Rightarrow 15x + 20 = 8x - 10 \Rightarrow 7x = {^{-}30}$

$\Rightarrow x = \frac{^{-}30}{7}$

(iii) $\frac{3x + 4}{4x - 5} = \frac{^{-}1}{2} \Rightarrow 2(3x + 4) = {^{-}1}(4x - 5) \Rightarrow 6x + 8 = {^{-}4x} + 5 \Rightarrow 10x = {^{-}3}$

$\Rightarrow x = \frac{^{-}3}{10}$

39. **(c)** The value of x that makes the denominator equal 0 is not in the domain. Thus if $4x - 5 = 0$ $\Rightarrow 4x = 5 \Rightarrow x = \frac{5}{4}$ makes the denominator 0, so $\frac{5}{4}$ is not in the domain.

41. This equality has the restriction $b \neq 0$ and is true only if:
(*i*) $c = 0$. Then $\frac{a}{b} = \frac{a+0}{b+0} = \frac{a}{b}$, or (*ii*) $a = b$. Then $\frac{a}{b} = \frac{a}{a} = \frac{a+c}{a+c}$.

43. **(a)** From the general form of an arithmetic sequence: $a_n = a_1 + (n - 1)d$, where a_n is the nth term of the sequence, a_1 is the first term, n is the number of terms, and d is the common difference, we have: $2 = 1 + (100 - 1)d \Rightarrow 1 = 99d \Rightarrow d = \frac{1}{99}$. Then $a_{50} = 1 + (50 - 1)\frac{1}{99} = 1\frac{49}{99}$.

(b) The sum of the first 50 terms is $1 + 1\frac{1}{99} + 1\frac{2}{99} + \cdots + 1\frac{48}{99} + 1\frac{49}{99}$. Rearranging gives: $(1 + 1\frac{49}{99}) + (1\frac{1}{99} + 1\frac{48}{99}) + \cdots + (1\frac{24}{99} + 1\frac{25}{99})$, or 25 pairs, each adding to $2\frac{49}{99}$. The sum is then $25 \cdot 2\frac{49}{99} = 62\frac{37}{99}$.

45. The portion of students that take one of the three foreign languages is $\frac{2}{3} + \frac{1}{9} + \frac{1}{18} = \frac{5}{6}$. The portion of students not taking one of the three is then $1 - \frac{5}{6} = \frac{1}{6}$. That number of students is then $\frac{1}{6} \cdot 720 = 120$ students.

Problem Set 6-4

1. **(a)** $>$. LCD = 24, so $\frac{7}{8} = \frac{21}{24}$ and $\frac{5}{6} = \frac{20}{24}$.

(b) $>$. LCD = 30, so $2\frac{4}{5} = 2\frac{24}{30}$ and $2\frac{3}{6} = 2\frac{15}{30}$.

(c) $<$. LCD = 40, so $\frac{^-7}{8} = \frac{^-35}{40}$ and $\frac{^-4}{5} = \frac{^-24}{40}$. (Note that $^-35 < ^-24$.)

(d) $<$. LCD = 56, so $\frac{1}{^-7} = \frac{^-1}{7} = \frac{^-8}{56}$ and $\frac{1}{^-8} = \frac{^-7}{56}$.

(e) $=$. $\frac{2}{5} = \frac{2 \cdot 2}{2 \cdot 5} = \frac{4}{10}$.

(f) $=$. $\frac{0}{7} = 0 = \frac{0}{17}$.

3. **(a)** $\frac{11}{13}, \frac{11}{16}, \frac{11}{22}$. When fractions have the same numerators, those with larger denominators have lesser value.

(b) $3, \frac{33}{16}, \frac{23}{16}$. $(3 = \frac{48}{16}.)$

(c) $\frac{^-1}{5}, \frac{^-19}{36}, \frac{^-17}{30}$. LCD = 180, so $\frac{^-1}{5} = \frac{^-36}{180}$, $\frac{^-19}{36} = \frac{^-95}{180}$, and $\frac{^-17}{30} = \frac{^-102}{180}$. Then $^-36 > ^-95 > ^-102$.

5. **(a)** No. $\frac{a}{b} > \frac{c}{d}$ if and only if $ad < bc$. To arrive at the second inequality both sides must be multiplied by bd (a negative number), thus reversing the direction of the inequality.

(b) Yes. Multiplying both sides by bd (a positive number) maintains the direction of the inequality.

7. **(a)** Over 7. $\frac{5}{8}$ and $\frac{5}{9}$ are both greater than $\frac{1}{2}$, so their sum is greater than 1. Added to $4 + 2$, the sum is greater than 7.

(b) Under 13. $7\frac{1}{10} + 5\frac{6}{11} < 7\frac{1}{10} + 5\frac{6}{10} = 12\frac{7}{10} < 13$.

(c) Under 1. Any number divided by a larger number results in a quotient of less than 1.

(d) Over 6. $6\frac{1}{10} \div \frac{11}{12} = 6\frac{1}{10} \cdot \frac{12}{11}$; i.e., a product of more than 6 and more than 1.

(e) Over 6. 10 reduced by less than 4 yields more than 6.

9. (a) $19\frac{8}{9} \cdot 9\frac{1}{10} \doteq 20 \cdot 9 = 180.$ (b) $80\frac{3}{4} \cdot 9\frac{1}{8} \doteq 81 \cdot 9 = 729.$

    (c) $77\frac{3}{5} \cdot 6\frac{1}{4} \doteq 78 \cdot 6 = 468.$ (d) $48\frac{2}{3} \div 8\frac{4}{9} \doteq 49 \div 8 \doteq 6.$

    (e) $5\frac{2}{3} \div 2\frac{1}{17} \doteq 6 \div 2 = 3.$

11. (a)   The square of a positive proper fraction is less than the original fraction.

    (b)   For a positive proper fraction $\frac{a}{b}$, $b > a > 0$ and $b^2 > a^2 > 0$. Then $\frac{a^2}{b^2} < \frac{a}{b}$ since $a^2 b < ab^2$.

    (c)   The square is greater.

    (d)   Similar to (b), but now $a > b > 0$, so $a^2 > b^2 > 0$. Thus $a^2 b > ab^2$ and $\frac{a^2}{b^2} > \frac{a}{b}$.

13. xy is greater. $x > 1$ and $y > 0$ implies $x \cdot y > 1 \cdot y$, or $xy > y$.

15. Answers may vary. One example is $\frac{3}{2}, \frac{4}{3}, \frac{5}{4}, \ldots$.

17. Answers may vary. One method is to convert the given fractions to equivalent fractions having larger common denominators, thus creating spaces between the two.

    (a) $\frac{3}{7} = \frac{9}{21}; \frac{4}{7} = \frac{12}{21}.$ Two rational numbers between them are $\frac{10}{21}$ and $\frac{11}{21}$.

    (b) $\frac{-7}{9} = \frac{-28}{36}; \frac{-8}{9} = \frac{-32}{36}.$ Numbers between them are $\frac{-30}{36}$ and $\frac{-31}{36}$.

    (c) $\frac{5}{6} = \frac{1000}{1200}; \frac{83}{100} = \frac{996}{1200}.$ Numbers between them are $\frac{997}{1200}$ and $\frac{998}{1200}$.

    (d)   There are many values between a negative fraction and a positive fraction. Two are 0 and $\frac{1}{2}$ in this case.

19. (a)   Answers may vary. Perhaps begin by pointing out the relevance of the denominator, and then illustrate with examples.

    (b)   Again, answers may vary. Point out the relevance, this time, of the numerator. Illustrate.

21. (a) $\frac{1}{3}, \frac{1}{3}, \frac{1}{3},$ and $\frac{1}{3}$.

    (b) $\frac{1+3+5+7+\cdots+201}{203+205+207+\cdots+403} = \frac{1}{3}.$ The numerator of the nth term follows the pattern $1 + 3 + 5 + \cdots$ for $n + 1$ numbers (up to the number $2n + 1$; e.g., in the 3rd term, up to $2(3) + 1 = 7$). The denominator picks up at this point with its 1st term $2n + 3$ (e.g., $2(3) + 3 = 9$ in the 3rd term) and last being $4n + 3$ (e.g., $4(3) + 3 = 15$).

    (c)   The sum of the first n terms of $1 + 3 + 5 + 7 + \cdots$ is given by n^2. The sum of the first $n + 1$ terms, as in each numerator, is $(n + 1)^2$. Thinking of the numerator and denominator as one sequence run together gives the first $2n + 2$ terms of the series, having a sum of $(2n + 2)^2 = 4(n + 1)^2$. To get the sum of the denominator alone, subtract the numerator; i.e., $4(n + 1)^2 - (n + 1)^2 = 3(n + 1)^2$. All terms of the sequence are then of the form:
    $$\frac{(n + 1)^2}{3(n + 1)^2} = \frac{1}{3}.$$

23. Less than. Consider $\frac{a}{b}$ and $\frac{a+n}{b+n}$, where $a < b$ (because $\frac{a}{b}$ is a proper fraction) and n can be any positive number. Then, because $ab + an < ab + bn$, $\frac{a}{b} < \frac{a+n}{b+n}$.

25. Distance is rate times time, so time is distance divided by rate. Thus $t = 28\frac{3}{4} \div 4\frac{1}{2} = 6\frac{7}{18}$ hours.

27. Altogether there were $3 \cdot 5 = 15$ practices lasting a total of $15 \cdot 1\frac{3}{4} = 26\frac{1}{4}$ hours.

1. (a) $\dfrac{\text{Poodles}}{\text{Cockers}} = \dfrac{18}{12} = \dfrac{3}{2}$ (b) $\dfrac{\text{Cockers}}{\text{Poodles}} = \dfrac{12}{18} = \dfrac{2}{3}$

3. (a) We know that $\frac{a}{b} = \frac{c}{d}$ only if $ad = bc$. Thus if $\frac{12}{x} = \frac{18}{45}$, then:
$18 \cdot x = 12 \cdot 45 \ \Rightarrow\ x = \frac{540}{18} = 30.$

   (b) $21 \cdot x = {}^{-}10 \cdot 7 \ \Rightarrow\ x = \frac{{}^{-}70}{21} = \frac{{}^{-}10}{3}.$

   (c) $7 \cdot 3x = 5 \cdot 98 \ \Rightarrow\ x = \frac{490}{21} = 23\frac{1}{3}.$

   (d) $\dfrac{3\frac{1}{2}}{5} = \dfrac{x}{15} \ \Rightarrow\ 5 \cdot x = 3\frac{1}{2} \cdot 15 \ \Rightarrow\ 5x = \frac{105}{2} \ \Rightarrow\ x = \frac{105}{10} = \frac{21}{2}.$

5. $\dfrac{5 \text{ adults}}{1 \text{ teen}} = \dfrac{12,345 \text{ adults}}{x \text{ teens}} \ \Rightarrow\ 5x = 12,345 \ \Rightarrow\ x = \frac{12345}{5} = 2469$ teenage drivers.

7. $\dfrac{1\backslash 3 \text{ inch}}{5 \text{ miles}} = \dfrac{18 \text{ inches}}{x \text{ miles}} \ \Rightarrow\ \frac{1}{3}x = 90 \ \Rightarrow\ x = 90 \div \frac{1}{3} \ \Rightarrow\ x = 270$ miles.

9. The candle has burned 5 inches in 12 minutes; thus $\dfrac{5 \text{ inches}}{12 \text{ minutes}} = \dfrac{30 \text{ inches}}{x \text{ minutes}} \ \Rightarrow\ 5x = 360 \ \Rightarrow\ x = 72$ minutes for 30 inches.

11. Let the width be represented by 5x and the length by 9x. Then the ratio of width to length will be 5x to 9x, or 5:9. We also know that the perimeter of a rectangle is twice the width plus twice the length. Thus: $2(5x) + 2(9x) = 2800 \ \Rightarrow\ 28x = 2800 \ \Rightarrow\ x = 100.$ Then the width is 5x = 500 feet and the length is 9x = 900 feet.

13. If the amount Sheila earned is $3\frac{1}{2}x$ and the amount Dora earned is $4\frac{1}{2}x$, then the ratio of Sheila's hours to Dora's hours is $3\frac{1}{2}x{:}4\frac{1}{2}x$. Thus:
$3\frac{1}{2}x + 4\frac{1}{2}x = 176 \ \Rightarrow\ 8x = 176 \ \Rightarrow\ x = 22.$ Then Sheila's earnings were $3\frac{1}{2} \cdot 22 = \$77$ and Dora's earnings were $4\frac{1}{2} \cdot 22 = \$99$.

15. (a) $\dfrac{\text{Rise}}{\text{Half-Span}} = \dfrac{10}{14}.$ The pitch is $\frac{5}{7}$, or 5:7.

   (b) $\dfrac{\text{Rise}}{\text{Half-Span}} = \dfrac{\text{Rise}}{8} = \dfrac{3}{4}.$ Thus $4 \cdot \text{Rise} = 24$, or the Rise is 6 feet.

17. $\dfrac{9 \text{ months}}{6 \text{ vacation days}} = \dfrac{12 \text{ months}}{x \text{ vacation days}} \ \Rightarrow\ 9x = 72 \ \Rightarrow\ x = 8$ days per year.

19. $\dfrac{\text{length}}{\text{wingspan}} = \dfrac{230 \text{ feet}}{195 \text{ feet}} = \dfrac{40 \text{ cm}}{W \text{ cm}}.$ Thus $230W = 7800$ and $W = \frac{7800}{230} = 33\frac{21}{23}$ cm, or about 34 cm.

21. (a) $\dfrac{\text{footprint length}}{\text{body length}} = \dfrac{40 \text{ cm}}{700 \text{ cm}} = \dfrac{2}{35}$, or 2:35.

   (b) $\dfrac{\text{footprint length}}{\text{body length}} = \dfrac{2}{35} = \dfrac{30}{x} \ \Rightarrow\ 2x = 1050$, or $x = 525$ cm long.

   (c) For the first set, $\dfrac{\text{footprint length}}{\text{thighbone length}} = \dfrac{40}{100} = \dfrac{20}{50}$; i.e., a 50 cm thighbone would correspond to a 20 cm footprint. Thus it is not likely that the 50 cm thighbone is from the animal which left the 30 cm footprint.

23. No. The price would be based on the area of pizza, which is not proportional to its diameter as is suggested by the given proportion. (Area is proportional to the square of the diameter.)

25. Sherwin can paint $\frac{1}{2}$ house per day; William $\frac{1}{4}$ house per day. Together they should paint $\frac{1}{2} + \frac{1}{4} = \frac{3}{4}$ house per day, so $\dfrac{\frac{3}{4} \text{ house}}{1 \text{ day}} = \dfrac{1 \text{ house}}{x \text{ days}} \ \Rightarrow\ \frac{3}{4}x = 1 \ \Rightarrow\ x = \frac{4}{3}$ days for the two together to paint the house.

27. $\frac{a}{b} = \frac{c}{d}$ implies that $ad = bc$, or $a = \frac{bc}{d}$. Then $\dfrac{b}{a} = \dfrac{b}{\left(\frac{bc}{d}\right)} = \frac{b}{1} \cdot \frac{d}{bc} = \frac{d}{c}.$

29. (a) The total number of men in all three rooms is $1 + 2 + 5 = 8$. The total number of women in all three rooms is $2 + 4 + 10 = 16$. Thus the ratio of men to women is $\frac{8}{16} = \frac{1}{2}$.

29. (b) If $\frac{a}{b} = \frac{c}{d} = \frac{e}{f}$, then $\frac{c}{d} = \frac{a \cdot m}{b \cdot m}$ and $\frac{e}{f} = \frac{a \cdot n}{b \cdot n}$. So $\frac{a+c+e}{b+d+f} = \frac{a+am+an}{b+bm+bn} = \frac{a(1+m+n)}{b(1+m+n)} = \frac{a}{b}$.

31. Dick can run $4\frac{9}{10} \div 5 = \frac{49}{50}$ as far as Tom. Harry can run $4\frac{4}{5} \div 5 = \frac{24}{25}$ as far as Dick. Thus Harry can run $\frac{24}{25} \cdot \frac{49}{50} = \frac{1176}{1250}$ as far as Tom, or, in a 5-mile race, $\frac{1176}{1250} \cdot 5 = \frac{588}{125}$ miles. The difference is $5 - \frac{588}{125} = \frac{37}{125}$ miles.

33. (a) $\frac{3}{4}x - \frac{5}{8} \geq \frac{1}{2} \Rightarrow 6x - 5 \geq 4 \Rightarrow 6x \geq 9 \Rightarrow x \geq \frac{9}{6} = \frac{3}{2}$

(b) $\frac{^-x}{5} + \frac{1}{10} < \frac{^-1}{2} \Rightarrow {}^-2x + 1 < {}^-5 \Rightarrow {}^-2x < {}^-6 \Rightarrow x > 3$

(c) $\frac{^-2}{5}(10x + 1) < 1 - x \Rightarrow {}^-4x - \frac{2}{5} < 1 - x \Rightarrow {}^-20x - 2 < 5 - 5x \Rightarrow {}^-15x < 7 \Rightarrow x > \frac{^-7}{15}$

(d) $\frac{2}{3}(\frac{1}{2}x - 7) \geq \frac{3}{4}x \Rightarrow \frac{1}{3}x - \frac{14}{3} \geq \frac{3}{4}x \Rightarrow 4x - 56 \geq 9x \Rightarrow {}^-56 \geq 5x \Rightarrow x \leq \frac{^-56}{5}$

Problem Set 6-6

1. (a) $3^{^-7} \cdot 3^{^-6} = 3^{^-7 + ^-6} = 3^{^-13} = \frac{1}{3^{13}}$ (b) $3^7 \cdot 3^6 = 3^{7+6} = 3^{13}$

(c) $5^{15} \div 5^4 = 5^{15 - 4} = 5^{11}$ (d) $5^{15} \div 5^{^-4} = 5^{15 - ^-4} = 5^{15+4} = 5^{19}$

(e) $(^-5)^{^-2} = \frac{1}{(^-5)^2} = \frac{1}{5^2} = \frac{1}{25}$ (f) $\frac{a^2}{a^{^-3}} = a^{2 - ^-3} = a^{2+3} = a^5$

(g) $\frac{a}{a^{^-1}} = a^{1 - ^-1} = a^{1+1} = a^2$ (h) $\frac{a^{^-3}}{a^{^-2}} = a^{^-3 - ^-2} = a^{^-1} = \frac{1}{a}$

3. (a) False. $2^3 \cdot 3^2 = 2^5 = 32 \neq (2 \cdot 3)^5 = 6^5 = 7776$ (The bases must be equal; they are not multiplied)

(b) False. The bases are not the same; when multiplying numbers with exponents the exponents are added and not multiplied.

(c) False. The bases must be the same for the exponents to be added. $a^m \cdot b^m = (ab)^m$.

(d) False. By definition, any number to the zero power is 1.

(e) False. $(a + b)^2 = (a + b)(a + b) = a^2 + 2ab + b^2 \neq a^2 + b^2$.

(f) False. $(a + b)^{^-m} = \frac{1}{(a + b)^m}$.

(g) False. $a^m \cdot a^n = a^{m+n}$; $a^{mn} = (a^m)^n$.

(h) True. $\left(\frac{a}{b}\right)^{^-1} = \frac{1}{(\frac{a}{b})} = \frac{b}{a}$

5. (a) Each cell has a "length" equal to twice its radius. The length of the line, then, would be twice the radius times the number of cells, or:
$2(4 \cdot 10^{^-3})(25 \cdot 10^{12}) = (2 \cdot 4 \cdot 25) \cdot (10^{^-3} \cdot 10^{12}) = 200 \cdot 10^9 = (2 \cdot 10^2) \cdot 10^9 = 2 \cdot 10^{11}$ mm.

(b) $2 \cdot 10^{11} \div 10^6 = 2 \cdot (10^{11 - 6}) = 2 \cdot 10^5$ km. There are 1.6 km per mile; thus the line of red blood cells would be $1.2 \cdot 10^5 = 120,000$ miles long.

7. (a) $x^{^-1} - x = \frac{1}{x} - x = \frac{1}{x} - \frac{x^2}{x} = \frac{1 - x^2}{x}$.

(b) $x^2 - y^{^-2} = x^2 - \frac{1}{y^2} = \frac{x^2 y^2}{y^2} - \frac{1}{y^2} = \frac{x^2 y^2 - 1}{y^2}$.

(c) $2x^2 + (2x)^2 + 2^2x = 2x^2 + 4x^2 + 4x = 6x^2 + 4x$.

(d) $y^{^-3} + y^3 = \frac{1}{y^3} + y^3 = \frac{1}{y^3} + \frac{y^6}{y^3} = \frac{1 + y^6}{y^3}$.

7. (e) $\dfrac{3a - b}{(3a - b)^{-1}} = (3a - b)(3a - b) = (3a - b)^2.$

(f) $\dfrac{a^{-1}}{a^{-1} + b^{-1}} = \dfrac{\frac{1}{a}}{\frac{1}{a} + \frac{1}{b}} = \dfrac{\frac{1}{a}}{\left(\frac{a + b}{ab}\right)} = \dfrac{1}{a}\cdot\dfrac{ab}{a + b} = \dfrac{b}{a + b}$

9. (a) $Q(0) = 10^{10}\left(\frac{6}{5}\right)^0 = 10^{10}\cdot 1 = 10^{10}$ bacteria when t = 0.

(b) $Q(2) = 10^{10}\left(\frac{6}{5}\right)^2 = 10^{10}\cdot\frac{36}{25}$ bacteria when t = 2 seconds.

11. (a) $f(0) = \frac{3}{4}\cdot 2^0 = \frac{3}{4}\cdot 1 = \frac{3}{4}$

(b) $f(5) = \frac{3}{4}\cdot 2^5 = \frac{3}{4}\cdot 32 = 24$

(c) $f(^-5) = \frac{3}{4}\cdot 2^{-5} = \frac{3}{4}\cdot\frac{1}{2^5} = \frac{3}{4}\cdot\frac{1}{32} = \frac{3}{128}.$

(d) We are looking for the largest integer n for which $\frac{3}{4}\cdot 2^n < \frac{3}{400}$, or simplifying, $\frac{3}{4}\cdot 2^n = \frac{3}{2^2}\cdot\frac{1}{2^{-n}} = \frac{3}{2^{2-n}}.$

For $\dfrac{3}{2^{2-n}} < \dfrac{3}{400}$, $2^{2-n} > 400$. $2^9 = 512$ is the first power of 2 greater than 400, so $2 - n \geq 9$ or

$^-n \geq 7$ or $n \leq {}^-7$. Thus $^-7$ is the largest integer for which the statement is true.

13. (a) $32^{50} = (2^5)^{50} = 2^{250}$, while $4^{100} = (2^2)^{100} = 2^{200}$. $2^{250} > 2^{200}$, so $32^{50} > 4^{100}$.

(b) $(^-27)^{-15} = [(^-3)^3]^{-15} = (^-3)^{-45} = \dfrac{1}{(^-3)^{45}} = {}^-\left[\dfrac{1}{3^{45}}\right].$ $(^-3)^{-75} = \dfrac{1}{(^-3)^{75}} = {}^-\left[\dfrac{1}{3^{75}}\right].$

$\dfrac{1}{3^{45}} > \dfrac{1}{3^{75}}$; their negatives reverse the direction of the inequality; thus $(^-3)^{-75}$ is the greater.

15. Look for a pattern:
$5^1 = 5$
$5^2 = 25$
$5^3 = 125$
$5^4 = 625$
$5^5 = 3125$
$5^6 = 15{,}625$
For $n > 2$, all powers have the last two digits equal to 25, preceded by 1 for odd powers and 6 for even powers. Since 127 is odd, the last three digits of 5^{127} are 125.

17. $\frac{3}{80} = \frac{d}{720} \Rightarrow 80d = 2160 \Rightarrow d = 27$ items defective.

19. (a) $\frac{^-3}{4}x = 1 \Rightarrow \frac{^-4}{3}\cdot\frac{^-3}{4}x = \frac{^-4}{3}\cdot 1 \Rightarrow x = \frac{^-4}{3}$

(b) $\frac{2}{3}x = \frac{^-3}{5} \Rightarrow \frac{3}{2}\cdot\frac{2}{3}x = \frac{3}{2}\cdot\frac{^-3}{5} \Rightarrow x = \frac{^-9}{10}$

(c) $\frac{1}{3}x - 5 = \frac{^-3}{4}x \Rightarrow 4x - 60 = {}^-9x \Rightarrow 13x = 60 \Rightarrow x = \frac{60}{13}$

(d) $\frac{x}{3} = \frac{^-3}{4} \Rightarrow 4x = {}^-9 \Rightarrow x = \frac{^-9}{4}$

(e) $\frac{x}{3} = \frac{27}{x} \Rightarrow x^2 = 81$. Since $9^2 = 81$ and $(^-9)^2 = 81$, $x = 9$ or $x = {}^-9$

(f) $\frac{x + 1}{3} = \frac{3}{4}x \Rightarrow 4(x + 1) = 9x \Rightarrow 4x + 4 = 9x \Rightarrow 4 = 5x \Rightarrow x = \frac{4}{5}$

21. The ratios will change since the additional students do not fit the ratio of existing students; e.g., if there were originally 6 boys and 16 girls (6 to 16 ratio), the new ratio would be a $6 + 2$ to $16 + 2$, or 8 to 18. In other words, $\frac{3x}{8x} < \frac{3x + 2}{8x + 2}.$

CHAPTER 7 - DECIMALS AND DECIMAL OPERATIONS

<u>Problem</u> <u>Set</u> <u>7-1</u>

1.　(a)　$0.023 = 0 \cdot \frac{1}{10^1} + 2 \cdot \frac{1}{10^2} + 3 \cdot \frac{1}{10^3} = 0 \cdot 10^{-1} + 2 \cdot 10^{-2} + 3 \cdot 10^{-3} = 2 \cdot 10^{-2} + 3 \cdot 10^{-3}$

　　(b)　$206.06 = 2 \cdot 10^2 + 0 \cdot 10^1 + 6 \cdot 10^0 + 0 \cdot 10^{-1} + 6 \cdot 10^{-2} = 2 \cdot 10^2 + 6 \cdot 1 + 6 \cdot 10^{-2}$

　　(c)　$312.0103 = 3 \cdot 10^2 + 1 \cdot 10^1 + 2 \cdot 10^0 + 1 \cdot 10^{-2} + 3 \cdot 10^{-4} = 3 \cdot 10^2 + 1 \cdot 10 + 2 \cdot 1 + 1 \cdot 10^{-2} + 3 \cdot 10^{-4}$

　　(d)　$0.000132 = 1 \cdot 10^{-4} + 3 \cdot 10^{-5} + 2 \cdot 10^{-6}$

3.　(a)　536.0076

　　(b)　3.008

　　(c)　0.000436

　　(d)　5,000,000.2

5.　(a)　Terminating decimal; the denominator contains only 5 as a prime factor.

　　(b)　Terminating decimal; the denominator contains no prime factors other than 2 and 5.

　　(c)　Terminating decimal; the reduced denominator contains only 2 as a prime factor.

　　(d)　Terminating decimal; the denominator contains only 2 as a prime factor.

　　(e)　Terminating decimal; the denominator contains only 5 as a prime factor.

　　(f)　Terminating decimal; the denominator contains only 5 as a prime factor.

　　(g)　Nonterminating decimal; the denominator contains 3 as a prime factor.

　　(h)　Terminating decimal; the denominator contains only 5 as a prime factor.

　　(i)　Nonterminating decimal; the denominator contains 13 as a prime factor.

7.　(a)　　36.812　(Note that we line up the decimal points)
　　　　　　 0.43
　　　　　+ 1.96
　　　　　‾‾‾‾‾‾
　　　　　 39.202

　　(b)　　200.010　(We add a zero to the end of 200.01)
　　　　　− 32.007
　　　　　‾‾‾‾‾‾
　　　　　 168.003

　　(c)　　 ⁻4.6120
　　　　　− 386.0193
　　　　　‾‾‾‾‾‾‾
　　　　　 ⁻390.6313

　　(d)　　　　　3.6 1　(Two digits after the decimal point)
　　　　　　× 0.4 1 3　(Three digits after the decimal point)
　　　　　　‾‾‾‾‾‾‾
　　　　　　 1 0 8 3
　　　　　　 3 6 1
　　　　　 1 4 4 4
　　　　　‾‾‾‾‾‾‾
　　　　　 1.4 9 0 9 3　$(2 + 3 = 5$ digits after the decimal point)

7. (e) $^-$2.6
             $\times$ 4
             $^-$1 0.4

    (f)   4.6 8 1
             2.3|$\overline{1\ 0.7\ 6\ 6\ 3}$ (Multiply divisor and dividend by 10)
                 9 2
                 $\overline{1\ 5\ 6}$
                 1 3 8
                 $\overline{\ \ 1\ 8\ 6}$
                   1 8 4
                   $\overline{\ \ \ 2\ 3}$
                     2 3
                     $\overline{\ \ \ 0}$

9. Maura bought a total of:
       $17.95
        13.59
        14.86
       179.98
         2.43
         2.43
    $\overline{\$231.24}$ in her shopping.

11. (a) $4.63 \cdot 10^8 = 4.63 \cdot 100,000,000 = 463,000,000.0$ (multiplying by 10^8 has the effect of moving the decimal point 8 places to the right)

    (b) $0.04 \cdot 10^8 = 0.04 \cdot 100,000,000 = 4,000,000.0$

    (c) $46.3 \cdot 10^8 = 46.3 \cdot 100,000,000 = 4,630,000,000.0$

    (d) $463.0 \cdot 10^8 = 463.0 \cdot 100,000,000 = 46,300,000,000.0$

    (e) $0.00463 \cdot 10^8 = 0.00463 \cdot 100,000,000 = 463,000.0$

    (f) $0.0000000463 \cdot 10^8 = 0.0000000463 \cdot 100,000,000 = 4.63$

    (g) $4.63 \cdot 10^{-4} = 4.63 \cdot \frac{1}{10^4} = 4.63 \cdot 0.0001 = 0.000463$ (multiplying by 10^{-4} has the effect of moving the

         decimal point 4 places to the left.

    (h) $0.04 \cdot 10^{-4} = 0.04 \cdot 0.0001 = 0.000004$

    (i) $46.3 \cdot 10^{-4} = 46.3 \cdot 0.0001 = 0.00463$

    (j) $0.0000463 \cdot 10^{-4} = 0.0000463 \cdot 0.0001 = 0.00000000463$

    (k) $4.63 \div 10^{-4} = 4.63 \div \frac{1}{10^4} = 4.63 \cdot \frac{10^4}{1} = 4.63 \cdot 10^4 = 4.63 \cdot 10,000 = 46,300.0$ (dividing by 10^{-4} has the

         effect of moving the decimal point 4 places to the right)

    (l) $0.04 \div 10^{-4} = 0.04 \cdot 10^4 = 0.04 \cdot 10,000 = 400.0$

    (m) $46.3 \div 10^{-4} = 46.3 \cdot 10^4 = 46.3 \cdot 10,000 = 463,000.0$

    (n) $0.0000463 \div 10^{-4} = 0.0000463 \cdot 10^4 = 0.0000463 \cdot 10,000 = 0.463$

13. (a) $(0.22)(0.35)$ on the calculator is 0.077. Multiplying by the rule in this section results in a product of 0.0770, but the calculator deletes the last zero because it is not a significant digit (i.e., it does not change the value of the number).

(b) $0.2436 \div 0.0006$ on the calculator is 406, with no decimal point. Dividing by the rule in this section results in a quotient of $406.\bar{0}$, but the calculator deletes the decimal point and all following zeros.

15. (2.082 lbs per quart)(29.922 quarts per cubic foot) $= 62.297604$. Rounding to the nearest thousandth, we have 62.298 pounds.

17. There would be a total of $30 + 20 + 10 = 60$ pounds of nuts. At an average price per pound of \$4.50, Keith would pay $(4.50)(60) = \$270.00$ for the 60 pounds.

He has already paid $(3.00)(30) + (5.00)(20) = 90.00 + 100.00 = \$190.00$ for nuts, so he has $270.00 - 190.00 = \$80.00$ left to pay for the additional 10 pounds.

$80.00 \div 10 = \$8.00$ per pound for the additional nuts.

19. (a) If there are 2.54 cm per inch, there are $(2.54)^3 = 16.387064$ cm^3 per cubic inch. (16.387064 cm^3 per in^3)(390 cubic inches) $= 6391$ cm^3 (rounded to the nearest cm^3) in the engine.

(b) $(3000 \text{ cm}^3) \div (16.387064 \text{ cm}^3 \text{ per in}^3) = 183$ in^3 (rounded to the nearest in^3) in the engine.

21. ($61.48 per share)(18 shares) $-$ (\$964 cost) $= \$142.64$ profit in the first group.
($85.35 per share)(350 shares) $-$ (\$27,422.50 cost) $= \$2450.00$ profit in the second group.
[(\$142.64 + \$2450.00) profit] $-$ (\$495.00 commission) $= \$2097.64$ profit, or \$2098 rounded.

23. (a) There is a difference of 0.9 between each element of the sequence, so it is arithmetic. Then $4.5 + 0.9 = 5.4$; $5.4 + 0.9 = 6.3$; $6.3 + 0.9 = 7.2$; ... .

(b) There is a difference of 0.2 between each element of the sequence, so it is arithmetic. Then $1.1 + 0.2 = 1.3$; $1.3 + 0.2 = 1.5$; $1.5 + 0.2 = 1.7$; ... .

(c) Each element of the sequence is 0.5 times the previous element, so it is geometric. Then $0.125 \cdot 0.5 = 0.0625$; $0.0625 \cdot 0.5 = 0.03125$; $0.0315 \cdot 0.5 = 0.015625$; ... .

(d) There is a difference of 1.3 between each element of the sequence, so it is arithmetic. Then $5.4 + 1.3 = 6.7$; $6.7 + 1.3 = 8.0$; $8.0 + 1.3 = 9.3$; ... .

25. We would divide 93,000,000 by 1565, or $\boxed{9}\boxed{3}\boxed{0}\boxed{0}\boxed{0}\boxed{0}\boxed{0}\boxed{0}\boxed{\div}\boxed{1}\boxed{5}\boxed{6}\boxed{5}\boxed{=}$. (It would take 59,425 hours, or about $6\frac{3}{4}$ years.)

27. (a) System A: (12 checks)(\$0.10 per check) $= \$1.20$.
System B: (12 checks)(\$0.07 per check) + \$0.75 $= \$1.59$.
System A is more economical for an average of 12 checks per month.

(b) System A: (52 checks)(\$0.10) $= \$5.20$.
System B: (52 checks)(\$0.07) + \$0.75 $= \$4.39$.
System B is more economical for an average of 52 checks per month.

27. (c) If we let n = the number of checks averaged per month, then we want 0.10n to equal 0.07n + 0.75:
$0.10n = 0.07n + 0.75$
$0.03n = 0.75$
$n = 25$, so the break-even point is 25 checks per month.

29. The alternate plan is a geometric sequence, with 1st term $0.01 and ratio 2. From Chapter 1 we learned the nth term of a geometric sequence with first term a and ratio r is given by ar^{n-1}. In this case, we have: $0.01 \cdot 2^{30-1} = 0.01 \cdot 536,870,912 = \$5,368,709$. The second option is more profitable by $\$5,368,709 - \$1,000,000 = \$4,368,709$.

Problem Set 7-2

1. (a) $4 \div 9 = 0.444\ldots = 0.\overline{4}$

   (b) $2 \div 7 = 0.285714285714\ldots = 0.\overline{285714}$

   (c) $3 \div 11 = 0.2727\ldots = 0.\overline{27}$

   (d) $1 \div 15 = 0.0666\ldots = 0.0\overline{6}$

   (e) $2 \div 75 = 0.2666\ldots = 0.2\overline{6}$

   (f) $1 \div 99 = 0.010101\ldots = 0.\overline{01}$

   (g) $5 \div 6 = 0.8333\ldots = 0.8\overline{3}$

   (h) $1 \div 13 = 0.076923076923\ldots = 0.\overline{076923}$

3. (a) All the sums obtained in this manner are 999.

   (b) $\frac{5}{13} = 0.\overline{384615}$. $384 + 615 = 999$, so the same result is obtained.

   (c) If there are an even number of digits in the repetend, the sums of the halves will always be a series of numbers divisible by 3, or a power of 10 less 1.

   (d) No. The repetend does not have an even number of digits.

5. (a) $n = 2.4\overline{5}$; $10n = 24.\overline{5}$. We now have a one-digit repetend, so:

$$10(10n) = 245.\overline{5}$$
$$\underline{-10n = -24.\overline{5}}$$
$$90n = 221 \qquad \text{and } n = \frac{221}{90}$$

   (b) $n = 2.\overline{45}$; we have a two-digit repetend, so:

$$100n = 245.\overline{45}$$
$$\underline{-n = -2.\overline{45}}$$
$$99n = 243 \qquad \text{and } n = \frac{243}{99} = \frac{27}{11}$$

   (c) $n = 2.4\overline{54}$; $10n = 24.\overline{54}$. We now have a two-digit repetend, so:

$$100(10n) = 2454.\overline{54}$$
$$\underline{-10n = -24.\overline{54}}$$
$$990n = 2430 \qquad \text{and } n = \frac{2430}{990} = \frac{27}{11}$$

   (d) $n = 0.2\overline{45}$; $10n = 2.\overline{45}$. We now have a two-digit repetend, so:

$$100(10n) = 245.\overline{45}$$
$$\underline{-10n = -2.\overline{45}}$$
$$990n = 243 \qquad \text{and } n = \frac{243}{990} = \frac{27}{110}$$

5. (e) $n = 0.02\overline{45}$; $100n = 2.\overline{45}$. We now have a two-digit repetend, so:

$$100(100n) = 245.\overline{45}$$
$$\underline{-100n = \quad -2.\overline{45}}$$
$$9900n = 243 \qquad \text{and } n = \tfrac{243}{9900} = \tfrac{27}{1100}$$

(f) $n = {}^{-}24.\overline{54}$; we have a two-digit repetend, so:

$$100n = {}^{-}2454.\overline{54}$$
$$\underline{-n = \quad +24.\overline{54}}$$
$$99n = {}^{-}2430 \qquad \text{and } n = \tfrac{{}^{-}2430}{99} = \tfrac{{}^{-}270}{11}$$

(g) $n = 0.\overline{4}$; we have a one-digit repetend, so:

$$10n = 4.\overline{4}$$
$$\underline{-n = -.\overline{4}}$$
$$9n = 4 \qquad \text{and } n = \tfrac{4}{9}$$

(h) $n = 0.\overline{6}$; we have a one-digit repetend, so:

$$10n = 6.\overline{6}$$
$$\underline{-n = -.\overline{6}}$$
$$9n = 6 \qquad \text{and } n = \tfrac{6}{9} = \tfrac{2}{3}$$

(i) $n = 0.5\overline{5}$; $10n = 5.\overline{5}$. We have a one-digit repetend, so:

$$10(10n) = 55.\overline{5}$$
$$\underline{-10n = -5.\overline{5}}$$
$$90n = 50 \qquad \text{and } n = \tfrac{50}{90} = \tfrac{5}{9}$$

(Note that $0.5\overline{5}$ is the same as $0.\overline{5}$)

(j) $n = 0.\overline{34}$; we have a two-digit repetend, so:

$$100n = 34.\overline{34}$$
$$\underline{-n = \quad -.\overline{34}}$$
$$99n = 34 \qquad \text{and } n = \tfrac{34}{99}$$

(k) $n = {}^{-}2.\overline{34}$; we have a two-digit repetend, so:

$$100n = {}^{-}234.\overline{34}$$
$$\underline{-n = \quad + 2.\overline{34}}$$
$$99n = {}^{-}232 \qquad \text{and } n = \tfrac{{}^{-}232}{99}$$

(l) $n = {}^{-}0.\overline{02}$; we have a two-digit repetend, so:

$$100n = {}^{-}2.\overline{02}$$
$$\underline{-n = \quad +.\overline{02}}$$
$$99n = {}^{-}2 \qquad \text{and } n = \tfrac{{}^{-}2}{99}$$

7. Answers to (a) through (d) may vary.

(a)   3.25 is between 3.2 and 3.3.

(b)   462.245 is between 462.24 and 462.25.

(c) $462.24\overline{3}$ is between $462.2\overline{4}$ and $462.\overline{24}$.

(d)   0.02 is between 0.003 and 0.03.

9. (a) $4\boxed{9}\boxed{7}3\boxed{6}.\boxed{5}\boxed{2}8\boxed{1}$ (b) $4\boxed{1}\boxed{2}3\boxed{5}.\boxed{6}\boxed{7}8\boxed{9}$

11. (224 miles) ÷ (12 gallons) = $18.\overline{6}$ = 19 mpg rounded to the nearest mile.

13. Camera — about \$25
     Film — about \$4
     Case — about \$8
     For a total estimated cost of about \$37.

15. (a) $3.325 \cdot 10^3$ (b) $4.632 \cdot 10^1$

     (c) $1.3 \cdot 10^{-4}$ (d) $9.30146 \cdot 10^5$

17. (a) The diameter of the earth is about $1.27 \cdot 10^7$ km.

     (b) The distance from Pluto to the sun is $5.797 \cdot 10^6$ km.

     (c) Each year, about $5 \cdot 10^7$ cans are discarded in the United States.

19. (a) $(8 \cdot 10^{12}) \cdot (6 \cdot 10^{15}) = 8 \cdot 6 \cdot 10^{12} \cdot 10^{15} = 48 \cdot 10^{27} = 4.8 \cdot 10^{28}$.

     (b) $(16 \cdot 10^{12}) \div (4 \cdot 10^5) = \frac{16}{4} \cdot 10^{12} \cdot 10^{-5} = 4 \cdot 10^7$.

     (c) $(5 \cdot 10^8) \cdot (6 \cdot 10^9) \div (15 \cdot 10^{15}) = \frac{5 \cdot 6}{15} \cdot 10^8 \cdot 10^9 \cdot 10^{-15} = 2 \cdot 10^2$

21. Light travels $(1.86 \cdot 10^5$ miles per sec$) \cdot (3.1536 \cdot 10^7$ secs per year$) \doteq 5.87 \cdot 10^{12}$ miles per year.
     $(5.87 \cdot 10^{12}$ miles per year$) \cdot (4$ years$) \doteq 2.35 \cdot 10^{13}$ miles that Alpha Centauri is away from the earth.

23. (a) We add $0.\overline{3}$ to each term to obtain the next term, so the continuing pattern is $1.\overline{6}$, 2, $2.\overline{3}$, ...

     (b) If we convert each of these terms to fractions, we have 0, $\frac{1}{2}$, $\frac{2}{3}$, $\frac{3}{4}$, $\frac{4}{5}$, and $\frac{5}{6}$; it can be seen that each term is arrived at by adding 1 to the numerator and denominator of the previous term. Thus, the next terms are $\frac{6}{7}$, $\frac{7}{8}$, $\frac{8}{9}$, ... Converting back to decimals, the next terms are $0.\overline{857142}$, 0.875, $0.\overline{8}$, ...

25. (a) $(0.18$ of body weight$) \cdot (120$ lbs$) = 21.6$ pounds of bones.

     (b) $(0.4$ of body weight$) \cdot (120$ lbs$) = 48$ pounds of muscle.

27. If the denominator of a fraction in its simplest form has no prime factors other than 2 or 5, it represents a terminating decimal.

Problem Set 7-3

1.   (a) $7.89 = (100 \cdot 7.89)\% = 789\%$.

     (b) $0.032 = (100 \cdot 0.032)\% = 3.2\%$.

     (c) $193.1 = (100 \cdot 193.1)\% = 19{,}310\%$.

     (d) $0.2 = (100 \cdot 0.2)\% = 20\%$.

     (e) $\frac{5}{6} = \left(100 \cdot \frac{5}{6}\right)\% = (100 \cdot 0.8\overline{3})\% = 83.\overline{3}\%$ or $83\frac{1}{3}\%$.

     (f) $\frac{3}{20} = \left(100 \cdot \frac{3}{20}\right)\% = (100 \cdot 0.15)\% = 15\%$.

     (g) $\frac{1}{8} = \left(100 \cdot \frac{1}{8}\right)\% = (100 \cdot 0.125)\% = 12.5\%$.

     (h) $\frac{3}{8} = \left(100 \cdot \frac{3}{8}\right)\% = (100 \cdot 0.375)\% = 37.5\%$ (or 3 times $12.5\% = 37.5\%$).

1.   (i) $\frac{5}{8} = \left(100 \cdot \frac{5}{8}\right)\% = (100 \cdot 0.625)\% = 62.5\%$ (or 5 times 12.5% = 62.5%).

      (j) $\frac{1}{6} = \left(100 \cdot \frac{1}{6}\right)\% = (100 \cdot 0.1\bar{6})\% = 16.\bar{6}\%$ or $16\frac{2}{3}\%$.

      (k) $\frac{4}{5} = \left(100 \cdot \frac{4}{5}\right)\% = (100 \cdot 0.8)\% = 80\%$.

      (l) $\frac{1}{40} = \left(100 \cdot \frac{1}{40}\right)\% = (100 \cdot 0.025)\% = 2.5\%$.

3.   (a)   <u>Four</u>   (b)   <u>Two</u>

      (c)   <u>25</u>   (d)   <u>200</u>

      (e)   <u>12.5</u>

5.   (a)   6% of 34 = 0.06 · 34 = 2.04.

      (b) $17 = n\% \cdot 34$
             $n\% = \frac{17}{34}$
             $n\% = \left(100 \cdot \frac{17}{34}\right)\% = (100 \cdot 0.5)\% = 50\%$

      (c) $18 = 0.3 \cdot n$
             $n = \frac{18}{0.3} = 60$

      (d)   7% of 49 = 0.07 · 49 = 3.43.

      (e) $61.5 = n\% \cdot 20.5$
             $n\% = \frac{61.5}{20.5}$
             $n\% = \left(100 \cdot \frac{61.5}{20.5}\right)\% = 300\%$

      (f) $16 = 0.40 \cdot n$
             $n = \frac{16}{0.40} = 40$

7.   6% of $16,000 is 0.06 · 16,000 = $960, which is the amount of the raise.
      She now makes 16,000 + 960 = $16,960.

9.   If C is the original cost, then 80% of C is $350, or 0.80 · C = 350.
      $C = \frac{350}{0.80} = \$437.50$ original cost.

11.   The amount of the discount is 35 − 28 = $7. We want to find out how much $7 is as a percentage of $35,
      or $\frac{7}{35} = 0.2 = 20\%$ discount.

13.   The number of eagles by which the population decreased was 728 − 594 = 134.
      The decrease as a percentage of the original population is $\frac{134}{728} \doteq 0.184 = 18.4\%$.

15.   The amount of Xuan's weight increase was 18 − 9 = 9 pounds.
      The increase as a percentage of his weight at birth is $\frac{9}{9} = 1.00 = 100\%$.

17.   The amount of the discount is 25% of $6.80, or 0.25 · 6.80 = $1.70.
      The sale price is 6.80 − 1.70 = $5.10.

19.   The amount of the tax is 5% of $320, or 0.05 · 320 = $16.
      Then the total cost is 320 + 16 = $336.

21.   4% of $80,000 is 0.04 · 80,000 = $3200 received.

23.   The house payment as a percentage of total income is $\frac{400}{2400} = 0.1\bar{6} = 16.\bar{6}\%$ or $16\frac{2}{3}\%$.

25. Let S be the salary of the previous year; then S + 10% of S = new salary.

S + 0.10S = 100,000 (this year); or 1.1S = 100,000; so S = $\frac{100,000}{1.1}$ ≐ \$90,909.09 (last year).

Last year, 1.1S = 90,909.09, so S = $\frac{90,909.09}{1.1}$ ≐ \$82,644.63 two years ago.

27. The amount of John's 20% profit is 0.20·330 = \$66, so the net price of the bike after a 10% discount must be 330 + 66 = \$396.

Now let L be the list price; then L − 10% of L = Net (or selling) price.

Thus L − 0.10L = 396; or 0.90L = 396; and L = $\frac{396}{0.90}$ = \$440. If John then prices the bike at \$440, he can offer a 10% discount of \$44 and still realize his \$66 profit.

29. Let M be the amount of money with which Howard enters the first store. If the owner then gives him as much money as he has with him, he will have M + M = 2M. He will spend 80% of that total, leaving him with 20%, or 0.20·2M = 0.4M.

In the second store, he will have left 20% of 2·0.4M, or 0.20·2·0.4M = 0.16M.

In the third store, he will have left 0.20·2·0.16M = 0.064M.

If 0.064M = \$12, then M = $\frac{12}{0.064}$ = \$187.50 in the beginning.

31. (a) 10% of 22 = \$2.20. 5% of 22 is half 10%, or \$1.10. Adding, we have 2.20 + 1.10 = \$3.30.

(b) 10% of 120 is \$12. 20% of 120 is twice 10%, or \$24.

(c) 10% of 38 is \$3.80. 5% of 38 is half 10%, or \$1.90.

(d) 25% is $\frac{1}{4}$, and 98·$\frac{1}{4}$ = 98÷4 = \$24.50.

33. (a) (*i*) Only the four corner blocks will have four faces painted; thus there are $\frac{4}{81}$ ≐ 0.049 = 4.9% painted.

(*ii*) The blocks along each edge, exclusive of the corner blocks, will have three faces painted. There are 7 of these along each edge, or 4·7 = 28 blocks; thus there are $\frac{28}{81}$ ≐ 0.346 = 34.6% painted.

(*iii*) Each of the interior blocks will have two faces painted. There are 81 − 4 − 28 = 49 of these; thus there are $\frac{49}{81}$ ≐ 0.605 = 60.5% painted.

(b) (*i*) $\frac{4}{64}$ = 6.25% painted.

(*ii*) $\frac{24}{64}$ = 37.5% painted.

(*iii*) $\frac{36}{64}$ = 56.25% painted.

(c) (*i*) $\frac{4}{49}$ ≐ 8.2% painted.

(*ii*) $\frac{20}{49}$ ≐ 40.8% painted.

(*iii*) $\frac{25}{49}$ ≐ 51.0% painted.

(d) (*i*) $\frac{4}{144}$ = 2.$\overline{7}$% painted.

(*ii*) $\frac{40}{144}$ = 27.$\overline{7}$% painted.

(*iii*) $\frac{100}{144}$ = 69.$\overline{4}$ painted.

35. (a) Answers may vary. If you are 20 years old, your range would be a rate of 60% of 220 − 20 = 120 to 80% of 220 − 20 = 160.

35. (b) (i) $\frac{15\ seconds}{41\ beats} = 0.\overline{36585}$ seconds between beats.

    (ii) $\frac{1/4\ minute}{41\ beats} = 0.00\overline{60975}$ minutes between beats.

37. A journeyman makes 200% of an apprentice's pay.
    A master makes 150% of a journeyman's pay = 150%·200% = 1.5·2 = 3 = 300% of an apprentice's pay.
    Thus the $4200 needs 1 + 2 + 3 = 6 shares, or $700 per share.
    The apprentice earns $700; the journeyman earns 200% of $700 = $1400; the master earns 150% of $1400 = $2100.

39. Dinner + 15% of dinner = $35; or 115% of dinner = $35. Dinner may thus be a maximum of $\frac{35}{1.15} \doteq$ $30.43.

41. (a) Marie owed $310 + 9% of ($16,250 − $5,000) = 310 + 0.09(11,250) = 310 + 1012.50 = $1322.50.

    (b) (i)   Filing separately: Peter owed 310 + 0.09(12,321 − 5000) = $968.89.
                                   Holly owed 310 + 0.09(6532 − 5000) = $447.88.
                         Together they owed 968.89 + 447.88 = $1416.77.

         (ii) Filing jointly: Total income was 12,321 + 6352 = $18,853.
                          Tax owed was 620 + 0.09(18,853 − 10,000) = $1416.77.

         Peter and Holly would pay the same tax either way.

43. $33.21 = 33\frac{21}{100} = \frac{3321}{100}$

45. If n = 31.0$\bar{5}$, then 10n = 310.$\bar{5}$ and we have a 1-digit repetend.
    $$10(10n) = 3105.\bar{5}$$
    $$\underline{-\ 10n = -310.\bar{5}}$$
    $$90n = 2795,\ \text{and } n = \frac{2795}{90} = \frac{559}{18}$$

47. (a) 32.015 $\doteq$ 32.0

    (b) 32.015 $\doteq$ 32

Problem Set 7-4

1. (a) 6% annually = $\frac{6}{2}$ = 3% per semiannual period.
        2 years compounded semiannually = 4 periods.
        A = 1000(1 + 0.03)^4 = 1000(1.03)^4 $\doteq$ 1000(1.12551) = $1125.51.
        Interest = 1125.51 − 1000 = $125.51.

   (b) 8% annually = $\frac{8}{4}$ = 2% per quarterly period.
        3 years compounded quarterly = 12 periods.
        A = 1000(1 + 0.02)^{12} $\doteq$ $1268.24.
        Interest = 1268.24 − 1000 = $268.24.

   (c) 10% annually = $\frac{10}{12}$ = 0.8$\bar{3}$% per monthly period.
        5 years compounded monthly = 60 periods.
        A = 1000(1 + 0.008$\bar{3}$)^{60} $\doteq$ $1645.31.
        Interest = 1645.31 − 1000 = $645.31.

1. (d) 12% annually $= \frac{12}{365}\%$ per daily period.
        4 years compounded daily $= 1460$ periods.
        $A = 1000(1 + \frac{0.12}{365})^{1460} \doteq 1615.95.$
        Interest $= 1615.95 - 1000 = \$615.95.$

3. Carolyn is compounding \$125 for 12 periods at 1.5% per period.
    Thus $A = 125(1 + 0.015)^{12} \doteq \$149.45$ (i.e., principal and interest) and interest owed $= 149.45 - 125 = \$24.45.$

5. In the expression for compound interest, $A = P(1 + i)^n$, the amount here is \$50,000 and P is what we need to find. Thus,
    $P = \dfrac{A}{(1 + i)^n}$, where $i = \frac{0.09}{4} = 0.0225$ and n = 20. We now have: $P = \dfrac{50,000}{(1.0225)^{20}} = \$32,040.82$ to be invested now.

7. For the 1st 3 years, P = 3000, $i = \frac{0.05}{4} = 0.0125$ and n = 12. Thus $A = 3000(1.0125)^{12} \doteq \$3482.26.$
    For the 2nd 3 years, P = 3482.26, $i = \frac{0.08}{4} = 0.02$, and n = 12. Thus $A = 3482.26(1.02)^{12} \doteq \$4416.35.$
    Thus the balance in the account after six years was \$4416.35.

9. P = 10,000, $i = \frac{0.14}{365}$, and n = 15·365 = 5475. Thus $A = 10,000(1 + \frac{0.14}{365})^{5475} \doteq \$81,628.82$ in the fund.

11. Suppose \$1 were to be invested in each institution. Then:

    For New Age, $i = \frac{0.09}{365}$ and n = 365; thus $A = 1(1 + \frac{0.09}{365})^{365} \doteq \$1.094162.$
    Subtracting the \$1 invested, we have earned about 9.4¢, corresponding to an effective rate of 9.4%.

    For Pay More, $i = \frac{0.105}{1}$ and n = 1; thus $A = 1(1 + 0.105) = \$1.105.$
    Subtracting the \$1 invested, we have earned 10.5¢, corresponding to an effective rate of 10.5%.

    The Pay More bank has a higher effective interest rate.

13. We are compounding at 11% annually for 6 years. Thus $A = 1.35(1 + 0.11)^6 = \$2.53.$ A hamburger would cost \$2.53 after six years if prices rise at 11% per year.

15. From problem 5, $P = \dfrac{A}{(1 + i)^n}.$ We have $i = \frac{0.065}{4} = 0.01625$, n = 16, and A = \$4650. Thus,

    $P = \dfrac{4650}{(1.01625)^{16}} \doteq \$3592.89$ initial investment.

17. At 1.1% per period (month) for 11 periods, $A = 300(1 + 0.011)^{11} \doteq \$338.36$, so Adrien and Jarrell will have \$338.36 in their account on December 1. Interest earned will be $338.36 - 300.00 = \$38.36.$
    Thus interest as a percentage of the amount deposited will be $\frac{38.36}{300} = 12.8\%$ effective annual yield.

19. We can develop a formula for compound decay:
        If we let A be the amount remaining after 1 year, r the rate of decay, and B the beginning amount, then after 1 year: $A = B - \text{decay} = B - rB = B(1 - r)$. After n periods, then, $A = B(1 - r)^n.$

    So in the rain forest, where $B = 2.34 \cdot 10^9$, $r = \frac{0.005}{12}$, and n = 20·12 = 240, we have:
    $A = 2.34 \cdot 10^9 (1 - \frac{0.005}{12})^{240} \doteq 2.12 \cdot 10^9$ trees remaining after 20 years.

Problem Set 7-5

1. Answers may vary. One such number could be 0.232233222333... .

3. We line up the decimal points:
$$0.9 = 0.90000000\ldots$$
$$0.\bar{9} = 0.99999999\ldots$$
$$0.\overline{98} = 0.98989898\ldots$$
$$0.9\overline{88} = 0.98888888\ldots$$
$$0.9\overline{98} = 0.99898989\ldots$$
$$0.\overline{898} = 0.89889889\ldots$$
From greatest to least, then, we have: $0.\bar{9}$, $0.9\overline{98}$, $0.\overline{98}$, $0.9\overline{88}$, 0.9, $0.\overline{898}$.

5. (a) $15 \cdot 15 = 225$, so $\sqrt{225} = 15$.

(b) $15.84 \cdot 15.84 \doteq 251$, so $\sqrt{251} \doteq 15.84$.

(c) $13 \cdot 13 = 169$, so $\sqrt{169} = 13$.

(d) $22^2 = 484$; $23^2 = 529$; so $\sqrt{512}$ is between 22 and 23.
$(22.6)^2 = 510.76$; $(22.7)^2 = 515.29$; so $\sqrt{512}$ is between 22.6 and 22.7.
Continue in this manner to find $\sqrt{512}$ to the desired accuracy ($\sqrt{512} \doteq 22.627$).

(e) $^-81$ has no square root. There is no number n such that $n^2 = {}^-81$.

(f) $25 \cdot 25 = 625$, so $\sqrt{625} = 25$.

7. (a)   False. $2 + \sqrt{2}$ is an irrational number.

(b)   False. $^-\sqrt{2} + \sqrt{2} = 0$, a rational number.

(c)   False. $\sqrt{2} \cdot \sqrt{2} = 2$, which is a rational number.

(d)   False. $\sqrt{2} - \sqrt{2} = 0$, a rational number.

9. Answers may vary. $\sqrt{2}$, $\sqrt{3}$, and $\sqrt{5}$ are three.

11. No. $\frac{22}{7}$ is a rational number that can be represented by the repeating decimal $3.\overline{142857}$.

13. (a)   We want the set of numbers that contains the set of rational numbers <u>or</u> the set of irrational numbers, <u>or</u> both. That set is R, the set of real numbers, or $Q \cup S = R$.

(b)   A rational number cannot be an irrational number, so $Q \cap S = \emptyset$.

(c)   The intersection of the set of rational numbers and the set of real numbers is the set of rational numbers (since Q is contained in R). Thus $Q \cap R = Q$.

(d)   No whole number can be irrational, so $S \cap W = \emptyset$.

(e)   The union of the set of whole numbers and the set of real numbers is the set of real numbers (since W is contained in R). Thus $W \cup R = R$.

(f)   Since the set of rational numbers is contained in the set of real numbers, $Q \cup R = R$.

15. (a) $x^2 + 1 = 5$
$x^2 = 4$
$x = 2$, and 2 belongs to N, I, Q, and R.

15. (b) $2x - 1 = 32$
           $2x = 33$
           $x = \frac{33}{2}$, and $\frac{33}{2}$ belongs to Q and R.

     (c) $x^2 = 3$
           $x = \sqrt{3}$, and $\sqrt{3}$ belongs to R and S.

     (d) $x^2 = 4$
           $x = 2$, and 2 belongs to N, I, Q, and R.

     (e) $\sqrt{x} = {}^-1$
           There is no solution to this equation, since by definition the principal square root of x is the nonnegative number a such that $a^2 = x$.

     (f) $\frac{3}{4}x = 4$
           $x = 4 \cdot \frac{4}{3} = \frac{16}{3}$, and $\frac{16}{3}$ belongs to Q and R.

17. The sides of the gate form the sides of a right triangle with the diagonal brace as the hypotenuse.
     If c is the length of the hypotenuse, then $c^2 = a^2 + b^2 = 4^2 + 5^2 = 16 + 25 = 41$.
     Thus the length of the brace $= \sqrt{41} \doteq 6.4$ feet.

19. The sequence 0.13, 0.1313, 0.131313, ... , can be represented by the repeating decimal $0.\overline{13} = \frac{13}{99}$.
     Since any term of the repeating decimal $0.\overline{13}$ is less than $\frac{13}{99}$, that is the rational number for which we are looking.

21. Suppose $\sqrt{p}$ is rational. If so, then $\sqrt{p} = \frac{a}{b}$, where a and b are integers and $b \neq 0$. Therefore $p = \frac{a^2}{b^2}$, or $pb^2 = a^2$. a^2 must have an even number of p's in its prime factorization, as must b^2. In pb^2, another factor of p is introduced, resulting in an odd number of p's in the prime factorization of pb^2 and hence of a^2. But p cannot appear both an odd number of times and an even number of times in the same prime factorization, so we have a contradiction. Consequently, $\sqrt{p}$ must be an irrational number.

23. (a) $0.5 + \frac{1}{0.5} = 0.5 + 2 = 2.5 \geq 2$.

     (b)   Suppose $x + \frac{1}{x} < 2$. Since $x > 0$, $x^2 + 1 < 2x$ so that $x^2 - 2x + 1 < 0$, or $(x - 1)^2 < 0$, which is false.

25. $0.00024 = \frac{24}{100,000} = \frac{3}{12,500}$

27. $\quad\quad 100n = 24.\overline{24}$
     $\quad\quad \underline{- n = -.\overline{24}}$
     $\quad\quad 99n = 24$, so $n = \frac{24}{99} = \frac{8}{33}$

29. 9% 0f $18,600 is $0.09 \cdot 18,600 = \$1674$ raise. $18,600 + 1674 = \$20,274$ as Joan's new salary.

Problem Set 7-6

1.   (a) $\sqrt{180} = \sqrt{36 \cdot 5} = \sqrt{36} \cdot \sqrt{5} = 6\sqrt{5}$

     (b) $\sqrt{529} = 23$

     (c) $\sqrt{363} = \sqrt{121 \cdot 3} = 11\sqrt{3}$

     (d) $\sqrt{252} = \sqrt{36 \cdot 7} = 6\sqrt{7}$

1. (e) $\sqrt{\frac{169}{196}} = \frac{\sqrt{169}}{\sqrt{196}} = \frac{13}{14}$

    (f) $\sqrt{\frac{49}{196}} = \frac{\sqrt{49}}{\sqrt{196}} = \frac{7}{14} = \frac{1}{2}$, or alternatively, $\sqrt{\frac{49}{196}} = \sqrt{\frac{1}{4}} = \frac{\sqrt{1}}{\sqrt{4}} = \frac{1}{2}$

3. (a) $2\sqrt{3} + 3\sqrt{2} + \sqrt{180} = 2\sqrt{3} + 3\sqrt{2} + 6\sqrt{5}$. (See problem 1(a) for $\sqrt{180}$) The sum cannot be simplified further.

    (b) $\sqrt[3]{4} \cdot \sqrt[3]{10} = \sqrt[3]{40} = \sqrt[3]{8 \cdot 5} = 2 \cdot \sqrt[3]{5}$

    (c) $\begin{aligned}(2\sqrt{3} + 3\sqrt{2})^2 &= (2\sqrt{3} + 3\sqrt{2}) \cdot (2\sqrt{3} + 3\sqrt{2}) \\ &= 2\sqrt{3} \cdot (2\sqrt{3} + 3\sqrt{2}) + 3\sqrt{2} \cdot (2\sqrt{3} + 3\sqrt{2}) \\ &= 4 \cdot 3 + 6\sqrt{6} + 6\sqrt{6} + 9 \cdot 2 \\ &= 12 + 12\sqrt{6} + 18 \\ &= 30 + 6\sqrt{6}\end{aligned}$

    (d) $\sqrt{6} \div \sqrt{12} = \sqrt{\frac{6}{12}} = \sqrt{\frac{1}{2}} = \frac{1}{\sqrt{2}}$

    (e) $\begin{aligned}5\sqrt{72} + 2\sqrt{50} - \sqrt{288} - \sqrt{242} &= 5\sqrt{36 \cdot 2} + 2\sqrt{25 \cdot 2} - \sqrt{144 \cdot 2} - \sqrt{121 \cdot 2} \\ &= 5 \cdot 6\sqrt{2} + 2 \cdot 5\sqrt{2} - 12\sqrt{2} - 11\sqrt{2} \\ &= 30\sqrt{2} + 10\sqrt{2} - 12\sqrt{2} - 11\sqrt{2} \\ &= 17\sqrt{2}\end{aligned}$

    (f) $\sqrt{8/7} \div \sqrt{4/21} = \sqrt{\frac{8}{7} \div \frac{4}{21}} = \sqrt{\frac{8}{7} \cdot \frac{21}{4}} = \sqrt{\frac{2}{1} \cdot \frac{3}{1}} = \sqrt{6}$

5. No. $\sqrt{x^2 + y^2} \neq x + y$. (Note, though, that $\sqrt{x^2 \cdot y^2} = x \cdot y$)

7. Recall from Section 1-1 that in a geometric sequence each successive term is obtained from its predecessor by multiplying by a fixed number r (ratio). The ratio may thus be derived by dividing the $(n + 1)$th term by the nth term, or, in this problem, $r = 3 \div 3^{3/4} = 3^{1-3/4} = 3^{1/4}$. Thus $3^{3/4}$ (the first term) times $3^{1/4}$ (the ratio) equals $3^1 = 3$ (the second term), and so on.

    We find the that exponents are now in an arithmetic sequence: $\frac{3}{4}$, 1, $\frac{5}{4}$, ... , 6 (the last exponent is 6 becuse $729 = 3^6$).

    In an arithmetic sequence (again, from Section 1-1), the nth term, where a is the 1st term, is $a + (n - 1)d$. In this case, the 1st term is $\frac{3}{4}$, the nth term is 6, and the difference, d, is $\frac{1}{4}$. Solving for n, we have:

    $$6 = \tfrac{3}{4} + (n - 1)\tfrac{1}{4}$$

    $$6 = \tfrac{3}{4} + \tfrac{1}{4}n - \tfrac{1}{4}$$

    $$6 = \tfrac{1}{2} + \tfrac{1}{4}n$$

    $\frac{11}{2} = \frac{1}{4}n$, so $n = 22$ and there are 22 terms in the sequence.

9. $(4/25)^{-1/3} = \dfrac{1}{(4/25)^{1/3}} = \dfrac{25^{1/3}}{4^{1/3}} = (25/4)^{1/3}$, and similarly, $(4/25)^{-1/4} = (25/4)^{1/4}$. Thus, in order from least to greatest, we have $(4/25)^{-1/4}$, $(4/25)^{-1/3}$, $(25/4)^{1/3}$.

11. $\sqrt{2\sqrt{2\sqrt{2}}} = \sqrt{2\sqrt{2 \cdot 2^{1/2}}} = \sqrt{2\sqrt{2 \cdot 2^{3/2}}} = \sqrt{2(2^{3/2})^{1/2}} = \sqrt{2 \cdot 2^{3/4}} = \sqrt{2^{7/4}} = (2^{7/4})^{1/2} = 2^{7/8}$

    and $2^{7/8} = \sqrt[8]{2^7}$.

13. $\sqrt[3]{(6 - 2)^{-2}} = \sqrt[3]{\frac{1}{16}} = \dfrac{1}{2 \cdot \sqrt[3]{2}}$

15.   (a) $\sqrt{2} - \frac{2}{\sqrt{2}} = 0$, which is rational.   (b)   Rational

     (c)   Irrational   (d) $\frac{1}{1 + \sqrt{2}} + 1 - \sqrt{2} = 0$; rational.

CHAPTER 8 - PROBABILITY

<u>Problem Set 8-1</u>

1. (a) S = {Clinton, Bush, Reagan, Carter, Ford, Nixon, Johnson, Kennedy, Eisenhower, Truman}

   (b) S = {C|C is one of my classmates}

   (c) S = {M|M is a member of the U. S. House of Representatives from my State}

3. (a) $P(1, 5, \text{or } 7) = \frac{1}{8} + \frac{1}{8} + \frac{1}{8} = \frac{3}{8}$.

   (b) $P(3 \text{ or } 6) = \frac{1}{8} + \frac{1}{8} = \frac{1}{4}$.

   (c) $P(2, 4, 6, \text{or } 8) = \frac{1}{8} + \frac{1}{8} + \frac{1}{8} + \frac{1}{8} = \frac{1}{2}$.

   (d) $P(6 \text{ or } 2) = \frac{1}{8} + \frac{1}{8} = \frac{1}{4}$.

   (e) $P(11) = 0$.

   (f) $P(4, 6, \text{or } 8) = \frac{1}{8} + \frac{1}{8} + \frac{1}{8} = \frac{3}{8}$.

   (g) P(Neither prime nor composite) $= P(1) = \frac{1}{8}$.

5. (a) There are 4 brown socks out of the total of 12 in the drawer, so $P(\text{Brown}) = \frac{n(\text{Brown})}{n(S)} = \frac{1}{3}$.

   (b) The events are mutually exclusive, so $P(\text{Black or green}) = \frac{n(\text{Black})}{n(S)} + \frac{n(\text{Green})}{n(S)} = \frac{6}{12} + \frac{2}{12} = \frac{2}{3}$.

   (c) There are no red socks in the drawer, so $P(\text{Red}) = 0$.

   (d) $P(\text{Not black}) = 1 - P(\text{Black}) = 1 - \frac{n(\text{Black})}{n(S)} = 1 - \frac{6}{12} = \frac{1}{2}$.

7. $P(\text{Missing flight}) = 1 - P(\text{Boarding flight}) = 1 - 0.2 = 0.8$.

9. (a) There are 36 equally likely outcomes when rolling two dice. Of these 36, a 7 may be obtained in six different ways: (1, 6), (2, 5), (3, 4), (4, 3), (5, 2), or (6, 1). 11 may be obtained in only two ways: (5, 6) or (6, 5). These events are mutually exclusive, so:

   $$P(7 \text{ or } 11) = \frac{n(7)}{n(S)} + \frac{n(11)}{n(S)} = \frac{6}{36} + \frac{2}{36} = \frac{2}{9}.$$

   (b) Two may be obtained in only one way: (1, 1); three may be obtained in two ways: (1, 2) or (2, 1); and twelve may be obtained in only one way: (6, 6). These events are mutually exclusive, so:

   $$P(\text{Loss on first roll}) = \frac{n(2)}{n(S)} + \frac{n(3)}{n(S)} + \frac{n(12)}{n(S)} = \frac{1}{36} + \frac{2}{36} + \frac{1}{36} = \frac{1}{9}.$$

   (c) A 4 may be rolled in three ways: (1, 3), (2, 2), (3, 1).
   A 5 may be rolled in four ways: (1, 4), (2, 3), (3, 2), (4, 1).
   A 6 may be rolled in five ways: (1, 5), (2, 4), (3, 3), (4, 2), (5, 1).
   A 8 may be rolled in five ways: (2, 6), (3, 5), (4, 4), (5, 3), (6, 2).
   A 9 may be rolled in four ways: (3, 6), (4, 5), (5, 4), (6, 3).
   A 10 may be rolled in three ways: (4, 6), (5, 5), (6, 4).
   These events are mutually exclusive, so:

   $$P(\text{Neither win nor loss}) = \frac{n(4)}{n(S)} + \frac{n(5)}{n(S)} + \frac{n(6)}{n(S)} + \frac{n(8)}{n(S)} + \frac{n(9)}{n(S)} + \frac{n(10)}{n(S)} = \frac{3}{36} + \frac{4}{36} + \frac{5}{36} + \frac{5}{36} + \frac{4}{36} + \frac{3}{36}$$

   $$P(\text{Neither win nor loss}) = \frac{2}{3}.$$

   (d) 6 or 8, with probabilities of $\frac{5}{36}$, have the highest probability of occurring again. (7 has a probability of $\frac{6}{36}$.)

   (e) It is not possible to roll a sum of 1 with two dice, so $P(1) = 0$.

   (f) The largest number which can be rolled with two dice is 12, so $P(< 13) = 1$.

9. (g) There is a $\frac{6}{36} = \frac{1}{6}$ probability of rolling 7 on any one roll; in 60 rolls one would expect $\frac{1}{6} \cdot 60 = 10$ sevens.

11. (a) There are 18 black slots on the roulette wheel, so $P(\text{Black}) = \frac{n(\text{Black})}{n(S)} = \frac{18}{38} = \frac{9}{19}$.

   (b) $P(0 \text{ or } 00) = \frac{n(0 \text{ or } 00)}{n(S)} = \frac{2}{38} = \frac{1}{19}$.

   (c) This problem is easier if we find the probability that the ball <u>does</u> land on a number 1 through 12, and then use the property of complementary events. Thus:

   $$P(\text{Not } 1\text{-}12) = 1 - P(1\text{-}12) = 1 - \frac{n(1\text{-}12)}{n(S)} = 1 - \frac{12}{38} = \frac{13}{19}.$$

   (d) Since there are no green numbers other than 0 and 00, the events are mutually exclusive. Thus:

   $$P(\text{Odd or green}) = \frac{n(\text{Odd})}{n(S)} + \frac{n(\text{Green})}{n(S)} = \frac{18}{38} + \frac{2}{38} = \frac{10}{19}.$$

13. (a) $P(\text{I win or you lose}) = P(H) + P(T) = \frac{1}{2} + \frac{1}{2} = 1$. Each player's probability of winning is not equal.

   (b) Equal. $P(\text{Heads I win}) = P(H) = \frac{1}{2}$; $P(\text{Tails you win}) = P(T) = \frac{1}{2}$.

   (c) Equal. $P(1; \text{I win}) = \frac{n(1)}{n(S)} = \frac{1}{6}$; $P(6; \text{you win}) = \frac{n(6)}{n(S)} = \frac{1}{6}$.

   (d) Equal. $P(\text{Even}; \text{I win}) = \frac{n(\text{Even})}{n(S)} = \frac{3}{6}$; $P(\text{Odd}; \text{you win}) = \frac{3}{6}$.

   (e) Not equal. $P(\geq 3; \text{I win}) = \frac{n(\geq 3)}{n(S)} = \frac{4}{6}$; $P(< 3; \text{you win}) = \frac{n(< 3)}{n(S)} = \frac{2}{6}$.

   (f) Equal. $P(1 \text{ on each}; \text{I win}) = \frac{1}{36}$; $P(6 \text{ on each}; \text{you win}) = \frac{1}{36}$.

   (g) Not equal. $P(3; \text{I win}) = \frac{n(3)}{n(S)} = \frac{2}{6}$; $P(2; \text{you win}) = \frac{n(2)}{n(S)} = \frac{1}{6}$.

   (h) Not equal. Red greater than white can occur in 15 ways:

Red	White
2	1
3	2, 1
4	3, 2, 1
5	4, 3, 2, 1
6	5, 4, 3, 2, 1

   There are also 15 ways in which the white die could be greater than the red die and 6 ways in which they could be equal. Thus: $P(\text{Red} > \text{white}; \text{I win}) = \frac{15}{36}$; $P(\text{White} \geq \text{red}; \text{you win}) = \frac{21}{36}$.

15. (a) The sample space, S, is $\{(H, H), (H, T), (T, H), (T, T)\}$. Exactly one head appears in two of the events, so:
   $$P(\text{Exactly 1 head}) = \frac{n(1 \text{ head})}{n(S)} = \frac{2}{4} = \frac{1}{2}.$$

   (b) At least one head means 1 head or 2 heads. $P(\text{At least 1}) = \frac{n(1 \text{ head})}{n(S)} + \frac{n(2 \text{ head})}{n(S)} = \frac{2}{4} + \frac{1}{4} = \frac{3}{4}$.

   (c) At most one head means 0 heads or 1 head. $P(\text{At most 1}) = \frac{1}{4} + \frac{1}{2} = \frac{3}{4}$.

17. No. $P(A) + P(B) > 1$, thus cannot be mutually exclusive.

1. (a) 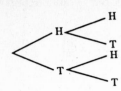 (b)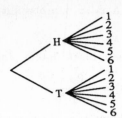

3. (a) $P(D) = \frac{1}{6}$; $P(A) = \frac{1}{6}$; $P(N) = \frac{1}{6}$. Thus $P(DAN) = \frac{1}{6} \cdot \frac{1}{6} \cdot \frac{1}{6} = \frac{1}{216}$.

    (b) $P(D) = \frac{1}{6}$; $P(A) = \frac{1}{5}$; $P(N) = \frac{1}{4}$. Thus $P(DAN) = \frac{1}{6} \cdot \frac{1}{5} \cdot \frac{1}{4} = \frac{1}{120}$.

5. This problem is similar to that of drawing colored marbles out of a box without replacement; i.e., three woman-colored marbles from a box with four woman-colored and six man-colored in it. Thus:
    $P(3 \text{ women}) = \frac{4}{10} \cdot \frac{3}{9} \cdot \frac{2}{8} = \frac{1}{30}$.

7. (a) This problem is best illustrated by a tree diagram showing four mutually exclusive paths for the probabilities of a white ball being drawn. For example, the first path would show probabilities of $\frac{1}{5}$ for drawing a white ball from the first box, $\frac{3}{5}$ of drawing a white ball from the second box given that white had been drawn from box one, and $\frac{2}{3}$ of drawing a white ball from the third box given that white had been drawn from boxes one and two. Other paths would be similarly drawn. Thus:
    $P(\text{White from 3}) = \frac{1}{5} \cdot \frac{3}{5} \cdot \frac{2}{3} + \frac{1}{5} \cdot \frac{2}{5} \cdot 1 + \frac{4}{5} \cdot \frac{2}{5} \cdot \frac{2}{3} + \frac{4}{5} \cdot \frac{3}{5} \cdot 1 = \frac{6}{75} \cdot \frac{2}{25} \cdot \frac{16}{75} \cdot \frac{12}{25} = \frac{64}{75}$

    (b) $P(\text{Black}) = 1 - P(\text{White}) = 1 - \frac{64}{75} = \frac{11}{75}$.

9. (a) $P(\text{White from box 1}) = \frac{3}{5}$; $P(\text{White from box 2}) = \frac{2}{6}$. $P(\text{Two whites}) = \frac{3}{5} \cdot \frac{2}{6} = \frac{1}{5}$.

    (b) "At least 1" means either one or two; i.e., black from 1 and black from 2, or, black from 1 and white from 2, or, white from 1 and black from 2. These events are mutually exclusive, so:
    $P(\text{At least 1 black}) = \frac{2}{5} \cdot \frac{4}{6} + \frac{2}{5} \cdot \frac{2}{6} + \frac{3}{5} \cdot \frac{4}{6} = \frac{8}{30} + \frac{4}{30} + \frac{12}{30} = \frac{4}{5}$.

    (c) "At most 1" means either zero or one. Since we can have a maximum of 2 black balls, it is easier to find the probability of 2 black balls and then use the property of complementary events. Thus:
    $P(\text{Two blacks}) = \frac{2}{5} \cdot \frac{4}{6} = \frac{4}{15}$. $P(\text{0 or 1 black}) = 1 - P(\text{Two blacks}) = 1 - \frac{4}{15} = \frac{11}{15}$.

    (d) $P(\text{Black-white or white-black}) = \frac{2}{5} \cdot \frac{2}{6} + \frac{3}{5} \cdot \frac{4}{6} = \frac{4}{30} + \frac{12}{30} = \frac{8}{15}$.

11. $P(\text{All boys}) = \frac{1}{2} \cdot \frac{1}{2} \cdot \frac{1}{2} \cdot \frac{1}{2} = \frac{1}{16}$.

13. Blond hair and blue eyes. Introducing another probability (red car) adds one more to the product of the probabilities; since each probability is less than 1 the product will be smaller.

15. Each question has a $\frac{1}{2}$ probability of being right, and the results of each question have no effect on subsequent questions. Thus $P(100\%) = \frac{1}{2} \cdot \frac{1}{2} \cdot \frac{1}{2} \cdot \frac{1}{2} \cdot \frac{1}{2} = \frac{1}{32}$.

17. (a) $P(\text{Paxson loses}) = P(\text{Rattlesnake wins})$. Thus $P(\text{4 Paxson loses}) = \frac{2}{3} \cdot \frac{2}{3} \cdot \frac{2}{3} \cdot \frac{2}{3} = \frac{16}{81}$.

    (b) There are six ways in which each school wins two games: $D = \{(PPRR), (PRPR), (PRRP), (RPPR), (RPRP), (RRPP)\}$. Each occurs with a probability $\frac{2}{3} \cdot \frac{2}{3} \cdot \frac{1}{3} \cdot \frac{1}{3} = \frac{4}{81}$.
    Thus $P(\text{Draw}) = 6 \cdot \frac{4}{81} = \frac{8}{27}$.

19. $P(\text{MISSISSIPPI}) = \frac{1}{11} \cdot \frac{4}{10} \cdot \frac{4}{9} \cdot \frac{3}{8} \cdot \frac{3}{7} \cdot \frac{2}{6} \cdot \frac{1}{5} \cdot \frac{2}{4} \cdot \frac{2}{3} \cdot \frac{1}{2} \cdot 1 = \frac{1152}{39916800} = \frac{1}{34650}$.

21. (a) Total area is 10 units by 10 units = 100 square units.

21.   (b)   (i) $P(\text{Area A}) = \frac{4}{100} = \frac{1}{25}$ (ii) $P(\text{Area B}) = \frac{12}{100} = \frac{3}{25}$

           (iii) $P(\text{Area C}) = \frac{20}{100} = \frac{1}{5}$ (iv) $P(\text{Area D}) = \frac{28}{100} = \frac{7}{25}$

           (v) $P(\text{Area E}) = \frac{36}{100} = \frac{9}{25}$

   (c)   20 points with two darts can only be scored if both land in Area A.
Thus $P(20 \text{ points}) = \frac{1}{25} \cdot \frac{1}{25} = \frac{1}{625}$.

   (d)   If the dart lands in neither D nor E, then it must land in either A, B, or C.
$P(A, B, \text{ or } C) = P(\text{Neither D nor E}) = \frac{4}{100} + \frac{12}{100} + \frac{20}{100} = \frac{9}{25}$.

23.   Assuming that we have an analog and not a digital display, the second hand will cover the distance between 3 and 4 in five seconds. Thus $P(\text{Between 3 and 4}) = \frac{5}{60} = \frac{1}{12}$.

25.   Set A covers 2 units; set B covers 5. Thus $P(B \in A) = \frac{2}{5}$.

27.   The board should be designed so that the portion in which it is desired to hit with probability $\frac{3}{5}$ will have $\frac{3}{5}$ of the total area.

29.   We want the probability that a randomly-selected patient has lung cancer, given that the patient smokes. We know that of the 30 smokers 25 have lung cancer, so :

$$P(\text{Cancer given smoker}) = \frac{n(\text{Cancer} \cap \text{Smoker})}{n(\text{Smoker})} = \frac{25}{30} = \frac{5}{6}.$$

31.   The probability of red or black on the 27th spin was the same as for each of the preceding 26. If the wheel is fair, the probability of red or black on any roll is unchanged by whatever may have previously occurred.

33.   As shown in Problem 29, the probability of an event given another happening, or $P(A \text{ given } B)$, is

$$P(A \text{ given } B) = \frac{P(A \cap B)}{P(B)}.$$ It follows, then, that $P(A \cap B) = P(B) \cdot P(A \text{ given } B)$. Thus:

$P(\text{Eaten} \cap \text{Sickly}) = P(\text{Sickly}) \cdot P(\text{Eaten given sickly}) = \frac{1}{20} \cdot \frac{1}{3} = \frac{1}{60}$;
$P(\text{Eaten} \cap \text{Not sickly}) = P(\text{Not sickly}) \cdot P(\text{Eaten given not sickly}) = \frac{19}{20} \cdot \frac{1}{150} = \frac{19}{3000}$;
and $P(\text{Eaten}) = \frac{1}{60} + \frac{19}{3000} = \frac{23}{1000}$.

35.   The probabilities of Abe's winning the game are summarized in the table below. Of the 12 possible games, only 8 result in choices with eqully likely outcomes, i.e., fair games.

		Abe's choice			
		HH	HT	TH	TT
	HH	--	.50	.75	.50
Your	HT	.50	--	.50	.25
choice	TH	.25	.50	--	.50
	TT	.50	.75	.50	--

37.   (a)   A certain event $\leftrightarrow$ (v)   (A certain event has a probability of 1)

   (b)   An impossible event $\leftrightarrow$ (iii)   (An impossible event has a probability of 0)

   (c)   A very likely event $\leftrightarrow$ (ii)   (A very likely event has a probability close to 1)

   (d)   An unlikely event $\leftrightarrow$ (i)   (An unlikely event has a probability close to 0)

   (e)   A 50% chance $\leftrightarrow$ (iv)   (A 50% chance has a probability of $\frac{1}{2}$)

1.   If trial 1 produces 2, 5, 1, 3, then Bridge #1 is open, Bridge #2 is closed, Bridge #3 is closed, and Bridge #4 is closed. There was no open route.

     If trial 2 produces 7, 4, 4, 6, then Bridge #1 is closed, Bridge #2 is open, Bridge #3 is open, and Bridge #4 is open. There was an open route.

     You may use a spinner, a random number generator, a table, or any other means of producing random numbers. Continue the experiment for 20 trials and record your results.

3.   (a)   Let rain be 1, 2, ... , 9 on a card; let no rain be a 10. Then shuffle the cards and draw randomly.

     (b)   Shuffle and draw a large number of times. Record the times a 10 occurs seven times in a row. Then

$$P(\text{No rain for 7 days}) = \frac{n(\text{No rain for 7 times})}{n(\text{Total experiments})}$$

     (c) $P(\text{No rain for 7 days}) = (0.1)^7 = 0.0000001.$

5.   Assuming an unbiased random sample of fish in the pond are caught, then $\frac{50}{300} = \frac{1}{6}$ of the total population is marked. Let n be the fish population; then $\frac{1}{6}n = 200$. Solving, n = 1200 fish.

7.   Pick a starting spot on the table and count the number of digits it takes before all the numbers 1 through 9 are obtained. Repeat this experiment many times and record the average number of boxes.

9.   Monday: Pick 10 random numbers; let those 0 to 7 represent rain and 8, 9 represent dry.

     Tuesday: Pick 10 random numbers. If it rained on Monday let 0 to 7 represent rain; if not, let 0 to 2 represent rain.

     Wednesday through Saturday: Repeat.

11.   (a)   Since it is possible for the losing team to win three games in a series, the maximum number that could be played is 7.

     (b)   Since the teams are evenly matched, use a table of random digits and let a number between 0 and 4 represent a win by Team A; let a number between 5 and 9 represent a win by Team B. Pick a starting spot and count the number of digits it takes before a Team A or Team B series win is recorded. Repeat the experiment many times and then base your answers on:

$$P(\text{4-game series}) = \frac{n(\text{4-game series})}{n(\text{Total series})} \text{ and } P(\text{7-game series}) = \frac{n(\text{7-game series})}{n(\text{Total series})}.$$

     Given evenly matched teams, the probability of a 4-game series would be expected to be low.

13.   In a random-number table, mark off 100 three-digit blocks. Let numbers 000-014 represent contraction of strep throat. Pick one at random from the block of 100; if it is within 000-014 it simulates having caught the disease. Do the experiment three times to represent three children. Now repeat this procedure many times and record the number of times one, two or all three children catch strep throat. Then:

$$P(\text{At least one}) = \frac{n(\text{1 child catches})}{n(\text{Total number of trials})} + \frac{n(\text{2 children catch})}{n(\text{Total number of trials})} + \frac{n(\text{3 children catch})}{n(\text{Total number of trials})}.$$

15.   (a) $\frac{1}{4}$ (b) $\frac{1}{52}$

     (c) $1 - \frac{4}{52} = \frac{48}{52} = \frac{12}{13}$ (d) $1 - \frac{1}{4} = \frac{3}{4}$

     (e) $\frac{1}{4} + \frac{1}{4} = \frac{1}{2}$ (f) $\frac{1}{52}$

     (g) $\frac{1}{13} + \frac{1}{4} - \frac{1}{13} \cdot \frac{1}{4} = \frac{4}{13}$ (h) $\frac{1}{2} + \frac{1}{2} = 1$

1. (a) $P(\text{Drawing a face card}) = \frac{12}{52} = \frac{3}{13}$, so Odds in favor $= \dfrac{P(\text{Face card})}{1 - P(\text{Face card})} = \frac{3}{13} \div \frac{10}{13} = 3{:}10$.

    (b)   Since the odds in favor are 3:10, the odds against are 10:3.

3. If $P(\text{Boy}) = \frac{1}{2}$, then $P(4 \text{ boys}) = (\frac{1}{2})^4 = \frac{1}{16}$. Thus odds against $= \dfrac{1 - P(4 \text{ boys})}{P(4 \text{ boys})} = \frac{15}{16} \div \frac{1}{16} = 15{:}1$.

5. $\dfrac{1 - P(\text{Win})}{P(\text{Win})} = \frac{3}{5}$, given that the odds against are 3:5. Solving for $P(\text{Win})$: $5[1 - P(\text{Win})] = 3[P(\text{Win})]$, or

    $P(\text{Win}) = \frac{5}{8}$.

7. Odds against raining $= \dfrac{1 - P(\text{Rain})}{P(\text{Rain})} = \dfrac{1 - 0.60}{0.60} = 2{:}3$.

9. The possible outcomes are HH, HT, TH, TT, so $P(2 \text{ heads}) = \frac{1}{4}$. Then E, the expected outcome, is $\$1.00(\frac{1}{4}) = 25\cent$; this is what should be paid to make a fair game.

11. $E = 1000(\frac{1}{500}) + 100(\frac{5}{500}) + 0(\frac{494}{500}) = \frac{1000}{500} + \frac{500}{500} = \$3.00$.

13. $\dfrac{P(\text{Broken arm})}{1 - P(\text{Broken arm})} = \frac{1000}{1}$. Solving for P, the probability of a broken arm: $1 \cdot P = 1000(1 - P)$, or

    $P = \frac{1000}{1001}$.

15. If the odds in favor of winning are 5:2, then $\dfrac{P(\text{Win})}{1 - P(\text{win})} = \frac{5}{2}$. Solving, we find $P(\text{Win}) = \frac{5}{7}$.
    Then $E = 14{,}000(\frac{5}{7}) = \$10{,}000$.

17. $P(2 \text{ heads}) = \frac{1}{4}$; $P(1 \text{ head}) = \frac{1}{2}$; $P(0 \text{ heads}) = \frac{1}{4}$. Accordingly, $E = 10(\frac{1}{4}) + 5(\frac{1}{2}) + 0(\frac{1}{4}) = \$5.00$.
    Because you pay the same as the expected gain, it is a fair game.

19. $\dfrac{1 - P(\text{Win})}{P(\text{Win})} = \frac{1{,}000{,}000{,}000}{1}$, or $1{,}000{,}000{,}000 \cdot P(\text{Win}) = 1 - P(\text{Win})$. Solving, $P(\text{Win}) = \frac{1}{1{,}000{,}000{,}001}$.

21. If the odds are 26:1 that Gameylegs will lose, then $\dfrac{P(\text{Loss})}{1 - P(\text{Loss})} = \frac{26}{1}$, or $P(\text{Loss}) = \frac{26}{27}$. Thus the probability of Gameylegs winning is $1 - \frac{26}{27} = \frac{1}{27}$.

23. The blue section must have $\frac{5}{6} \cdot 360° = 300°$; the red section must have $360° - 300° = 60°$.

Problem Set 8-5

1. Answers may vary. The fundamental counting principal says that if an event can occur in a fixed number of ways, and after it has occurred another event can happen in a fixed number of ways, then the total number of ways the two events can occur is the product of the number of ways of each. Permutations are the number of ways different arrangements of things can happen, if the order of the things is distinct. Combinations are the number of ways different arrangements of things can happen if the order of the things is not distinct.

3. (a)   There are $10^6 = 1{,}000{,}000$ possible license plates.

    (b)   The 1990 census showed Montana, Wyoming, Alaska, Delaware, North and South Dakota, and Vermont with less than 1,000,000 automobiles.

    (c)   Answers may vary; one is to use numbers plus letters of the alphabet.

5. Each coin toss will result in two possible outcomes (H or T). Five tosses will then result in $2^5 = 32$ different combinations of heads and tails.

7.   Assuming all letters after the first can be repeated, there are $2 \cdot 26 \cdot 26 = 1352$ three-letter call signs available (the factor 2 represents either K or W). There are $2 \cdot 26 \cdot 26 \cdot 26 = 35,152$ four-letter call signs available.

9.   (a)   True. $6 \cdot 5! = 6 \cdot (5 \cdot 4 \cdot 3 \cdot 2 \cdot 1) = 6!$.

      (b)   False. $3! + 3! = 3 \cdot 2 \cdot 1 + 3 \cdot 2 \cdot 1 \neq 6!$.

      (c)   False. $\frac{6!}{3!} = \frac{6 \cdot 5 \cdot 4 \cdot 3 \cdot 2 \cdot 1}{3 \cdot 2 \cdot 1} = 6 \cdot 5 \cdot 4 \neq 2!$.

      (d)   False. $\frac{6!}{3} = \frac{6 \cdot 5 \cdot 4 \cdot 3 \cdot 2 \cdot 1}{3} \neq 2!$

      (e)   True. See (c).

      (f)   True. $\frac{6!}{4!2!} = \frac{6 \cdot 5 \cdot 4 \cdot 3 \cdot 2 \cdot 1}{(4 \cdot 3 \cdot 2 \cdot 1)(2 \cdot 1)} = \frac{6 \cdot 5}{2 \cdot 1} = 15$.

      (g)   True. $(n + 1) \cdot n! = (n + 1) \cdot n \cdot (n - 1) \cdot (n - 2) \cdot \ \cdots \ \cdot 3 \cdot 2 \cdot 1 = (n + 1)!$.

11.   Since order is not distinct, the number of two-person committees is a combination of six things taken two at a time, or $_6C_2$. $_6C_2 = \frac{6!}{2!(6 - 2)!} = 15$ different committees.

13.   (a)   Since order is distinct, this is a permutation of 30 things taken 3 at a time: $_{30}P_3 = \frac{30!}{27!} = 24,360$ ways.

      (b)   In this case order is not distinct; this is a combination: $_{30}C_3 = \frac{30!}{27!3!} = 4060$ ways.

15.   There are $9! = 362,880$ different ways of arranging the nine books.

17.   We want the number of ways of choosing 10 points, 2 at a time. Since a line may be drawn either way, order is not distinct; i.e., we have a combination. $_{10}C_2 = \frac{10!}{8!2!} = 45$ straight lines.

19.   Sally can run $\frac{9!}{4!3!2!} = 1260$ nine-flag signals up the pole.

21.   If there were n people at the party, there were n combinations of people two at a time shaking hands. That is, $_nC_2 = \frac{n!}{(n - 2)!2!} = \frac{n \cdot (n - 1)}{2!} = 28$. If $n \cdot (n - 1) = 56$, $n = 8$ and there were 8 people at the party.

23.   (a) $_5C_3 = $ the third number in row 5, or 10.   (b) $_5C_5 = $ the fifth number in row 5, or 1.

      (c) $_6C_0 = $ the 0th number in row 6, or 1.   (d) $_3C_2 = $ the second number in row 3, or 3.

25.   If we treat this as 5 people to be seated in 5 chairs (since the couples cannot be separated), there are $5! = 120$ different ways of being seated. Each couple, though, can be alternated, and there are $2^5 = 32$ ways of doing this. $120 \cdot 32 = 3840$ possible combinations.

CHAPTER 9 - STATISTICS: AN INTRODUCTION

Problem Set 9-1

1.

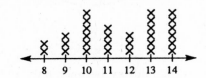

Glasses of Lemonade Sold

represents 10 glasses

3.   Student Ages at Washington School

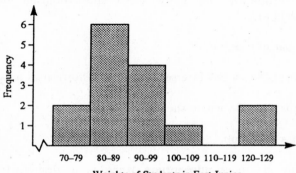

5.

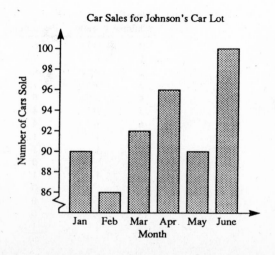

Weights of Students in East Junior
High Algebra I Class

7.   (a)   Novenber, with approximately 30 cm of rain.

(b)   15 (October) + 25 (December) + 10 (January) = 50 cm.

9.   (a)   The Mississippi is approximately 3800 km long.

(b)   The Columbia is approximately 1900 km long.

11.

Car Sales for Johnson's Car Lot

13. (a)

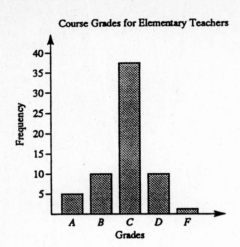

Course Grades for Elementary Teachers

(b)

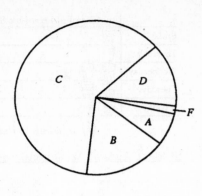

15. The line graph is more helpful, since we can approximate the point midway between 8:00 and 12:00 noon and then draw a vertical line upward until it hits the line graph. An approximation for the 10:00 temperature can then be obtained from the vertical axis.

17. (a) The chicken. It's graph has the shortest bar of the graph.

(b) 10 miles per hour, where the length of the chicken's bar intersects 10 on the horizontal axis.

(c) The cheetah. Twice the rabbit's 35 mph is 70 mph, where the cheetah's bar ends.

(d) Yes. The lion's speed is 50 mph; the zebra's 40 mph.

19. Answers may vary, but a circle graph would be more appropriate when it is desired to emphasize proportions.

21. Answers may vary, but a stem-and-leaf plot is more informative when exact data is needed.

23. (a) Asia.

(b) Africa.

(c) It is about two-thirds as large.

(d) Asia and Africa.

(e) About 5:16.

(f) Approximately 58.6 million square miles.

25. (a)

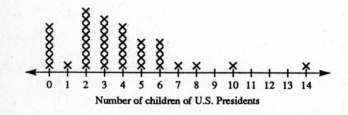

Number of children of U.S. Presidents

(b)

No. of Children	Tally	Frequency
0	JHT I	6
1	I	1
2	JHT III	8
3	JHT II	7
4	JHT I	6
5	IIII	4
6	IIII	4
7	I	1
8	I	1
9		0
10	I	1
11		0
12		0
13		0
14	I	1
		40

(c) The most frequent number of children is two.

1.   (a)   Ordering the data, we have 2, 5, 5, 7, 8, 8, 8, 10.

       (*i*)   Mean $= \frac{2 + 5 + 5 + 7 + 8 + 8 + 8 + 10}{8} = \frac{53}{8} = 6.625.$

       (*ii*)   Median: The midpoint is between 7 and 8, or $\frac{7 + 8}{2} = 7.5.$

       (*iii*)   Mode: 8 occurs most frequently, so the mode $= 8.$

   (b)   Ordering the data, we have 10, 11, 12, 12, 12, 14, 14, 16, 20.

       (*i*)   Mean $= \frac{10 + 11 + 12 + 12 + 12 + 14 + 14 + 16 + 20}{9} = \frac{121}{9} = 13.\overline{4}.$

       (*ii*)   Median: The midpoint is at 12, so the median $= 12.$

       (*iii*)   Mode: 12 occurs most frequently, so the mode $= 12.$

   (c)   Ordering the data, we have 12, 17, 18, 18, 22, 22, 30.

       (*i*)   Mean $= \frac{12 + 17 + 18 + 18 + 22 + 22 + 30}{7} = \frac{139}{7} \doteq 19.9.$

       (*ii*)   Median: The midpoint is at 18, so the median $= 18.$

       (*iii*)   Mode: 18 and 22 occur most frequently, so we have dual modes of 18 and 22.

   (d)   Ordering the data, we have 63, 75, 80, 80, 80, 80, 82, 90, 92, 92.

       (*i*)   Mean $= \frac{63 + 75 + 80 + 80 + 80 + 80 + 90 + 92 + 92}{10} = \frac{814}{10} = 81.4.$

       (*ii*)   Median: The midpoint is between 80 and 80, or the median $= 80.$

       (*iii*)   Mode: 80 occurs most frequently, so the mode $= 80.$

   (e)   (*i*)   Mean $= \frac{5 + 5 + 5 + 5 + 5 + 10}{6} = \frac{35}{6} = 5.8\overline{3}.$

       (*ii*)   Median: The midpoint is between 5 and 5, or the median $= 5.$

       (*iii*)   Mode: 5 occurs most frequently, so the mode $= 5.$

3.   Since mean $= \frac{\text{sum of test scores}}{\text{number of test scores}},$ then $75 = \frac{\text{sum}}{20}$ or sum $= 20 \cdot 75 = 1500.$

5.   If the mean of 28 scores is 80, then the sum of the scores is $28 \cdot 80 = 2240.$ Adding 60 and 50, the new sum is 2350. The new mean is thus $\frac{2350}{28 + 2} = 78.\overline{3}.$

7.   Select the mode; it is the size which sold most frequently.

9.   Total lineman weight is $7 \cdot 230 = 1610$ pounds; total backfield weight is $4 \cdot 190 = 760$ pounds. Total player weight is $1610 + 760 = 2370$ pounds. The mean weight is thus $\frac{2370}{11} \doteq 215.5$ pounds per player.

11.   (a)   The total of salaries, in thousands of dollars, is:
       $18 \cdot 2 + 22 \cdot 4 + 26 \cdot 4 + 35 \cdot 3 + 38 \cdot 12 + 44 \cdot 8 + 50 \cdot 4 + 80 \cdot 2 + 150$
       $= 36 + 88 + 104 + 105 + 456 + 352 + 200 + 160 + 150 = 1651,$ or \$1,651,000.
       There are a total of 40 players, so the mean annual salary is $\frac{1651000}{40} = \$41,275.$

   (b)   The median is between the 20th and 21st (in order, from smallest to largest) salaries. Since salaries between the 13th and 25th are all at \$38,000, the median is \$38,000.

11.   (c)   The largest number of salaries is 12 at \$38,000, so the mode is \$38,000.

13.   The total miles of the trip were $43,390 - 42,800 = 590$ miles. The total amount of gasoline used was $12 + 18 = 30$ gallons. Her fuel mileage was thus $\frac{590 \text{ miles}}{30 \text{ gallons}} = 19\frac{2}{3}$ miles per gallon.

15.   Mean hours per day was $\dfrac{5\frac{1}{2} + 3\frac{1}{2} + 5\frac{1}{4} + 6\frac{3}{4} + 8}{5} = \frac{29}{5} = 5\frac{4}{5}$ hours.

17.   (a)   Set A: mean is $\frac{24}{4} = 6$; range is 9 - 3 = 6.

      (b)   Set B: all elements are 11, so mean, median, and mode are all 11.
                Set C: mean $= \frac{77}{7} = 11$; median and mode are each 11.

      (c)   Set C: mean $= \frac{12}{4} = 3$; median $= \frac{2+4}{2} = 3$; there is no mode, since no value occurs more than once.

19.   (a)   Answers may vary; one set would be 10, 30, 70, and 90.

      (b)   The smaller numbers are the same amount below the mean as the larger numbers are above it. That is, their mean is also 50.

      (c)   The mean of 10, 30, 70, and 90 is 50. See (b) above.

21.   The mean is increased by the value of the number added; all values have been shifted the same amount. The standard deviation is unchanged; the spread between the numbers has remained constant.

23.   (a) $\bar{x} = \dfrac{96+71+43+77+75+76+61+83+71+58+97+76+74+91+74+71+77+83+87+93+79}{21} \doteq 76.8.$

      (b)   Ordering, the scores are:
                43, 58, 61, 71, 71, 71, 74, 74, 75, 76, 76, 77, 77, 79, 83, 83, 87, 91, 93, 96, 97.
                The median is the 11th score, or 76.

      (c)   The mode is 71, or the most frequent score.

      (d)

x	$x - \bar{x}$	$(x - \bar{x})^2$
96	19.2	368.64
71	⁻5.8	33.64
43	⁻33.8	1142.44
77	0.2	0.04
75	⁻1.8	3.24
76	⁻0.8	0.64
61	⁻15.8	249.64
83	6.2	38.44
71	⁻5.8	33.64
58	⁻18.8	353.44
97	20.2	408.04
76	⁻0.8	0.64
74	⁻2.8	7.84
91	14.2	201.64
74	⁻2.8	7.84
71	⁻5.8	33.64
77	0.2	0.04
83	6.2	38.44
87	10.2	104.04
93	16.2	262.44
79	2.2	4.84
		$\overline{3293.24}$

$v = \dfrac{3293.24}{21} \doteq 156.8$

23. (e) $s = \sqrt{156.8} \doteq 12.5$

25. If we let Ginny's three scores be represented by F (first), S (second), and T (third), then:
  S = 90 (the median);

  $$\frac{F + S + T}{3} = 92 \text{ (the mean), or } F + S + T = 376;$$

  F − T = 6 (the range).
  Solving as a system of equations, we find: F = 96, S = 90, and T = 90.

27. No. To find the average speed we divide the distance traveled by the time it takes to drive it. The first part of the trip took $\frac{5 \; miles}{30 \; mph} = \frac{1}{6}$ hours. The second part of the trip took $\frac{5 \; miles}{50 \; mph} = \frac{1}{10}$ hours. To find the

  average speed we then compute $\dfrac{5 \text{ miles} + 5 \text{ miles}}{\frac{1}{6} \text{ hour} + \frac{1}{10} \text{ hour}} = 37.5$ mph.

29. (a) The median in a box plot is the middle line through the box. The median of Theater A is thus 25; that of Theater B is 50.

  (b) The greatest range is that of Theater B: 80 − 15 = $65.

  (c) The highest price of either is the upper value at Theater B, $80.

  (d) Answers may vary. Some observations are that there is significantly more variation and generally higher prices at Theater B.

31. (a) Minneapolis: Lower extreme = 366   Los Angeles: Lower extreme = 516
            Lower quartile = 416   Lower quartile = 571
            Median = $\frac{447 + 561}{2}$ = 504   Median = $\frac{620 + 625}{2}$ = 622.5
            Upper quartile = 668   Upper quartile = 735
            Upper extreme = 950   Upper extreme = 858
  The box plot is shown below:

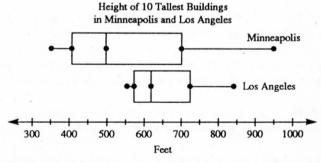

Height of 10 Tallest Buildings
in Minneapolis and Los Angeles

  (b) In Minneapolis, the IQR = 668 − 416 = 252. There are no values more than 1.5·IQR = 378 feet above the upper quartile or more than 378 feet below the lower quartile, so there are no outliers. In Los Angeles there are no values more than 1.5·IQR = 1.5(735 − 571) = 246 feet above the upper quartile or more than 246 feet below the lower quartile, so there are no outliers.

33. (a) (i) Mean = $\frac{1 + 3 + 5 + 7 + 9}{5}$ = 5. Median is the middle value, or 5.

      (ii) 199 = 1 + (n − 1)2, so n = 100; i.e., there are 100 terms in the sequence.
           The sum of 100 terms of this sequence is $\frac{100}{2}(1 + 199)$ = 10,000.
           The 50th term is 1 + (50 − 1)2 = 99.

           Thus the mean = $\frac{10,000}{100}$ = 100; the median is between term 50 and 51, or $\frac{99 + 101}{2}$ = 100.

33. (a) (*iii*) $607 = 7 + (n - 1)3$, so $n = 201$ and there are 201 terms in the sequence.
The sum of 201 terms of this sequence is $\frac{201}{2}(7 + 607) = 61{,}707$.
The 101st term is $7 + (101 - 1)3 = 307$.

Thus the mean $= \frac{61{,}707}{201} = 307$; the median is the 101st term, or 307.

(b) The mean and median of an arithmetic sequence are the same.

35. (a) Mount Everest is the highest mountain, at approximately 8500 meters.

(b) Mounts Aconcagus, Everest, and McKinley.

Problem Set 9-3

1. (a) 85 is one standard deviation below the mean; 115 is one standard deviation above the mean. That is:
$Z_{85} = \frac{85 - 100}{15} = {}^-1$, and $Z_{115} = \frac{115 - 100}{15} = 1$.
Since $34 + 34 = 68\%$ of the area under the curve lies within ± 1 standard deviation from the mean, 68% of the students will have IQ's between 85 and 115. 68% of 1500 is 1020 students in that range.

(b) 70 is two standard deviations below the mean; 130 is two standard deviations above the mean. 95% of the area under the curve lies within ± 2 standard deviations from the mean, and 95% of 1500 = 1425 students with IQ's between 70 and 130.

(c) 145 is three standard deviations above the mean; only 0.1% of the area under the curve is more than three standard deviations from the mean. 0.01% of 1500 = 1.5, so one or two students will have an IQ of more than 145.

3. $Z_{4.50} = \frac{4.50 - 5.00}{0.50} = {}^-1$ and $Z_{5.50} = \frac{5.00 - 5.00}{0.50} = 1$.
The amount of data between ± 1 standard deviations is 68%, so there is a 68% chance that a worker picked at random will earn between \$4.50 and \$5.50 per hour.

5. $Z_{2\ min} = \frac{2 - 4}{2} = {}^-1$. Only $50 - 34 = 16\%$ of the data under the curve is less than 2 standard deviations below the mean, so 16% of the calls will last less than 2 minutes.

7. (a) $Z_{130} = \frac{130 - 100}{15} = 2$. $34 + 13.5 = 47.5\%$ of the data under the curve lies within 2 standard deviations above the mean, so 47.5% of the population will have IQ's between 100 and 130.

(b) $Z_{85} = \frac{85 - 100}{15} = {}^-1$. $50 - 34 = 16\%$ of the data under the curve is less than 1 standard deviation below the mean, so 16% of the population will have IQ's of less than 85.

9. $Z_{1.4} = 91.92$; $Z_{1.5} = 93.32$. The percentage of scores between $Z = 1.4$ and 1.5 is thus $93.32 - 91.92 = 1.4\%$.

11. $Z = {}^-1.25 = \frac{53 - 63}{s} = \frac{10}{s}$, or ${}^-1.25s = 10$. Solving, s (standard deviation) = 8.

13. 95% of all data under a normal curve is within ± 2 standard deviations of the mean. The range corresponding to ± 2 standard deviations is between $65.5 - 2 \cdot 2.5 = 60.5$ inches to $65.5 + 2 \cdot 2.5 = 70.5$ inches.

15. $Z_{440} = \frac{440 - 500}{60} = {}^-1$. A z-score of ${}^-1$ represents the 16th percentile, so $0.16 \cdot 10{,}000 = 1600$ students rated deficient.

17. (a) The trend of the line slopes downward to the right, so there is a negative correlation.

(b) Approximately 10.   (c) Approximately 22 years old.

19. If the mean is 27, then the total of the scores is $36 \cdot 27 = 972$. Adding the two additional scores, the new total is 1054. Mean $= \frac{1054}{38} \doteq 27.74$.

21. Men's <u>Olympic</u> <u>100-m</u> <u>Gold</u> <u>Medal</u> <u>Times</u>

10	0 2 3 3 3 4 5 6 8 8 8 8
11	0 0
12	0

10|8 represents 10.8 seconds.

Problem Set 9-4

1. Answers may vary.

   (a) The claim cannot be substantiated without knowing more about the noise characteristics of the car and glider in question. Many gliders are quite noisy.

   (b) There is no way of knowing whether or not this claim is true. It may be that 95% of its cycles sold in the United States were sold in the last year.

   (c) 10% more than 10% is not very much.

   (d) Fresher than what?

   (e) "Up to" can cover a multitude of sins.

   (f) Brighter than what?

   (g) How many dentists responded? Who paid them?

   (h) This is an example of carrying an argument to a ridiculous extreme.

   (i) Is there another airline flying to the city?

3. She could have taken a different number of quizzes during the first part of the quarter than in the second part.

5. The horizontal axis does not have uniformly-sized intervals, and neither the horizontal axis nor the graph are labeled.

7. No. It could very well be that most of the pickups sold in the past 10 years were actually sold during the last two years. In such a case most of the pickups have been on the road for only two years, and therefore the given information would not imply that the average life of a pickup is around ten years.

9. The three-dimensional drawing distorts the graph. The result of doubling the radius and the height of the can are to increase the volume by a factor of 8.

11. One would need more information; e.g., is the graph in percentage or actual numbers?

13. (a) This bar graph would have perhaps 20 accidents as the baseline. Then 38 in 1992 would appear to be almost double the 24 of 1988, when in fact it is only 58% higher.

    (b) This bar graph would have 0 accidents as its baseline.

15. It is not clear what is meant by "margin" and it is not clear whether the dollar amounts are for units or some other quantity (such as thousands of dollars).

CHAPTER 10 - INTRODUCTORY GEOMETRY

Problem Set 10-1

1. (a) $\overleftrightarrow{AB}$ (b) $\overline{AB}$

   (c) $\overline{AB}$ (d) $\overrightarrow{AB}$

   (e) $\overleftrightarrow{AB} \| \overleftrightarrow{CD}$ (f) $\overline{AB}$

   (g) $\overleftrightarrow{AB} \perp \overleftrightarrow{CD}$ (h) $m(\angle ABC) = 30°$

3. No. The symbol is a finite collection of points.

5. (a) True   (b) True

   (c) False. Three points may define a plane with the fourth not on that plane.

   (d) False. They may be skew.   (e) True

   (f) True

   (g) False. In fact, no plane contains both, which is what makes them skew.

   (h) False. Think of the baseboard and a horizontal window sill on the same wall. They are parallel lines both parallel to the ceiling, yet their plane (the wall) is in this case perpendicular to the ceiling.

   (i) False. Three points may define a plane, but try putting a line through three corners of a table top.

   (j) True   (k) True

   (l) True

7. 20 pairs. Adjacent angles share a common vertex and a common side, and have nonoverlapping interiors.

9. (a) Yes. l and m cannot intersect since $\alpha \| \beta$, and they cannot be skew since γ contains both.

   (b) No. The sloped sides of any A-frame structure would intersect the ground in two parallel lines, but the sides are not parallel to each other.

   (c) Yes. If the planes were not parallel they would intersect in a line m and at least one of the given lines would intersect m and would then intersect plane α, which contradicts the fact that the given lines are parallel to α.

11. (a) Approximately 36°   (b) Approximately 120°

13. (a) Draw a line with 3 points labeled A, B, and C. Then there are four rays determined by the three points: $\overrightarrow{AB}$, $\overrightarrow{BC}$, $\overrightarrow{CB}$, and $\overrightarrow{BA}$ (remember that $\overrightarrow{AB} = \overrightarrow{AC}$, but $\overrightarrow{AB} \neq \overrightarrow{BA}$).

   (b) Draw a line with 4 points labeled A, B, C, and D. Then there are six rays: $\overrightarrow{AB}$, $\overrightarrow{BC}$, $\overrightarrow{CD}$, $\overrightarrow{DC}$, $\overrightarrow{CB}$, and $\overrightarrow{BA}$.

   (c) With 5 colinear points A, B, C, D, and E, there are eight rays: $\overrightarrow{AB}$, $\overrightarrow{BC}$, $\overrightarrow{CD}$, $\overrightarrow{DE}$, $\overrightarrow{ED}$, $\overrightarrow{DC}$, $\overrightarrow{CB}$, $\overrightarrow{BA}$

   (d) There are 4, 6, and 8 rays for 3, 4, and 5 points, respectively. The general term for the number of rays given n points is thus $2(n - 1)$.

15. (a)

		Number of Intersection Points					
		0	1	2	3	4	5
Number of lines	2			Not Possible	Not Possible	Not Possible	Not Possible
	3					Not Possible	Not Possible
	4			Not Possible			
	5			Not Possible	Not Possible		
	6			Not Possible	Not Possible	Not Possible	

(b) The maximum number of intersections is the number of possible pairings of two lines: $\frac{n(n-1)}{2}$, or $_nC_2$.

17. (a) No. If $\angle$ BDC were a right angle, then both $\overleftrightarrow{BD}$ and $\overleftrightarrow{BC}$ would be perpendicular to $\overleftrightarrow{DC}$ and thus be parallel.

(b) No. Consider some line $\overleftrightarrow{QP}$ with $\overrightarrow{QP} \perp \alpha$ and Q on the same side of α as D. Then $\angle$ QPC is a right angle. PD divides $\angle$ QPC into two angles ($\angle$ QPD and $\angle$ DPC) which then must both be less than a right angle.

(c) Yes. Two planes are perpendicular if and only if one plane contains a line perpendicular to the other plane.

19. (a)

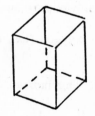

(b)

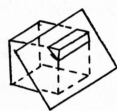

(c)

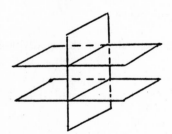

(d)

21. (*i*) (b) is empty because lines cannot be both skew and coplanar.

(*ii*) (d) is empty because lines cannot be both skew and parallel.

(*iii*) (e) is empty; lines cannot be skew, coplanar, and parallel.

(*iv*) (g) is empty because lines cannot be parallel without being coplanar.

23. (a) No. Skew lines do not intersect, thus cannot be perpendicular.

(b) No. Obtuse angles are greater than 90°, so their sum is greater than $90 + 90 = 180°$.

(c) No. As in (b), but "less than 90°" and "less than 180°."

25.   Segments do not extend beyond their endpoints and can be separate without being parallel.

27.   By definition, a point has no size; i.e., there is no "smallest" point. No matter how close the two points are, another point can be placed between them, leading to an infinite number of points on a segment.

29.   Suppose the lines of intersection are not parallel. They cannot be skew since they are both in the third plane. They must then intersect at some point x which must be in both parallel planes. But since parallel planes cannot have a common point, this too is impossible. Thus the lines must be parallel.

Problem Set 10-2

1.   (a)   By definition, polygonal curves are made entirely of line segments. Thus 1, 2, 3, 6, 7, 8, 9, 11, and 12 are polygonal curves.

     (b)   "Simple" adds the restriction that the polygonal curves may not cross themselves, leaving 1, 2, 7, 8, 9, and 11.

     (c)   Closed polygonal curves are those that when traced have the same starting and stopping points. Thus the closed polygonal curves are 1, 2, 3, 6, 7, 8, 9, and 11.

     (d)   Polygons are polygonal curves which are both simple and closed. The polygons are then 1, 2, 7, 8, 9, and 11.

     (e)   If all segments connecting any two points of a polygon are inside the polygon (i.e., the region is not dented inwards anywhere) then the polygon is a convex polygon. The convex polygons are 7 and 8.

     (f)   If part of any segment joining two points of a polygon is outside the polygon (i.e., it is "caved in" somewhere), then it is concave. The concave polygons are 1, 2, 9, and 11.

3.   (a)   The straight path from X crosses the curve six times (an even number). This indicates that X is outside the curve.

     (b)   The straight path from X crosses the curve twice; it is outside the curve.

5.   A segment can pass through at most two sides of a triangle. With each side of the quadrilateral passing through two sides of the triangle, there can be eight intersections.

7.   Answers may vary.

(a)   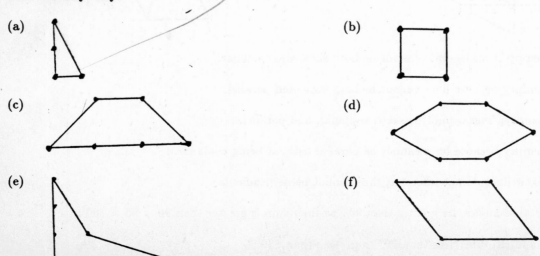   (b)

(c)   (d)

(e)   (f)

9. From "Looking Back" in Section 10-2 example problem 2, the number of diagonals is $\frac{n(n-3)}{2}$.

(a) $\frac{10(7)}{2} = 35$ diagonals

(b) $\frac{20(17)}{2} = 170$ diagonals

(c) $\frac{100(97)}{2} = 4850$ diagonals

11. (a) False. Isosceles triangles might have only two congruent sides.

(b) True. If three sides are congruent, then "at least two" are.

(c) True. A square is a rectangle with all sides congruent.

(d) True. Those that are squares are rhombuses.

(e) True. All have four sides.

(f) False. Though all sides are congruent, angles may not be.

(g) True. A trapezoid is a quadrilateral with at least one pair of parallel sides.

(h) False. Equilateral triangles have three congruent sides; scalene triangles have none.

(i) True. A kite is a quadrilateral with two distinct pairs of consecutive sides congruent.

(j) True; those with four congruent sides.

(k) False. In fact, all squares are rectangles.

(l) False. Some trapezoids are parallelograms, because the set of parallelograms is a proper subset of the set of trapezoids.

(m) True. Right triangles may have two congruent sides.

(n) False. An isosceles trapezoid that is a square is also a kite.

(o) False. (See (n) above)

13. Angles must also be congruent as is the case only in special rhombuses; i.e., squares.

15. (a) T, Q, R, H, G, I, F, J

(b) Y, Z, E

(c) W, D, A, Z, U, E

(d) Q, J, F, G, H

(e) Y

Answers may vary.

The angles are formed by any two rays. The number of angles is the number of pairs of rays; i.e., the combinations of all rays taken two at a time.

a) $_{10}C_2 = \frac{10!}{2!(10-2)!} = 45.$

$_nC_2 = \frac{n(n-1)(n-2)\cdots(1)}{2\cdot1\cdot[(n-2)(n-3)\cdots(1)]} = \frac{n(n-1)}{2}.$

{C} is the only point of intersection.

(b) $\overline{BD}$; $\overline{CD}$ adds nothing to $\overline{BD}$.

21.   (c) $\overline{AB}$, $\overline{AC}$, and $\overline{AD}$ all contain {A}.   (d)   {D} is the only point of intersection.

<u>Problem Set 10-3</u>

1.   (a)   ∠ 1 and ∠ 2 are adjacent; ∠ 3 and ∠ 4 are vertical.

     (b)   ∠ 1 and ∠ 2 are vertical; ∠ 3 and ∠ 4 are adjacent.

     (c)   ∠ 1 and ∠ 2 are neither vertical nor adjacent, since they are not formed by two intersecting lines and
             do not have a common side.

     (d)   ∠ 1 and ∠ 2 are adjacent.

3.   (a)   (b)
     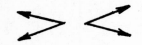   

     (c)   (d)

     (e)

5.   The angles of every triangle add to 180°; subtract the given angles to find the third angle.

     (a) $60° \left(180 - (70 + 50) = 60\right)$ (b) $45° \left(180 - (90 + 45) = 45\right)$

     (c) $60° \left(180 - (90 + 30) = 60\right)$ (d) $60° \left(180 - (60 + 60) = 60\right)$

7.   (a)   No. Two or more obtuse angles would produce a sum of more than 180°, the sum of all angles in a
             triangle.

     (b)   Yes. For example, each angle may have measure 60°.

     (c)   No. The sum of the measures of the three angles would be more than 180°.

     (d)   No. It may have an obtuse or right angle as well.

9.   (a)   Using congruent vertical angles, x = 40°. y = 180 − (90 + 40) = 50°.

     (b)   Using complementary interior angles, x + 4x = 90; x = 18°.

     (c)   Using supplementary interior angles formed by parallel lines, m∠ ACD = 110°. m∠ BCD = 50°
             from vertical angles. Thus y = 110 − 50 = 60°, so x = 180 − (70 + 60) = 50°.

     (d)   Using supplementary angles, one vertex of the triangle = 180 − 125 = 55°. Using vertical angles, the
             other vertex of the triangle = 42°. Thus the interior angle of the triangle vertical to x is
             180 − (55 + 42) = 83°, so, using vertical angles, x = 83°.

11. The ratio could be written 7x:2x. The angles must add to 90°, so 7x + 2x = 90 ⇒ x = 10. The angles are
     7(10) = 70° and 2(10) = 20°.

13. (a) The six angles surrounding the center point add to 360°. The angles contained by triangles equal those not contained (vertical angles); the contained angles must then add to $\frac{1}{2}(360) = 180°$. The three triangles total $3(180) = 540°$. The numbered angles must then add to $540 - 180 = 360°$.

(b) $m\angle 1 + m\angle 3 + m\angle 5 = 180°$ (the sum of a triangle's interior angles); likewise, $m\angle 2 + m\angle 4 + m\angle 6 = 180°$. The sum of the angles is $180 + 180 = 360°$.

(c) 360° (same as (b)).

15. (a) Each exterior angle is $180 - 162 = 18°$. Since exterior angles add to 360°, there must be $360 \div 18 = 20$ angles and hence 20 sides.

(b) A dodecagon has 12 exterior angles so each is $360 \div 12 = 30°$. The interior angles are then $180 - 30 = 150°$ each.

17. (a) Drawing diagonals from one vertex gives three triangles, for a total of $3 \cdot 180 = 540°$.

(b) There are always two less triangles than sides, so the sum of the measures of the angles is $(n - 2 \text{ triangles}) \cdot (180° \text{ each}) = (n - 2) \cdot 180°$.

19. (a) The measures of the angles are the same.

(b) $m(\angle 4) + m(\angle 3) = 180°$ (straight line). $[m(\angle 1) + m(\angle 2)] + m(\angle 3) = 180°$ (the sum of the angles in a triangle). Since both $m(\angle 4)$ and $[m(\angle 1) + m(\angle 2)]$ plus $m(\angle 3) = 180°$, they must be equal.

21. Vertical angles are formed by two intersecting lines. In this case, angle 1 is formed by a line and a ray.

23. The measure of an octogon's interior angle is $\frac{(n - 2)180}{n} = \frac{(6)180}{8} = 135°$. By using supplementary angles, the measure of each of the triangle's interior angles is $180 - 135 = 45°$. Since the two interior angles of the isosceles triangle are each 45°, $\angle 1 = 180 - (45 + 45) = 90°$.

25. The angles must be supplementary.

27. $m(\angle 1) = 90 - 30 = 60°$. $m(\angle 2) = 180 - (90 + 60) = 30°$. $m(\angle 3) = 180 - (30 + 40) = 110°$.

29. (*i*) Theorem 10-1(a):
Let both $\angle 2$ and $\angle 3$ be supplements of $\angle 1$.
Then: $m(\angle 2) + m(\angle 1) = 180°$
$\quad\quad m(\angle 3) + m(\angle 1) = 180°$
$\quad\quad m(\angle 2) + m(\angle 1) = m(\angle 3) + m(\angle 1)$
$\quad\quad m(\angle 2) = m(\angle 3)$, so $\angle 2 \simeq \angle 3$.
Let $\angle 3$ be the supplement of $\angle 1$, and $\angle 4$ be the supplement of $\angle 2$, and $\angle 1 \simeq \angle 2$.
Then: $m(\angle 3) + m(\angle 1) = 180°$
$\quad\quad m(\angle 4) + m(\angle 2) = 180°$
$\quad\quad m(\angle 3) + m(\angle 1) = m(\angle 4) + m(\angle 2)$
$\quad\quad \angle 1 \simeq \angle 2$ implies $m(\angle 1) = m(\angle 2)$
$\quad\quad m(\angle 3) + m(\angle 2) = m(\angle 4) + m(\angle 2)$
$\quad\quad m(\angle 3) = m(\angle 4)$, so $\angle 3 \simeq \angle 4$.

(*ii*) The proof of Theorem 10-1(b) is similar to that of Theorem 10-1(a), using 90° in place of 180° and complement in place of supplement.

31. Mark point F on ray $\overrightarrow{AB}$ past point B, and mark point E on ray $\overrightarrow{CB}$ past point B, as shown below:

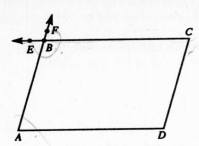

(a)   m(∠ A) = m(∠ FBC) (corresponding angles)
      m(∠ FBE) + m(∠ FBC) = 180° (supplementary angles)
      m(∠ FBE) = m(∠ ABC) (vertical angles)
      Then m(∠ ABC) + m(∠ A) = 180° (substitution)

(b)   m(∠ A) = m(∠ ABE) (alternate interior angles)
      m(∠ ABE) = m(∠ C) (corresponding angles)
      Then m(∠ A) = m(∠ C), and likewise m(∠ B) = m(∠ D).

33. Answers may vary.

(a)   TO PARALLELOGRAM :L :W :A
        REPEAT 2[FD :L RT 180 — :A FD :W RT :A]
      END

(b)   TO RECTANGLE :L :W
        PARALLELOGRAM :L :W 90
      END

(c)   TO RHOMBUS :L :L :A
        PARALLELOGRAM :L :L :A
      END

(d)   Execute PARALLELOGRAM 50 50 90.

(e)   Execute RHOMBUS 50 90.

35. No. The union of two rays will always extend indefinitely in at least one direction.

37. Crease a large piece of cardboard and lay it on the roof with the crease along $\overline{BC}$ and extending past B. Measure the dihedral angle of the folded cardboard.

39. (a)   Hexagon.   (b)   Rectangle or pentagon.

     (c)   Two intersecting segments.   (d)   Rectangle.

     (e)   Square or rectangle.

1. (a) Quadrilateral pyramid.   (b) Quadrilateral prism.

    (c) Pentagonal pyramid.

3. Answers may vary, but examples are: square prism (saltine crackers), rectangular prism (cereal), circular cylinder (canned corn), triangular prism (candy bar).

5. (a) True. This is the definition of a right prism.

    (b) False. No pyramid is a prism; e.g., a pyramid has one base and a prism two bases.

    (c) True. The definition of a pyramid starts with the fact that it is a polyhedron.

    (d) False. They lie in parallel planes.

    (e) False. The base can be any simple closed curve.

    (f) False. They have two bases.

    (g) False. They are parallelograms; if they were rectangles they would be right prisms.

    (h) True, by definition.

7. (a)   (b)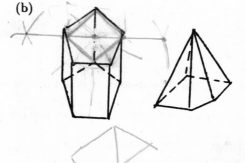

    (c)

9. (a) Hexagonal pyramid.   (b) Quadrilateral (square) pyramid.

    (c) Cube.   (d) Rectangular prism.

    (e) Hexagonal prism.

11. (a) (*iv*)   (b) (*ii*)

13.
Prism	Vertices per Base	Diagonals per Vertex	Total Number of Diagonals
Quadrilateral	4	1	4
Pentagonal	5	2	10
Hexagonal	6	3	18
Heptagonal	7	4	28
Octagonal	8	5	40
⋮			
n-gonal	n	$(n - 3)$	$n(n - 3)$

15. (a) 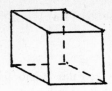   (b)

(c) 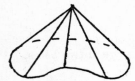   (d)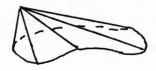

17. (a)   Object 2. Note the relationship between numbered faces.

(b)   Object 4. The two figures cannot be on adjoining faces.

19. (a) $V = 5$; $E = 8$; $F = 5$. $V + F - E = 5 + 5 - 8 = 2$.

(b) $V = 8$; $E = 12$; $F = 6$. $8 + 6 - 12 = 2$.

(c) $V = 6$; $E = 10$; $F = 6$. $6 + 6 - 10 = 2$.

21. Using Euler's formula to find the missing value:

(a)   6 vertices   (b)   48 edges

(c)   11 faces

23. (a)   A cone might be described as a many-sided pyramid.

(b)   A cylinder might be described as a many-sided prism.

25. A parallelogram. Try it and see.

27. A nonogon has nine sides. Thus the interior angle measurement is $\frac{(9 - 2)180}{9} = 140°$.

29. (a)   A right triangle.

(b)   The sum of the measures of complementary angles is 90°. Thus the measure of the third angle must be 90° and the triangle is a right triangle.

Problem Set 10-5

1. (a)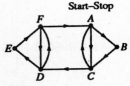

Path:
ABCACDEFDFA;
any point can be a
starting point.

(b)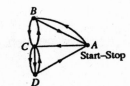

Path:
ABACBCDCDA;
any point can be a
starting point.

1.   (c)

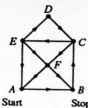

Start   Stop

Path:
ABCFAEDCEFB;
only points *A* and *B*
can be starting points.

(d)   Not traversable; has more than two odd
       vertices.

(e)

Start

Path:
ABCBDCAD;
only points *A* and *D*
can be starting points.

(f)   Not traversable; has more than two odd
       vertices.

(g)

Start   Stop

Path:
FADABCBGFEDCHEHG;
only points *F* and *G*
can be starting points.

(h)

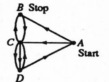

Path:
ACBCDCDAB;
only points *A* and *B*
can be starting points.

(i)   Not traversable; has more than two odd
       vertices.

(j)

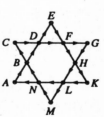

3.

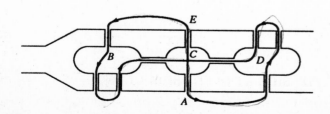   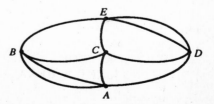

5.   Yes. See figure.

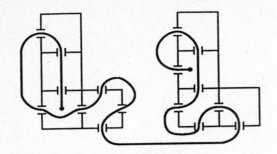

7. | Network | R | V | A | R + V − A |
      |---------|---|---|---|-----------|
      | (a) | 6 | 6 | 10 | 2 |
      | (b) | 7 | 4 | 9 | 2 |
      | (c) | 6 | 6 | 10 | 2 |
      | (d) | 4 | 4 | 6 | 2 |
      | (e) | 5 | 4 | 7 | 2 |
      | (f) | 8 | 8 | 14 | 2 |
      | (g) | 9 | 8 | 15 | 2 |
      | (h) | 6 | 4 | 8 | 2 |
      | (i) | 7 | 7 | 12 | 2 |
      | (j) | 8 | 12 | 18 | 2 |

9.   To be non-traversable, a network must have more than two odd vertices. An example is below.

Problem Set 10-6

1.   (a)   TO RECTANGLE :LENGTH :WIDTH
                PARALLELOGRAM :LENGTH :WIDTH 90
             END

      (b)   TO RHOMBUS :SIDE :ANGLE
                PARALLELOGRAM :SIDE :SIDE :ANGLE
             END

3.   TO CUBE :SIDE
        REPEAT 3 [RHOMBUS :SIDE 60 RIGHT 120]
      END

5.   Execute on the computer.

7.   Answers may vary.

      (a)   TO HEXSTACK :SIDE
                REPEAT 3 [LEFT 30 HEXAGON :SIDE FD :SIDE RT 60 FD :SIDE LT 60]
             END
             TO HEXAGON :SIDE
                REPEAT 6 [FD :SIDE RIGHT 60]
             END

7. (b)   TO HONEYCOMB :SIDE
                REPEAT 3 [HEXAGON :SIDE RT 120]
            END

9. Answers may vary.

    (a)   TO SEG
                RT 45 FD 50 BK 100
                FD 50 LT 45
            END

    (b)   TO PAR
                PENUP FD 50 PENDOWN
                SEG
            END

11. Answers may vary.
    TO FILL.RECT :WIDTH :LENGTH
      IF :WIDTH < 0 STOP
      REPEAT 4[FD :WIDTH RT 90 FD :LENGTH RT 90]
      FILL.RECT :WIDTH − 1 :LENGTH − 1
      HT
    END

13. Answers may vary.
    TO COUNT.ANGLES :NUMBER
      IF :NUMBER = 1 OUTPUT 0 STOP
      OUTPUT :NUMBER − 1 + COUNT.ANGLES :NUMBER − 1
    END

CHAPTER 11 - CONSTRUCTIONS, CONGRUENCE, AND SIMILARITY

Problem Set 11-1

1. (a) One such triangle is:

   Then BC > AC.

   (b) The triangle in (a) satisfies the condition. The angle opposite $\overline{BC}$ is larger than the angle opposite $\overline{AC}$ [m($\angle$ A) > m($\angle$ B)].

   (c) The side of greater length is opposite the angle of greater measure.

3. (b) Yes; SSS.   (c) Yes; SSS.

   (d) No triangle.   (e) Yes; SSS.

   (f) Yes; SAS.   (g) No; SSA can be ambiguous.

   (h) Yes; SAS. With one angle given in an isosceles triangle, others are determined.

   (i) Yes; SAS.

5. (a) Yes. The given information satisfies SAS.

   (b) Yes; SSS.

   (c) No. Not SAS since the angles are non-included. SSA is not sufficient to ensure a congruent triangle.

7. The lengths must be the same since they are corresponding parts of congruent triangles.

9. (a) See Figure 11-11.

   (b) Use the procedure in Figure 11-9 with all sides the length of $\overline{AB}$.

   (c) Any angle in an equilateral triangle is 60°. Follow the procedure in (b) to construct a 60° angle.

   (d) Copy $\angle$ A, the mark off the desired length for the congruent sides on each side of the angle. Connect the two marked points.

11. (a) $\triangle$ ABC $\simeq$ $\triangle$ ABC; $\triangle$ ACB $\simeq$ $\triangle$ ABC; $\triangle$ BAC $\simeq$ $\triangle$ ABC; $\triangle$ BCA $\simeq$ $\triangle$ ABC; $\triangle$ CAB $\simeq$ $\triangle$ ABC; $\triangle$ CBA $\simeq$ $\triangle$ ABC.

    (b) Consider the correspondence $\triangle$ BCA $\simeq$ $\triangle$ ABC. Then $\angle$ B $\simeq$ $\angle$ A, $\angle$ C $\simeq$ $\angle$ B, and $\angle$ A $\simeq$ $\angle$ C; i.e., all angles are congruent to each other. Thus, $\triangle$ ABC (and any equilateral triangle) is equiangular.

13. If the non-included angles of existing triangles are obtuse or right. When the non-included angle is acute, it is sometimes possible to construct two triangles satisfying the given measures. With obtuse and right angles, only one triangle is possible.

15. (a) Parallelogram.

15. (b)   Let QRST be the quadrilateral; point N be the intersection of the diagonals. $\triangle$ QRN $\simeq$ $\triangle$ STN and $\triangle$ RSN $\simeq$ $\triangle$ TQN by SAS (congruent sides from bisection and vertical angles). Then $\angle$ RQN $\simeq$ $\angle$ TSN and $\angle$ SRN $\simeq$ $\angle$ QTN by CPCTC. With these alternate interior angles congruent, the opposite sides must be parallel.

17. (a)   Parallelogram.

     (b)   Let QRST be the parallelogram. $\triangle$ SRT $\simeq$ $\triangle$ QTR by SSS. Then $\angle$ SRT $\simeq$ $\angle$ QTR and $\angle$ QRT $\simeq$ $\angle$ STR by CPCTC. With these alternate interior angles congruent, the opposite sides must be parallel.

19. Answers may vary.
     TO EQUITRI :SIDE
       REPEAT 3 [FD :SIDE RT 120]
     END

21. They produce basically the same results.

Problem Set 11-2

1.   (a) 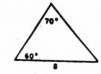   (b)

     (c)   (d)   Infinitely many are possible.

3.   (a)   Yes. The triangles are congruent by ASA.

     (b)   Yes. The triangles are congruent by AAS.

     (c)   No. SSA does not assign congruence.

     (d)   No. AAA does not assure congruence.

5.   If diagonals of a quadrilateral besect each other, it must be a parallelogram. Connecting the legs at their midpoint will then ensure that the board and the floor are opposite sides of the parallelogram and are thus parallel to each other.

7.   (a)   True.   (b)   True.

     (c)   True.   (d)   True.

     (e)   True.

     (f)   False. A trapezoid may have only one pair of parallel sides.

7.   (g)   True.

    (h)   False. A square is both a rectangle and a rhombus.

    (i)   False. A square can be a trapezoid.

    (j)   True. In fact, all are.

9.   There are five possibilities; one parallelogram and four kites.

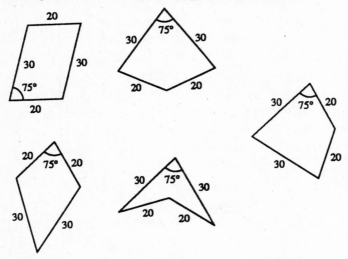

11. (a) $\overline{OP} \simeq \overline{OQ}$

    (b) $\angle$ PDO $\simeq$ $\angle$ QBO; alternate interior angles formed by the transversal $\overleftrightarrow{DB}$ and parallel lines $\overleftrightarrow{DC}$ and $\overleftrightarrow{AB}$. $\angle$ DPO $\simeq$ $\angle$ BQO because $\overleftrightarrow{PQ}$ is a transversal of $\overleftrightarrow{CD}$ and $\overleftrightarrow{AB}$. $\overline{DO} \simeq \overline{BO}$; diagonals of a parallelogram bisect each other. $\triangle$ POD $\simeq$ $\triangle$ QOB by AAS. Thus $\overline{PO} \simeq \overline{QO}$ by CPCTC.

13. Let ABCD be an isosceles trapezoid with $\angle$ A $\simeq$ $\angle$ D and $\overline{BC} \| \overline{AD}$.

    (a)   Sides opposite congruent angles in an isosceles trapezoid are congruent.

    (b)   The diagonals are congruent.

    (c)   (*i*)   Draw $\overline{BX}$ and $\overline{CY}$ perpendicular to $\overline{AD}$. Since $\overline{BC} \| \overline{AD}$, the distances between them must be constant; i.e., $\overline{BC} \simeq \overline{CY}$. Then $\triangle$ ABX $\simeq$ $\triangle$ DCY by AAS, so $\overline{AB} \simeq \overline{DC}$ by CPCTC.

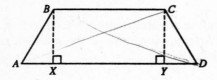

          (*ii*) $\triangle$ ABD $\simeq$ $\triangle$ DCA by SAS (given $\angle$ BAD $\simeq$ $\angle$ CDA, $\overline{AB} \simeq \overline{DC}$, and $\overline{AC}$ common). Thus $\overline{BD} \simeq \overline{AC}$ by CPCTC.

15. (a)   Rhombus.

    (b)   Use SAS to prove that $\triangle$ ECF $\simeq$ $\triangle$ GBF $\simeq$ $\triangle$ EDH $\simeq$ $\triangle$ GAH.

    (c)   Parallelogram.

15. (d)   Suppose ADCB in part (a) is a parallelogram.   By SAS $\triangle$ EDH $\simeq$ $\triangle$ GBF which implies that $\overline{EH} \simeq \overline{GF}$. Similarly, $\triangle$ ECF $\simeq$ $\triangle$ GAH and thus $\overline{EF} \simeq \overline{GH}$. By SSS $\triangle$ EFG $\simeq$ $\triangle$ GHE. Therefore $\angle$ GEH $\simeq$ $\angle$ EGF and consequently $\overline{FG} \| \overline{EH}$. Similarly, $\overline{EF} \| \overline{HG}$.

    (e)   Parallelogram.

17. (a) $\angle$ ABD $\simeq$ $\angle$ CDB and $\angle$ CBD $\simeq$ $\angle$ ADB (alternate interior angles with respect to parallel lines), so $\triangle$ ABD $\simeq$ $\triangle$ CDB (ASA). Thus $\angle$ BAD $\simeq$ $\angle$ DCB (CPCTC); similarly, $\angle$ ABC $\simeq$ $\angle$ CDA.

    (b) $\triangle$ ABD $\simeq$ $\triangle$ CDB, so $\overline{AB} \simeq \overline{CD}$ and $\overline{AD} \simeq \overline{CB}$.

    (c) $\angle$ BAC $\simeq$ $\angle$ DCA and $\angle$ ABD $\simeq$ $\angle$ CDB (alternate interior angles), and $\overline{AB} \simeq \overline{DC}$ (from (b)), so $\triangle$ BAF $\simeq$ $\triangle$ DCF and thus $\overline{AF} \simeq \overline{CF}$ and $\overline{BF} \simeq \overline{DF}$.

    (d)   As for any triangle, in $\triangle$ ABD m($\angle$ BAD) + m($\angle$ ABD) + m($\angle$ ADB) = 180°.
          From (a), $\angle$ CBD $\simeq$ $\angle$ ADB; substitution gives m($\angle$ BAD) + m($\angle$ ABD) + m($\angle$ CBD) = 180°.
          Since m($\angle$ ABC) = m($\angle$ ABD) + m($\angle$ CBD), then m($\angle$ BAD) + m($\angle$ ABC) = 180°.
          Thus $\angle$ ABC and $\angle$ BAD are supplementary.

19. (a)   Answers may vary.
          TO RHOMBUS :SIDE :ANGLE
            REPEAT 2 [FD :SIDE RT (180 − :ANGLE) FD :SIDE RT :ANGLE]
          END

    (b)   They are congruent.

    (c)   TO SQ. RHOM :SIDE
            RHOMBUS :SIDE 90
          END

21. Use the procedure in Figure 11-9.

23. (a)   Yes; SAS.   (b)   Yes; SSS.

    (c)   No; SSA is not a congruous relation.

Problem Set 11-3

1.   (a) and (b).   Use Figure 11-23.

3.   (a)   See Figure 11-25.

     (b)   See Figure 11-27.

     (c)   See Figure 11-26.

5.   Given ∠ BAC, put one strip of tape so that an edge of the tape is along $\overline{AB}$ and another strip of tape so that one of its edges is on $\overline{AC}$. Two edges of the strips of tape intersect in the interior of the angle; connect A with this point and you will have the angle bisector.

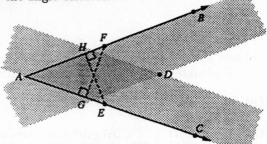

7.   (a)   The perpendicular bisectors meet at a point inside the triangle.

      (b)   The perpendicular bisectors meet at the midpoint of the hypotenuse of the right triangle.

      (c)   The perpendicular bisectors meet at a point outside the triangle.

9.   Construct as described.

11.   Answers may vary. One possibility is to:
      (i)   Draw a line segment (10¢).
      (ii)   Draw two intersecting arcs (20¢) to construct a perpendicular segment (10¢).
      (iii) With compass point at the intersection of the two segments, sweep a wide arc (10¢) intersecting both segments.
      (iv)   Maintain the same compass setting and measure an arc from each of these points to determine the fourth point (20¢).
      (v)   Draw the two segments to complete the square (20¢).
      The total is 90¢.

13.   (a) $\overrightarrow{PQ}$ is the perpendicular bisector of $\overline{AB}$.

      (b)   Q is on the perpendicular bisector of $\overline{AB}$ because $\overline{AQ} \simeq \overline{QB}$. Similarly, P is on the perpendicular bisector of $\overline{AB}$. Because a unique line contains two points, the perpendicular bisector contains $\overrightarrow{PQ}$.

      (c) $\overrightarrow{PQ}$ is the angle bisector of ∠ APB; $\overrightarrow{QC}$ is the angle bisector of ∠ AQB.

      (d)   △ APQ $\simeq$ △ BPQ by SSS; thus ∠ APQ $\simeq$ ∠ BPQ by CPCTC. Similarly, △ AQC $\simeq$ △ BQC so so ∠ AQC $\simeq$ ∠ BQC.

15.   (a)   Construct a 60˚ angle (equilateral triangle) and bisect it.

      (b)   Bisect a 30˚ angle.

      (c)   Add 30˚ and 15˚ angles.

      (d)   Add 60˚ and 15˚ angles.

      (e)   Add 90˚ and 15˚ angles.

17.   (a)   Since the triangles are congruent, the acute angles formed by the hypotenuse and the line are congruent. Since the corresponding angles are congruent, the hypotenuses are parallel and the line is the transversal.

      (b)   Beginning with the given line containing the hypotenuse, slide the triangle along the ruler until the hypotenuse passes through P.

19. Let *l* be the given line and P a point not on *l*. Through P draw any line k intersecting *l*. That line forms ∠ 1 with *l*. Construct ∠ 2 congruent to ∠ 1 so that the two angles are alternate interior angles. Line *m* (which contains a side of ∠ 2) is parallel to *l*.

21. Answers may vary.

(a)   TO ANGBIS :MEAS
          REPEAT 3 [FD 75 BK 75 RT :MEAS/21]
       END

(b)   TO PERBIS :SIZE
          FD :SIZE/2 RT 90 FD :SIZE BK
          :SIZE/2 FD :SIZE RT 90 FD
          :SIZE/2
       END

(c)   TO PARALLEL :SEG1 :SEG2
          FD :SEG1 PENUP RT 90
          FD 20 RT 90 PENDOWN
          FD :SEG2
       END

23. (a)   Copy the angle, then measure off each side along a side of the angle. Connect.

(b)   Copy $\overline{AB}$. Make arcs from A and B, one with radius AC, the other with radius BC. Their intersection is C. Connect.

(c)   Copy the side; copy the angles at opposite ends, extending their sides until they meet to form the triangle.

Problem Set 11-4

1. Folding the circle over on itself in two different directions will locate the center.

3. (a)   90°   (b)   90°

(c)   90°

(d)   Any angle with its vertex on a circle and sides intersecting the endpoints of a diameter of that circle is a right angle.

(e)   △ AOC and △ BOC are isosceles (radii are congruent), with ∠ OAC ≃ OCA and ∠ OAC ≃ ∠ OBC. All angles of a triangle add to 180°; here then ∠ OAC + ∠ OCA + ∠ OCB + ∠ OBC = 180°. Substituting for the congruent angles gives ∠ OCA + ∠ OCA + ∠ OCB + ∠ OCB = 180°, or 2(∠ OCA + ∠ OCB) = 180°; thus ∠ OCA + ∠ OCB (i.e., ∠ ACB) = 90°.

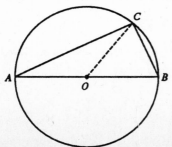

5.   Inscribe a square as described in Figure 11-39. Then bisect either the vertical angles or the sides (both processes result in the same lines) to locate the additional vertices in the circle.

7.   The circle will touch the midpoints of all sides. Bisect two opposite sides to locate the center of the circle; measure from the located center to the midpoint of a side for the radius.

9.   Construct a perpendicular from O to *l* to obtain the radius. Then draw the circle with the compass. (Construct the perpendicular as in Figure 11-28)

11. (a)   Isosceles.

     (b) $m(\angle 1) + m(\angle 2) = m(\angle 3)$. Angles 1 and 2 add with $\angle$ BOC to 180° (total of angles of a triangle), and $\angle$ 3 also adds with $\angle$ BOC to 180° (straight line). The two quantities must then be equal.

     (c) $m(\angle 1) = \frac{1}{2}m(\angle 3)$. $m(\angle 1) + m(\angle 2) = m(\angle 3)$, and $m(\angle 1) = m(\angle 2)$ (base angles of isosceles triangle OBC).

     (d)   In (c), $\angle$ 1 is formed by two chords and $\angle$ 3 is formed by radii from O to points opposite $\angle$ 1. In both circles (a) and (b), α and β have the same relationship. Thus in each case, $\alpha = \frac{1}{2}\beta$.

     (e)   Angles 1, 2, and 3 are all formed by chords intersecting the same points on the major arc. Thus $m(\angle 1) = m(\angle 2) = m(\angle 3)$.

13. (a)   270° (three right angles).

     (b)   180° (two right angles).

15. The radius *r* of the circle is half the distance between the parallel lines. The center of the circle is on line *n* parallel to the given lines and equidistant from these lines. The center of the circle can be obtained by finding the point of intersection of line *n* with the circle whose center is at P and whose radius is *r*.

17. Answers may vary.
     TO DIAMETER
       REPEAT 360 [FD 1 RT 1] RT 90 FD 100
     END

19. In $\triangle$ ABC, $\angle$ B is included between $\overline{AB}$ and $\overline{BC}$.

21. The bisector of one of a pair of vertical angles bisects the other if extended, forming two new pairs of vertical angles.

Problem Set 11-5

1.   (a)   Similar by AAA, since all angles are 60°.

     (b)   Similar. Sides are proportional and angles congruent.

     (c)   Not always similar.   (d)   Not always similar.

     (e)   Similar; radii are proportional.

     (f)   Not always similar.

1. (g) Similar. Sides are proportional and angles congruent.

3. Yes. The scale factor is 1 and the angles are congruent.

5. (a) and (b) Construct triangles as outlined.

    (c) The triangles are similar when, for example, in $\triangle$ ABC and $\triangle$ DEF, $\frac{AB}{DE} = \frac{AC}{DF}$ and $\angle A \simeq \angle D$.

7. The ratio of the perimeters is the same as the ratio of the sides.

9. (a) $\frac{\text{short side}}{\text{long side}} = \frac{5}{10} = \frac{x}{x+7}$. Solving, $5(x + 7) = 10x$, or $x = 7$.

    (b) $\frac{3}{x} = \frac{7}{8}$. Solving, $7x = 3 \cdot 8$, or $x = \frac{24}{7}$.

    (c) $\frac{x}{6} = \frac{x+4}{14}$. Solving, $14x = 6(x + 4)$, or $x = 3$.

    (d) $\frac{x}{12 - x} = \frac{8}{5}$. Solving, $8(12 - x) = 5x$, or $x = \frac{96}{13}$.

11. Lay the licorice diagonally on the paper so that it spans a number of spaces equal to the number of children. Cut on the lines. Equidistant parallel lines will divide any transversal into congruent segments.

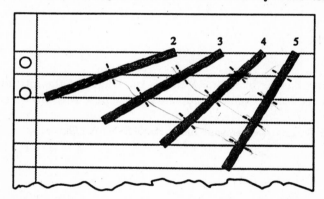

13. No. The maps are similar and even though the scales may change, the actual distances do not.

15. The setup forms similar triangles with proportional sides satisfying $\frac{150}{300} = \frac{x}{1800}$, where x is the height of the tree. Solving, $300x = 150 \cdot 1800$, or $x = 900$ cm. We could have as easily converted all measurements to meters, finding $x = 9$ m.

17. Converting all measurements to inches (3 feet = 36 inches; 7 feet = 84 inches) and using similar triangles gives $\frac{36}{13} = \frac{x}{84}$. Solving, $13x = 36 \cdot 84$, or $x \doteq 232.6$ inches $\doteq 19.38$ feet.

19. CF = 13 m; AE = 12 m.
    Construct $\overline{BP}$ perpendicular to $\overline{CF}$. $\triangle$ CBP $\simeq$ $\triangle$ DFE by AAS because $\overline{BC} \simeq \overline{FD}$ (opposite sides of a rectangle) and $\angle$ DEF $\simeq \angle$ CPB (right angles). From $\angle$ FDE $\simeq \angle$ CFD (alternate interior angles between the parallels $\overleftrightarrow{CF}$ and $\overleftrightarrow{DE}$ and the transversal $\overleftrightarrow{DF}$) and $\angle$ CFD $\simeq \angle$ BCP (alternate interior angles between $\overleftrightarrow{FD} \| \overleftrightarrow{BC}$ and the transversal $\overleftrightarrow{CF}$) it follows that $\angle$ FDE $\simeq \angle$ BCP. By CPCTC, $\overline{CP} \simeq \overline{DE}$ and hence CP = DE = 4 m. CF = PF + CP; because ABPF is a rectangle, PF = BA = 9 m, and thus CF = 9 + 4 = 13 m. $\overline{AF} \simeq \overline{BP}$ (ABPF is a rectangle) and $\overline{FE} \simeq \overline{BP}$ (CPCTC in $\triangle$ CBP and $\triangle$ DFE). Consequently $\overline{AF} \simeq \overline{FE}$. $\triangle$ ABF $\sim$ $\triangle$ EFD (by AA since $\angle$ AFB and $\angle$ FDE are complements of $\angle$ DFE and each triangle has a right angle.) Consequently AF:EF = AF:ED, or 9:EF = AF:4, or EF $\cdot$ AF = 36. Because $\overline{EF} \simeq \overline{AF}$, we have $(EF)^2 = 36$, or EF = 6. Because AE = 2(EF), AE = 12 m.

19.

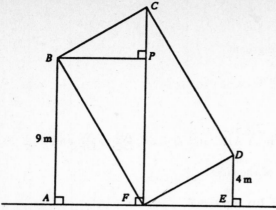

21.   Answers may vary.

(a)   TO TRISECT :LEN
          REPEAT 3 [MARK FD :LEN/3]
       END

       TO MARK
         RT 90 FD 5 BK 5 LT 90
       END

(b)   TO PARTITION :LEN :NUM
          REPEAT :NUM [MARK FD :LEN/:NUM]
       END

23.   Copy the base and construct its perpendicular bisector. Measure the length of the altitude and mark it off on the bisector from the midpoint of the base. Connect endpoints of the base with the end of the altitude.

No solutions exist for Problem Set 11-6, for answers see your Instructor's Resource Guide.

CHAPTER 12 - MOTION GEOMETRY AND TESSELLATIONS

1. (a) A skier skiing straight down a slope moves in a translation because there is no accompanying twisting or turning.

   (b) A floating leaf would include both translation and rotating.

3. Reverse the translation so that the image completes a slide from X′ to X (to what is called its pre-image). Then check by carrying out the given motion in the "forward" direction; i.e., see if $\overline{AB}$ goes to A′B′.

   (a)
   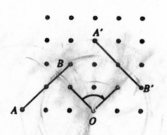

   (b)
   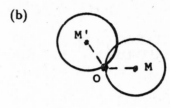

5. Answers may vary. Some are ceiling fans, clock hands, or compact discs.

7. Reverse the rotation (to the counterclockwise direction) to locate $\overline{AB}$; i.e., the pre-image.

   (a)
   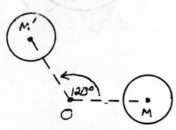

   (b)

9. (a)
   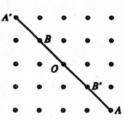

   (b)

11. Step 1: Draw $\overline{PP'}$. Step 2: Find the midpoint of $\overline{PP'}$ — call this midpoint X. Step 3: Draw the line through Q and X. Step 4: Measure off the distance from Q to X, then mark off the same distance on the opposite side of Q. Call this point Q′. Q′ is the image of Q under the half-turn.

13. (a) A circle.

    (b) The vertices A and B trace an identical path if and only if OA = OB; i.e., if and only if O is on the perpendicular bisector of $\overline{AB}$. Thus all points O for which two vertices trace an identical path are the points on the perpendicular bisectors of the sides of the triangle.

    (c) Yes. The intersection of the perpendicular bisectors (center of the circumscribed circle).

15. (a) $l' = l$ (b) $l' \parallel l$

15. (c) $l' \perp l$ (d) l' and l intersect at a 60° angle.

17. (a)   Execute the program.

    (b)   TO SLIDE :DIRECTION :DISTANCE :SIDE
            EQUILATERAL :SIDE
            SETHEADING :DIRECTION
            FORWARD :DISTANCE
            PENDOWN
            SETHEADING 0
            EQUILATERAL :SIDE
          END

          TO EQUILATERAL :SIDE
           REPEAT 3 [FORWARD :SIDE RIGHT 120]
          END

19. (a)   TO TURN.CIRCLE :A
            CIRCLE
            LEFT :A
            CIRCLE
          END

          TO CIRCLE
           REPEAT 360 [FORWARD 1 RT 1]
          END

          To produce the desired transformation, execute TURN.CIRCLE 180.

    (b)   To produce the desired transformation, execute TURN.CIRCLE 90.

Problem Set 12-2

1.   Locate the image of vertices directly across (perpendicular to) l on the geoboard.

     (a)   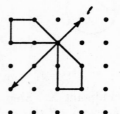   (b)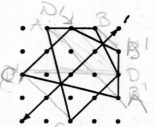

3.   Find the image of the center of the circle and one point on the circumference of the circle to determine the image of the circle.

5.   As directed.

7.   The images are congruent but in different locations.

9.

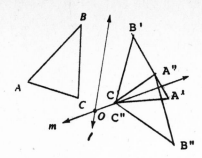

11. (a) If AB = BC then the perpendicular bisector of $\overline{AC}$ is the required line. Because a point is on the perpendicular bisector of $\overline{AC}$ if and only if it is equidistant from A and C, the image of B when reflected in l is B and the image of A is C. Hence the image of △ ABC is △ CBA.

(b) Equilateral triangles. Each side could be considered as the base.

(c) No. Since no sides (or angles) are congruent, bisecting any side or angle will leave non-congruent portions of the triangle on opposite sides of the bisector.

(d) All lines containing diameters will satisfy this situation. Diameters divide a circle into two congruent semicircles.

13. (a) For glide reflections with the translation parallel to the reflection line, the images are the same regardless of order.

(b) Reflections and translations are commutative only for the conditions described in (a).

15. Construct as suggested.

17. Reflect A about road 1 to locate A′, and B about road 2 to locate B′. Align A′ and B′ to locate P and Q. This is an extension of the problem illustrated in Figure 12-31. Reflecting A and B creates the straight-line (i.e., shortest) path $\overline{A'B'}$, which by construction is equal to the distance (AP + PQ + QB) for the actual roads.

19. (a) ⁻150° rotation about the turtle's starting point.

(b) Reflection about a vertical line containing the turtle's starting point.

(c) 45° rotation and slide.

21. (a) TO EQTRI :SIDE
    REPEAT 3 [FORWARD :SIDE RIGHT 120]
END

(b) TO EQTRI2 :SIDE
    REPEAT 3 [FORWARD :SIDE LEFT 120]
END

(c) A reflection in a vertical line through the turtle's home.

(d) A half-turn with the turtle's home as center.

23. H, I, N, O, S, Z.

25. (a) A rotation of any angle about the center of the circle will result in the same circle.

25.   (b)   Reflections about lines containing diameters.

Problem Set 12-3

1.   (a) and (b). Changing the order of reflection leads to a different final image in both cases. The only case in which the images will not be different is when $l \perp m$.

3.   (a)   (4, 3) reflects about m to (4, 1); (4, 1) reflects about n to (2, 1).

      (b)   (0, 1) → (0, 3) → (6, 3)

      (c)   (⁻1, 0) → (⁻1, 4) → (7, 4)

      (d)   (0, 0) → (0, 4) → (6, 4).

5.   (a)   Slide the small triangle down three units (translation), then complete a size transformation with scale factor 2 using the top right vertex as the center.

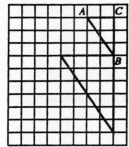

      (b)   Slide right 5, up 1, then complete the size transformation as in (a).

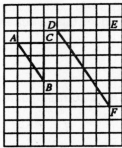

      (c)   Rotate 90° counterclockwise with the lower right vertex of the small triangle as the center of rotation. Then size transformation with scale factor 2 using the same point as center.

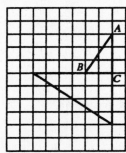

7.   (a)   Translation taking B to B' followed by a size transformation with center B' (and scale factor approximately 2).

7. (b) Rotate 90° counterclockwise using center B, translate to take B to B′, and then a size translation with a scale factor of approximately $\frac{1}{2}$.

(c) Half-turn with the midpoint of $\overline{AA'}$ as center, followed by a size transformation with scale factor approximately $\frac{1}{2}$ and center A′.

(d) Half-turn about C followed by a size transformation with center C and scale factor approximately $\frac{3}{2}$.

Problem Set 12-4

1. (a) (i) Yes. A geometrical figure has line symmetry if it is its own image under a reflection in some line. A line may be drawn through the center circle, either horizontally or vertically, about which the figure is its own image. The line may also be drawn through any of the sets of arrows.

(ii) Yes. The figure will match the original figure after rotations of 90°, 180°, or 270°.

(iii) Yes. Any figure having 180° rotational symmetry has point symmetry about the turn center.

(b) (i) Yes. A vertical line through the middle of the bulb is a line of symmetry.

(ii) No. The figure will not match the original under rotations of less than 360°.

(iii) No. The figure does not have 180° rotational symmetry.

(c) (i) Yes. A vertical line through the stem is a line of symmetry.

(ii) No.   (iii) No.

(d) (i) Yes. A horizontal line through the middle of the plane is a line of symmetry.

(ii) No.   (iii) No.

3. Reflect the given portions about l.

(a) 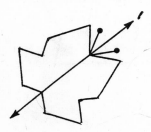   (b)

5. (a) One line of symmetry; vertically through the center.

(b) One; vertically through the center.

(c) None.

(d) One; vertically through the center.

(e) Five; one through each vertex and its opposite face.

5.   (f)   One; vertically through the center.

7.   Answers may vary, but examples include the letter S and the Chevrolet logo.

9.   (a)   (b)

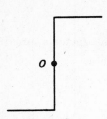   

11. TO TURN.SYM :S :N :A
       REPEAT :N [SQUARE :S RIGHT :A]
     END

     TO SQUARE :S
       REPEAT 4 [FORWARD :S RIGHT 90]
     END

     (a)   Execute TURN.SYM 50 6 60   (b)   Execute TURN.SYM 50 3 120

     (c)   Execute TURN.SYM 50 2 180   (d)   Execute TURN.SYM 50 3 240

     (e)   Execute TURN.SYM 50 6 300

13. (a), (b), and (c): One method is to trace over the figure heavily, then fold at *l* and trace along the figure (as seen through the paper), copying the image with a "carbon paper" process.

Problem Set 12-5

1.   (a)   (b)

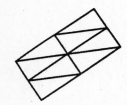   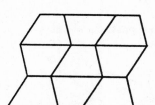

3.   Experimentation by cutting shapes out and moving them about is one way to learn about these types of problems.

     (a)

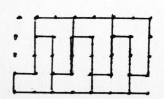

3. (b)   Cannot be tessellated.

    (c)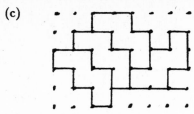

    (d)   Tessellate as in (a).

5. Hint: Consider figures like a pentagon formed by combining a square and an equilateral triangle, or the figure in Problem 7 on page 669 of the text.

7.  ```
    TO TILESTRIP :S
       REPEAT 4 [TILE :S PENUP RIGHT 180 FORWARD 3*:S PENDOWN]
    END

    TO TILE :S
     RIGHT 180
     REPEAT 3 [REPEAT 4 [FORWARD :S LEFT 60] RIGHT 120]
    END
    ```

Problem Set 12-6

1.  ```
    TO WALL3 :XPT :YPT :SIDE
       DRAW
       SETUP :XPT :YPT
       WALLPAPER3 :YPT :SIDE
    END

    TO SETUP :XPT :YPT
     PENUP
     SETXY :XPT :YPT
     PENDOWN
    END

    TO WALLPAPER :YPT :SIDE
     TRISTRIP :SIDE
     PENUP
     SETUP (:XPT + :SIDE*(SORT 3)/2) :YPT
     PENDOWN
     WALLPAPER3 :YPT :SIDE
    END
    ```

1.  ```
    TO TRISTRIP :SIDE
      IF XCOR + :SIDE > 120 TOPLEVEL
      IF (ANYOF (XCOR < −120)
      (XCOR + :SIDE*(SQRT 3)/2 > 120)
      (YCOR < −100)(YCOR + :SIDE > 100))
      STOP
      TRIANGLE :SIDE
      FORWARD :SIDE
      RIGHT 60
      TRIANGLE :SIDE
      LEFT 60
      TRISTRIP :SIDE
    END

    TO TRIANGLE :SIDE
      REPEAT 3 [FORWARD :SIDE RIGHT 120]
    END
    ```

3.  ```
    TO WALL4 :XPT :YPT :SIDE
      DRAW
      SETUP :XPT :YPT
      WALLPAPER4 :YPT :SIDE
    END

    TO SETUP :XPT :YPT
      PENUP
      SETXY :XPT :YPT
      PENDOWN
    END

    TO WALLPAPER4 :YPT :SIDE
      MAKE "X XCOR
      HEXSTRIP :SIDE
      PENUP
      SETUP (XCOR + :SIDE*(SQRT 3)) :YPT
      PENDOWN
      WALLPAPER4 :YPT :SIDE
    END

    TO HEXSTRIP :SIDE
      IF XCOR + :SIDE > 120 TOPLEVEL
      IF (ANYOF (XCOR < −120) (XCOR + :SIDE*(SQRT 3)) > 120)
      (YCOR < −100) (YCOR + :SIDE*3 > 100)) STOP
      HEXAGON :SIDE
      FORWARD :SIDE RIGHT 60 FORWARD :SIDE LEFT 60
      HEXSTRIP :SIDE
    END

    TO HEXAGON :SIDE
      REPEAT 6 [FORWARD :SIDE RIGHT 60]
    END
    ```

5. Yes. Once the figures fit between two parallel lines, then one could make a rubber stamp of the parallel lines and the drawings between them and stamp them all across the plane.

7.
```
TO WALL6 :XPT :YPT :SIDE
  DRAW
  SETUP :XPT :YPT
  WALLPAPER6 :YPT :SIDE
END

TO SETUP :XPT :YPT
  PENUP
  SETXY :XPT :YPT
  PENDOWN
END

TO WALLPAPER6 :YPT :SIDE
  CHEVRONSTRIP :SIDE
  PENUP
  SETUP (XCOR + :SIDE) :YPT
  PENDOWN
  WALLPAPER6 :YPT :SIDE
END

TO CHEVRONSTRIP :SIDE
  IF  XCOR + :SIDE > 120  TOPLEVEL
  IF (ANYOF (XCOR − :SIDE < −120) (XCOR + :SIDE > 120)
   (YCOR − :SIDE*(SQRT 2)/2 < −100) (YCOR + :SIDE > 100)) STOP
  CHEVRON :SIDE
  FORWARD :SIDE
  CHEVRONSTRIP :SIDE
END

TO CHEVRONSTRIP :SIDE
  FORWARD :SIDE RIGHT 135
  FORWARD :SIDE*(SQRT 2)/2 LEFT 90
  FORWARD :SIDE*(SQRT 2)/2 RIGHT 135
  FORWARD :SIDE RIGHT 45
  FORWARD :SIDE*(SQRT 2)/2 RIGHT 90
  FORWARD :SIDE*(SQRT 2)/2 RIGHT 45
END
```

CHAPTER 13 - CONCEPTS OF MEASUREMENT

<u>Problem Set 13-1</u>

1. (a) AB = 1.0 cm − 0.1 cm = 0.9 cm or 9 mm   (b) DE = 4.5 cm − 3.6 cm = 0.9 cm or 9 mm

   (c) CJ = 10.0 − 2.0 = 8.0 cm or 80 mm   (d) EF = 5.0 − 4.5 = 0.5 cm or 5 mm

   (e) IJ = 10.0 − 9.3 = 0.7 cm or 7 mm   (f) AF = 5.0 − 0.1 = 4.9 cm or 49 mm

   (g) IC = 9.3 − 2.0 = 7.3 cm or 73 mm   (h) GB = 6.2 − 1.0 = 5.2 cm or 52 mm

3. (a) ——

   (b) ————————————————————————

   (c) ———

   (d) ————————————————————

   (e) ——

   (f) ————————————————————————————————————

   (g) ————————————————————

   (h) ————————

5. (a) Cm; a new pencil measures about 19 cm.   (b) Mm; the diameter is about 21 mm.

   (c) Cm or m; the width is about 120 cm or 1.2 m.

   (d) Cm or mm; the thickness is about 2 cm or 20 mm.

   (e) Cm; about 23 cm.

   (f) M or cm; the height is about 1.9 m or 190 cm.

   (g) M or cm; an average man's height is about 1.75 m (175 cm); an average woman's about 1.65 m (165 cm).

   (h) Cm or mm; about 15-20 cm or 150-200 mm.

7. In each case, note that:
   From m to cm move decimal point two places to the right.
   From cm to mm move decimal point one place to the right.
   From mm to cm move decimal point one place to the left.
   From cm to m move decimal point two places to the left.

   (a) 0.35 m → $\boxed{35 \text{ cm}}$ → 350 mm

   (b) $\boxed{1.63 \text{ m}}$ → 163 cm → 1630 mm

   (c) 0.035 m → 3.5 cm → $\boxed{35 \text{ mm}}$

   (d) 0.1 m → 10 cm → $\boxed{100 \text{ mm}}$

   (e) $\boxed{2 \text{ m}}$ → 200 cm → 2000 mm

9. Convert each to cm: 8cm; 521.8 cm; 245 cm; 9.1 cm; 600 cm; 70 cm. In decreasing order, then, we have: 6 m; 5218 mm; 245 cm; 700 mm; 91 mm; 8 cm.

11. (a)   8 cm   (b)   12 cm

    (c)   9 cm   (d)   20 cm

13. (a), (b), (c).   The sum of the lengths of any two sides of a triangle is greater than the length of the third side alone.

15. (a)   Yes. A rhombus with 120° and 60° angles satisfies this condition. The shorter diagonal divides the triangle into two equilateral triangles; thus the sides of the rhombus must be the same length as the diagonal.

    (b)   No. Either diagonal is the hypotenuse of a right triangle and must be longer than the legs (i.e., the sides of the square). The perimeter has to be less than 4 times the diagonal.

17. (a)   The maximum perimeter is attained when the longer sides are part of the perimeter; e.g.:

    (b)   The minimum perimeter is attained when the longer sides are not part of it; e.g., the original rectangle.

19. Circumference is 2π times the radius (C = 2πr), so $r = \frac{C}{2\pi}$:

    (a) $r = \frac{12\pi}{2\pi} = 6$ cm.   (b) $r = \frac{6}{2\pi} = \frac{3}{\pi} \doteq 0.955$ m.

    (c) $r = \frac{0.67}{2\pi} = \frac{0.335}{\pi} \doteq 0.107$ m.   (d) $r = \frac{92\pi}{2\pi} = 46$ cm.

21. The circumference doubles; the relationship between the two measures is linear.

23. The height is 3 tennis-ball-diameters. The perimeter is given by the circumference of a tennis ball, πd, and is thus about 3.14 tennis-ball-diameters.

25. (a) $\left(\frac{300,000 \text{ km}}{\text{sec}}\right)\left(\frac{60 \text{ sec}}{\text{min}}\right)\left(\frac{60 \text{ min}}{\text{hr}}\right)\left(\frac{24 \text{ hr}}{\text{day}}\right)\left(\frac{365 \text{ days}}{\text{year}}\right) \doteq 9.5 \cdot 10^{12}$ km per year.

    (b)   (4.34 light years)(9.5·10^{12} km per year) $\doteq 4.1 \cdot 10^{13}$ km.

    (c) $\left(\frac{4.1 \cdot 10^{13} \text{ km}}{60,000 \text{ km/hr}}\right) \doteq 6.8 \cdot 10^{8}$ hours, or about 78,000 years.

    (d)   Light travels (8·60 + 19)(300,000) $\doteq 1.5 \cdot 10^{8}$ km in 8 min 19 sec. $\left(\frac{1.5 \cdot 10^{8} \text{ km}}{60,000 \text{ km\hr}}\right) \doteq 2495$ hours, or about 104 days.

27. Perimeter = $2 \cdot 19 + 12 + \frac{1}{2} \cdot \pi \cdot 12 = 50 + 6\pi \doteq 68.8$ feet.

29. The outer curve has a greater radius and a correspondingly greater distance (i.e., arc length) to run. To compensate for the extra distance, the outer lane is given an apparent head start.

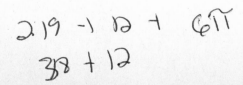

31. A straight line of squares gives minimum area. A square, or the closest thing possible, gives the maximum area; e.g., for perimeter = 22, a 1 by 10 rectangle gives least area while a 5 by 6 rectangle has greatest area.

Perimeter	Minimum Area	Maximum Area
4	1	1
6	2	2
8	3	4
10	4	6
12	5	9
14	6	12
16	7	16
18	8	20
20	9	25
22	10	30
24	11	36
26	12	42
2n	n − 1	*

* Let q be the whole number quotient when 2n is divided by 4. If 2n is a multiple of 4, then the maximum area is q^2; otherwise it is $q(q + 1)$.

Problem Set 13-2

1. (a) cm^2; in^2 (b) cm^2; in^2

    (c) cm^2; in^2 (d) m^2, yd^2

    (e) m^2; yd^2 (f) km^2; mi^2

3. In each case, note that:
    From m^2 to cm^2, move the decimal point 4 places to the right.
    From cm^2 to mm^2, move the decimal point 2 places to the right.
    From mm^2 to cm^2, move the decimal point 2 places to the left.
    From cm^2 to m^2, move the decimal point 4 places to the left.

    0.0588 → 588 → 58,800
    0.000192 → 1.92 → 192
    1.5 → 15,000 → 1,500,000
    0.01 → 100 → 10,000
    0.0005 → 5 → 500

5. (a)   444.4   (b)   0.32

    (c)   6400   (d)   130,680

7. (a)   This figure is a triangle with base 3 and height 2, so $A = \frac{1}{2}(3)(2) = 3$ units^2.

7. (b)   Total area = $(4)(3) = 12$ units^2.

Area A = $\frac{1}{2}(3)(2) = 3$ units^2.
Area B = $\frac{1}{2}(2)(1) = 1$ unit^2.
Area C = $\frac{1}{2}(3)(2) = 3$ units^2.
Area D = $(1)(2) = 2$ units^2.

So the area of the figure is $12 - (3 + 1 + 3 + 1) = 3$ units^2.

(c)   This figure is a triangle with base 2 and height 2, so A = $\frac{1}{2}((2)(2) = 2$ units^2.

(d)   Total area = $(3)(3) = 9$ units^2

Area A = $\frac{1}{2}(1)(1) = \frac{1}{2}$ unit^2
Area B = $(2)(1) = 2$ units^2
Area C = $\frac{1}{2}(1)(1) = \frac{1}{2}$ unit^2
Area D = $\frac{1}{2}((1)(2) = 1$ unit^2

So the area of the figure is $9 - (\frac{1}{2} + 2 + \frac{1}{2} + 1) = 5$ units^2

(e)   Total area = $(4)(4) = 16$ units^2

Area A = $(2)(1) = 2$ units^2
Area B = $\frac{1}{2}(2)(1) = 1$ unit^2
Area C = $\frac{1}{2}(1)(3) = 1\frac{1}{2}$ units^2
Area D = $\frac{1}{2}(1)(3) = 1\frac{1}{2}$ units^2
Area E = $\frac{1}{2}(4)(2) = 4$ units^2

So the area of the figure is $16 - (2 + 1 + 1\frac{1}{2} + 1\frac{1}{2} + 4) = 6$ units^2

(f)   Total area = $(3)(3) = 9$ units^2

Area A = $\frac{1}{2}(1)(2) = 1$ unit^2
Area B = $\frac{1}{2}(1)(1) = \frac{1}{2}$ unit^2
Area C = $(1)(1) = 1$ unit^2
Area D = $(1)(1) = 1$ unit^2
Area E = $\frac{1}{2}(1)(1) = \frac{1}{2}$ unit^2
Area F = $\frac{1}{2}(1)(1) = \frac{1}{2}$ unit^2

So the area of the figure is $9 - (1 + \frac{1}{2} + 1 + 1 + \frac{1}{2} + \frac{1}{2}) = 4\frac{1}{2}$ units^2

9. (a)   A = $\frac{1}{2}bh = \frac{1}{2}(10)(4) = 20$ cm^2.

(b)   A = $\frac{1}{2}(6$ m$)(3$ cm$) = \frac{1}{2}(6$ m$)(0.03$ m$) = 0.09$ m^2, or A = $\frac{1}{2}(600$ cm$)(3$ cm$) = 900$ cm^2.

(c)   A = $\frac{1}{2}(3)(5) = 7\frac{1}{2}$ m^2.

(d)   Place point D at the intersection of the two dashed lines. Then:
          Area $\triangle$ ABD = $\frac{1}{2}(8)(6) = 24$ cm^2; area $\triangle$ CBD = $\frac{1}{2}(10)(3) = 15$ cm^2.
          Adding, area $\triangle$ ABC = area $\triangle$ ABD + area $\triangle$ CBD = $24 + 15 = 39$ cm^2.

(e)   Let $\overline{AB}$ be the base; $\overline{BC}$ be the height. Then A = $\frac{1}{2}(30)(40) = 600$ cm^2.

11. (a)   A = $l^2 = 3^2 = 9$ cm^2.   (b)   A = $l \cdot w = (8)(12) = 96$ cm^2.

11. (c)   Using the Pythagorean theorem, the height of the small triangle is $\sqrt{3^2 - 2^2} = \sqrt{5}$. The height of the large triangle is $\sqrt{5^2 - 2^2} = \sqrt{21}$. The area of the large triangle is thus $\frac{1}{2}(4)(\sqrt{5}) = 2\sqrt{5}$; the area of the small triangle is $\frac{1}{2}(4)(\sqrt{21}) = 2\sqrt{21}$. The area of the figure, then, is $2\sqrt{21} - 2\sqrt{5} = 2\left(\sqrt{21} - \sqrt{5}\right)$, or about 256 cm^2.

    (d) $A = b{\cdot}h = (5)(4) = 20$ cm^2

    (e) $A = \frac{1}{2}h(b_1 + b_2) = \frac{1}{2}(7)(10 + 14) = 84$ cm^2.

    (f) $A = \frac{1}{2}(6)(27 + 8) = 105$ cm^2.

13. (a)   True.

    (b)   The area would be 60 cm^2 only if the parallelogram were to be a rectangle.

    (c)   The area cannot be more than 60 cm^2, since the height cannot be more than 6 cm (if the base is 10 cm).

    (d)   Since we do not know the height, the area can only be expressed as "less than 60 cm^2."

15.   The diagonals of a rhombus are perpendicular. The height of $\triangle ABC$ in the diagram below is thus $\frac{b}{2}$, and $\triangle ABC$ has area $\frac{1}{2}a(\frac{b}{2}) = \frac{ab}{4}$. Since there are two such triangles, the area of the rhombus is $2{\cdot}\frac{ab}{4} = \frac{ab}{2}$.

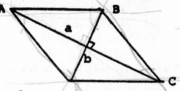

17. (a) $A = \pi r^2 = \pi(5^2) = 25\pi$ cm^2.

    (b) $A = \frac{\theta}{360°}{\cdot}\pi r^2 = \frac{60}{360}{\cdot}\pi(4^2) = \frac{8}{3}\pi$ cm^2.

    (c) $A = \frac{36}{360}{\cdot}\pi(6^2) = \frac{18}{5}\pi$ cm^2.

    (d)   Since this is a half-circle, $A = \frac{1}{2}\pi r^2 = \frac{1}{2}\pi(3^2) = \frac{9}{2}\pi$ cm^2.

    (e)   First find θ. The angle is related to a full circle as the arc length is related to the circumference; i.e., $\frac{\theta}{360} = \frac{\text{arc length}}{2\pi r}$, or $\frac{\theta}{360} = \frac{20}{2\pi(10)}$. Solving, $\theta \doteq 114.59°$. Finally, $A = \frac{114.59}{360}{\cdot}\pi(10^2) = 100$ cm^2.

19.   The plot is $(22\text{ m})(28\text{ m}) = 616$ m^2. It will take $\dfrac{616\text{ m}^2}{85\text{ m}^2\text{ per bag}} = 7.25$ bags (so 8 bags must be bought).

21. (a)   The area of a regular polygon is given by $A = \frac{1}{2}(\text{apothem})(\text{perimeter})$. Here a (the apothem) is $2\sqrt{3}$ and the perimeter is $6{\cdot}4 = 24$. Thus $A = \frac{1}{2}\left(2\sqrt{3}\right)(24) = 24\sqrt{3} \doteq 41.57$ cm^2.

    (b) $A = \frac{1}{2}bh = \frac{1}{2}(6)\left(3\sqrt{3}\right) = 9\sqrt{3} \doteq 15.59$ cm^2.

23. (a)   The radius of the large circle is 2 cm. Its area is $\pi{\cdot}2^2 = 4\pi$ cm^2. Each small circle has area $\pi{\cdot}1^2 = \pi$ cm^2. The shaded area is thus $4\pi - 2(\pi) = 2\pi$ cm^2.

    (b)   The area of the semicircle is $\frac{1}{2}(\pi r^2) = \frac{1}{2}\pi(1^2) = \frac{1}{2}\pi$ cm^2. The area of the triangle is $\frac{1}{2}bh = \frac{1}{2}(2)(2) = 2$ cm^2. The shaded area is thus $\left(\frac{1}{2}\pi + 2\right)$ cm^2.

23. (c)   If the 1 cm radius were extended, it would be the diameter of the large circle, cutting off a small shaded semicircle the same size as the small white semicircle. The shaded area is thus equal to half the large circle, whose radius is 2 cm. The shaded area is thus $\frac{1}{2}(\pi \cdot 2^2) = 2\pi$ cm^2.

    (d)   Consider half the figure, as shown below. Areas A + B = Area C. Areas A + B = Rectangle − Semicircle $= 5 \cdot 10 - \frac{1}{2}(\pi \cdot 5^2) = 50 - \frac{25}{2}\pi$. A + B + C is twice this, or $100 - 25\pi$. Considering both halves of the figure, the total unshaded area is $2(100 - 25\pi) = 200 - 50\pi$. The shaded area is that of the square less the unshaded area, or $10^2 - (200 - 50\pi) = (50\pi - 100)$ cm^2.

    (e)   The square has sides of length 20 cm and area of $20^2 = 400$ cm^2. Each circle has area $\pi \cdot 5^2 = 25\pi$ cm^2. The shaded area is thus $400 - 4(25\pi) = (400 - 100\pi)$ cm^2.

    (f)   The two shaded areas form a circle with radius $\frac{r}{2}$, so their area is $\pi(\frac{r}{2})^2 = \frac{\pi r^2}{4}$.

    (g)   The four shaded areas form two circles each having radius $\frac{r}{4}$, so their area is $2\pi(\frac{r}{4})^2 = \frac{\pi r^2}{8}$.

    (h)   The eight shaded areas form four circles each having radius $\frac{r}{8}$, so their area is $4\pi(\frac{r}{8})^2 = \frac{\pi r^2}{16}$.

25. (a)   If we let r = radius of each circle, then the length of the rectangle is 12r and the width is 6r. Thus the area of the rectangle is $72r^2$. The area of each circle is πr^2 and there are 18 circles, so the total area used for lids is $18\pi r^2$. The wasted area is $72r^2 - 18\pi r^2$, and so the ratio of waste to total area is $\frac{72r^2 - 18\pi r^2}{72r^2} = \frac{18r^2(4 - \pi)}{72r^2} = \frac{4 - \pi}{4}$, or about 21.4%.

    (b)   (i)   The length of the rectangle would be 24r and the width 12r, for an area of $288r^2$. The total area of lids would be $72\pi r^2$. Thus the waste would be:

$$\frac{288r^2 - 72\pi r^2}{288r^2} = \frac{72r^2(4 - \pi)}{288r^2} = \frac{4 - \pi}{4}, \text{ or about 21.4\% (as before).}$$

         (ii)   Regardless of the radius of the circles, if the rectangle remains the same size the amount of waste will be the same.

27. (a)   4:9. $\frac{A_1}{A_2} = \frac{s_1^2}{s_2^2}$, and $\frac{s_1}{s_2} = \frac{2}{3}$. Thus $\frac{A_1}{A_2} = \left(\frac{2}{3}\right)^2 = $ 4:9.

    (b)   4:9. By the Pythagorean theorem, $d^2 = s^2 + s^2 = 2s^2$. If $d_1:d_2 = 2:3$, then $d_1^2:d_2^2 = 4:9$ But $d_1^2:d_2^2 = 2s_1^2:2s_2^2 = s_1^2:s_2^2$, or the ratio of areas is 4:9.

29. (a)   As developed in problems 27 and 28, the ratio of the areas of any two similar objects may be found by squaring the ratio of any corresponding lengths. So for diagonals in the ration 20:27, areas have the ratio $20^2:27^2$, or 400:729. This ratio is less than that of the prices (400:600); i.e., there is less area in the smaller screen in comparison to price. The 27-inch set is a better buy.

    (b)   Let d be the diagonal of the specified set. The areas of the sets have the same ratio as that of the squared diagonals. Thus $20^2:d^2 = 1:2$, or $\frac{400}{d^2} = \frac{1}{2}$. Solving, $d \doteq 28.3$ inches.

31.   The new figure is a parallelogram that has twice the area of the trapezoid. The area of the parallelogram is $A = \frac{1}{2}(AB + DC)h$, where h is the height of the parallelogram. Thus the area of the trapezoid is $\frac{1}{2}(AB + DC)h$.

33.   One possibility would be to mark off perpendicular diameters, then make arcs with the radius of the circle from the endpoints of the diameters.

35. Removing the same amount from all sides of the original square will form another square. Its area is given by $s^2 = 64$, so $s = 8$ inches. Thus 1 inch should be removed from each side ($10 - 1 - 1 = 8$, or 1 inch from the left and right, top and bottom). Therefore, $x = 1$.

37. (a) 10   (b) 104

     (c) 0.35   (d) 40

     (e) 8000   (f) 6.504

39. By construction, $\triangle ABC \simeq \triangle BAC'$. Then congruent alternate interior angles $\angle ABC \simeq \angle BAC'$ and $\angle ABC' \simeq \angle BAC$ imply $\overline{AC} \| \overline{BC'}$ and $\overline{BC} \| \overline{AC'}$; i.e., $BCAC'$ is a parallelogram (by definition).

Problem Set 13-3

1. (a) $x^2 + 8^2 = 10^2 \Rightarrow x^2 + 64 = 100 \Rightarrow x^2 = 36 \Rightarrow x = 6.$

  (b) $2^2 + 2^2 = x^2 \Rightarrow 4 + 4 = x^2 \Rightarrow x^2 = 8 \Rightarrow x = \sqrt{8} = 2\sqrt{2}.$

  (c) $(3a)^2 + (4a)^2 = x^2 \Rightarrow 9a^2 + 16a^2 = x^2 \Rightarrow 25a^2 = x^2 \Rightarrow x = 5a.$

  (d) $x^2 + 5^2 = 13^2 \Rightarrow x^2 + 25 = 169 \Rightarrow x^2 = 144 \Rightarrow x = 12.$

  (e) $x^2 + (\frac{s}{2})^2 = s^2 \Rightarrow x^2 + \frac{s^2}{4} = s^2 \Rightarrow x^2 = \frac{3s^2}{4} \Rightarrow x^2 = \sqrt{\frac{3s^2}{4}} = \frac{s\sqrt{3}}{2}.$

  (f) $x^2 + x^2 = 4^2 \Rightarrow 2x^2 = 16 \Rightarrow x^2 = 8 \Rightarrow x = \sqrt{8} = 2\sqrt{2}.$

  (g) $8^2 + a^2 = 17^2 \Rightarrow 64 + a^2 = 289 \Rightarrow a^2 = 225 \Rightarrow a = 15.$
     $8^2 + b^2 = 10^2 \Rightarrow 64 + b^2 = 100 \Rightarrow b^2 = 36 \Rightarrow b = 6.$
     Thus $x = 15 - 6 = 9.$

  (h) $5^2 + 12^2 = x^2 \Rightarrow 25 + 144 = x^2 \Rightarrow x^2 = 169 \Rightarrow x = 13.$

  (i) $4^2 + 4^2 = (2x)^2 \Rightarrow 16 + 16 = 4x^2 \Rightarrow 32 = 4x^2 \Rightarrow x^2 = 8 \Rightarrow x = 2\sqrt{2}.$

  (j) $3^2 + 6^2 = x^2 \Rightarrow 9 + 36 = x^2 \Rightarrow x^2 = 45 \Rightarrow x = \sqrt{45} = 3\sqrt{5}.$

  (k) $3^2 + 3^2 = d^2 \Rightarrow 9 + 9 = d^2 \Rightarrow d^2 = 18 \Rightarrow d = \sqrt{18}.$
     Then $3^2 + d^2 = x^2 \Rightarrow 9 + 18 = x^2 \Rightarrow x^2 = 27 \Rightarrow x = \sqrt{27} = 3\sqrt{3}.$

  (l) $3^2 + 4^2 = y^2 \Rightarrow 9 + 16 = y^2 \Rightarrow y^2 = 25 \Rightarrow y = 5.$
     Using similar triangles: $\frac{x}{5} = \frac{1}{3} \Rightarrow 3x = 5 \Rightarrow x = \frac{5}{3}.$

3. For the answer to be yes, the numbers must satisfy the Pythagorean theorem (with largest measure $= c$).

  (a) $10^2 + 16^2 \neq 24^2 \Rightarrow$ not a right triangle.

  (b) $16^2 + 30^2 = 34^2 \Rightarrow$ a right triangle.

  (c) $(\sqrt{2})^2 + (\sqrt{2}) = 2^2 \Rightarrow$ a right triangle.

  (d) $1^2 + (\sqrt{3})^2 = 2^2 \Rightarrow$ a right triangle.

  (e) $(\sqrt{2})^2 + (\sqrt{3})^2 = (\sqrt{5})^2 \Rightarrow$ a right triangle.

3. (f) $\left(\frac{3}{2}\right)^2 + \left(\frac{4}{2}\right)^2 = \left(\frac{5}{2}\right)^2 \Rightarrow$ a right triangle.

5. (a)   Based on 4 and $4\sqrt{3}$ leg lengths, this is a 30°-60°-90° triangle with special relationships. Using this knowledge, x = 8 and $y = 2\sqrt{3}$. (Otherwise, use the Pythagorean theorem for x and similar triangles for y.)

    (b)   Using the special relationship for 45°-45°-90° triangles, $x = \sqrt{2}\left(2\sqrt{2}\right) = 4$. $\sqrt{2}$ y = $2\sqrt{2}$, or y = 2.

7. The distances form the legs of a right triangle. The southbound plane travels (3.5 hr)·(376 km/hr) = 1316 km; the westbound plane travels (3.5 hr)·(648 km/hr) = 2268 km. The distance apart is given by $d^2 = (1316)^2 + (2268)^2 \Rightarrow d = \sqrt{6{,}875{,}680} \doteq 2622$ km.

9. Yes. Knowing that they are right triangles, the third sides (legs) are fixed by the Pythagorean theorem. The triangles are congruent by SSS.

11. (a)   Drawing radii to consecutive vertices of the hexagon forms an equilateral triangle (central angle is $\frac{1}{6}\cdot 360 = 60°$). Each side of the hexagon is thus 5 cm. Drawing an apothem forms 30°-60°-90° triangles, whose special relationships tell us that the apothem (the longer leg of the 30°-60°-90° triangle in this case) is $\left(\frac{5}{2}\right)\sqrt{3}$. The area for any regular polygon is A = $\frac{1}{2}$(apothem)(perimeter), so here A = $\frac{1}{2}\left[\left(\frac{5}{2}\right)\sqrt{3}\right](6\cdot 5) = 37.5\sqrt{3}$ cm^2.

    (b)   Substituting r for 5 above gives the area of an inscribed regular hexagon as A = $\frac{1}{2}\left[\left(\frac{r}{2}\right)\sqrt{3}\right](6\cdot r)\right]$, or A = $\frac{3r^2}{2}\cdot\sqrt{3}$ cm^2.

13. (a)   The altitude forms 30°-60°-90° triangles. Its height is thus $\frac{s}{2}\cdot\sqrt{3}$, and A = $\frac{1}{2}$bh = $\frac{1}{2}(s)\left(\frac{s}{2}\cdot\sqrt{3}\right)$, or

    A = $\frac{s^2\sqrt{3}}{4}$.

    (b)   The triangle is isosceles with height = base = s. A = $\frac{1}{2}(s)(s) = \frac{s^2}{2}$.

15. Draw and lable the rhombus as shown:

    $DF^2 + BF^2 = BD^2$, or $DF^2 + 144 = 400 \Rightarrow DF = 16$. Then CF = 16 − DC, so $(16 - DC)^2 + 12^2 = BC^2$. But BC = DC, so $(16 - DC)^2 + 12^2 = DC^2$. Thus $256 - 32\cdot DC + DC^2 + 144 = DC^2 \Rightarrow 400 = 32\cdot DC \Rightarrow DC = 12.5$ cm. $DE^2 + EC^2 = DC^2$, or $10^2 + EC^2 = 12.5^2 \Rightarrow EC^2 = 56.25 \Rightarrow EC = 7.5$. Thus AC = 15 cm.

17. From the "special triangles" section, the hypotenuse of any 45°-45°-90° triangle is $\sqrt{2}$ times a leg. Thus here, $c = \sqrt{2}\cdot l$, or $l = \frac{c}{\sqrt{2}}$.

19. The sides of squares made in this fashion will always be hypotenuses of right triangles (as shown in (a)). As such, the relationship $s^2 = a^2 + b^2$ must hold, with *a* and *b* whole numbers, since they are given by spaces between dots. Only numbers representable this way can be areas of such squares (since s^2 is the area of a square).

19. (a)   Here $1^2 + 2^2 = 5 = s^2$, so the relationship exists.

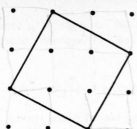

(b)   Not possible.

(c)   Here $2^2 + 2^2 = 8 = s^3$, so the relationship exists.

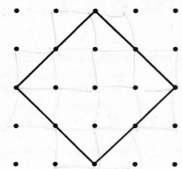

(d)   Not possible.   (e)   Not possible.

21.   The included angle between sides of length c is 90°. Adding the areas of the three triangles gives $A = \frac{1}{2}ba + \frac{1}{2}ab + \frac{1}{2}cc = ab + \frac{1}{2}c^2$. Using the formula for area of a trapezoid gives

$A = \frac{1}{2}(a + b)(a + b) = \frac{1}{2}(a^2 + 2ab + b^2)$. These represent the same area, so

$ab + \frac{1}{2}c^2 = \frac{1}{2}(a^2 + 2ab + b^2) \Rightarrow 2ab + c^2 = a^2 + 2ab + b^2 \Rightarrow c^2 = a^2 + b^2$.

23.   (a)   Yes.

(b)   The area of an equilateral triangle with side s is $\frac{s^2}{4} \cdot \sqrt{3}$. Let the sides of the right triangle be a, b, and

c, with c the hypotenuse. The areas of the equilateral triangles are thus $\frac{a^2}{4} \cdot \sqrt{3}$, $\frac{b^2}{4} \cdot \sqrt{3}$, and $\frac{c^2}{4} \cdot \sqrt{3}$.

We must now answer the question, "Does $\frac{a^2}{4}\sqrt{3} + \frac{b^2}{4}\sqrt{3} = \frac{c^2}{4}\sqrt{3}$?" Multiplying both sides by $\frac{4}{\sqrt{3}}$ gives

$a^2 + b^2 = c^2$, which must be true since the triangle is right.

25.   There is a 6 foot (or meter) vertical rise in a horizontal distance of 100 feet (or meters).

27.   The brace will be a hypotenuse. Then $3^2 + 5^2 = x^2$, or $x = \sqrt{34}$. This must be the diagonal distance of the bracing board. Its length is given by $(0.5)^2 + l^2 = x^2$, or $l \doteq 5.81$ feet. The excess length is $8 - 5.81$, or 2.19 feet.

29.   Form a right triangle with a diameter, height, and length of spaghetti (the hypotenuse) that just fits. Then $d^2 + h^2 = s^2$, or $4^2 + 10^2 = h^2 \Rightarrow h = \sqrt{116} \doteq 10.77$ inches.

31.   (a)   Change all measurements to mm and draw horizontal lines to form three rectangles. The rectangles will have dimensions 75 mm by 25 mm, 25 mm by 30 mm, and 35 mm by 20 mm. The areas are 1875 mm^2, 750 mm^2, and 700 mm^2, for a total of 3325 mm^2 = 33.25 cm^2.

(b)   The area is $\frac{1}{2}(10)(6) = 30$ cm^2.

31. (c)   Change 600 cm to 6 m. The area is then $\frac{1}{2}(6 + 10)(4) = 32$ m^2.

33.   The area has a circumference of 10 m; i.e., $2\pi r = 10$. Then $r = \frac{10}{2\pi} = \frac{5}{\pi}$. The area is πr^2, or
   $\pi(\frac{5}{\pi})^2 = \frac{25}{\pi}$ m^2.

Problem Set 13-4

1.   (a)   SA of a cube $= 6e^2$ (where $e =$ the length of each edge). SA $= 6(4)^2 = 96$ cm^2.

   (b)   SA of a right circular cylinder $= 2\pi r^2 + 2\pi rh$ (where r is the radius of the top and bottom circles and h is the height of the cylinder). SA $= 2\pi(6)^2 + 2\pi(6)(12) = 72\pi + 144\pi = 216\pi$ cm^2.

   (c)   SA of a right triangular prism $= ph + 2B$ (where p is the perimeter, h is the height, and B is the area of the base). $p = 2l + 2w = 2(8) + 2(5) = 26$ cm; $B = lw = (8)(5) = 40$ cm^2. $h = 6$ cm.
   SA $= (26)(6) + 2(40) = 156 + 80 = 236$ cm^2.

   (d)   SA of a sphere $= 4\pi r^2$ (where r is the radius). SA $= 4\pi(4)^2 = 64\pi$ cm^2.

   (e)   SA of a right circular cone $= \pi r^2 + \pi rl$ (where r is the radius of the base and l is the slant height from any point on the base to the vertex of the cone). To find l, use the Pythagorean theorem:

   $l = \sqrt{4^2 + 3^2} = 5$ cm. SA $= \pi(3)^2 + \pi(3)(5) = 9\pi + 15\pi = 24\pi$ cm^2.

   (f)   SA of a right square pyramid $= B + \frac{1}{2}pl$ (where B is the area of the base, p is the perimeater of the base, and l is slant height from the base to the apex). $B = b^2$ (where b is the length of a face of the base) $= 5^2 = 25$ cm^2; $p = 4b = 4(5) = 20$ cm. SA $= 25 + \frac{1}{2}(20)(6.5) = 25 + 65 = 90$ cm^2.

   (g)   The width of the slanted roof is given by: $w = \sqrt{8^2 + 15^2} = 17$ feet. Roof area is then given by $2(17 \cdot 40) = 1360$ ft^2. The triangular area is $2(\frac{1}{2})(30)(8) = 240$ ft^2. The side wall area is $2(20 \cdot 30) + 2(20 \cdot 40) = 2800$ ft^2. The base area is $(30)(40) = 1200$ ft^2.
   Total surface area is $1360 + 240 + 2800 + 1200 = 5600$ ft^2.

   (h)   Hemispherical area is $\frac{1}{2}(4\pi r^2) = \frac{1}{2}(4\pi \cdot 10^2) = 200\pi$ ft^2.
   Base area is $\pi r^2 = \pi(10^2) = 100\pi$ ft^2.
   Lateral area of cylinder $= 2\pi rh = 2\pi(10)(60) = 1200\pi$ ft^2.
   Total surface area $= 200\pi + 100\pi + 1200\pi = 1500\pi$ ft^2.

   (i)   Slant height is given by: $l = \sqrt{4^2 + 8^2} = 4\sqrt{5}$ cm. Conical area $= \pi rl = \pi(4)(4\sqrt{5}) = 16\sqrt{5}\pi$ cm^2.
   Hemispherical area $= \frac{1}{2}(4\pi r^2) = \frac{1}{2}(4)\pi(4)^2 = 32\pi$ cm^2.

   Total surface area $= (32 + 16\sqrt{5})\pi$ cm^2.

3.   Change all units to mm. The ring then has an inner radius of 20 mm and a height of 30 mm.
   The outer ring has a radius of 22 mm and a height of 30 mm; SA $= 2\pi rh = 2\pi(22)(30) = 1320\pi$ mm^2.
   The inner ring has a radius of 20 mm and a height of 30 mm; SA $= 2\pi(20)(30) = 1200\pi$ mm^2.
   The area of the top and bottom rings is each the area of a circle with radius 22 mm minus the area of a circle with radius 20 mm.
   There are two base rings, so SA $= 2[\pi(22^2) - \pi(20^2)] = 2[484\pi - 400\pi] = 168\pi$ mm^2.
   The total surface area $= 1320\pi + 1200\pi + 168\pi = 2688\pi$ mm^2, or 26.88π cm^2.

5.   SA (large cube) $= 6e^2 = 6(6)^2 = 216$ cm^2. SA (small cube) $= 6(4^2) = 96$ cm^2.
   Ratio of surface areas $= \frac{96}{216} = \frac{4}{9} = 4:9$.
   Note that the ratio of the surface areas is the ratio of the squares of the sides.

7.   SA of a right pyramid = B + $\frac{1}{2}pl$, where B is the area of the base, p is the perimeter of the base, and l is the slant height from the base to the apex.
     B = $\frac{1}{2}ap$, where a is the apothem. Since a hexagon is composed of equilateral triangles about the center, the distance from each vertex to the center is the same as each edge. Thus

$$a = \sqrt{12^2 - 6^2} = \sqrt{108} = 6\sqrt{3}. \text{ Then B} = \frac{1}{2}\left(6\sqrt{3}\right)(6 \cdot 12) = 216\sqrt{3}.$$

Since the apothem is $6\sqrt{3}$ and the altitude is 9, $l = \sqrt{9^2 + \left(6\sqrt{3}\right)^2} = \sqrt{189} = 3\sqrt{21}$.

Finally, SA = $216\sqrt{3} + \frac{1}{2}(6 \cdot 12)\left(3\sqrt{21}\right) = \left(216\sqrt{3} + 108\sqrt{21}\right)$ m^2.

9.   For any figure, if all dimensions have the same percentage change, the change of the area is the square of the change in a side. Thus:

(a)   The surface area is quadrupled.   (b)   The surface area is multiplied by 9.

(c)   The surface area is multiplied by k^2.

11. (a)   SA of a sphere is proportional to the square of the radius, so if radius is doubled SA is increased by a factor of 4.

(b)   The SA is multiplied by 9.

13. Answers may vary. One possibility is to form a regular square pyramid with base sides of 2 cm and triangle slant heights of 1.5 cm. Then SA = B + $\frac{1}{2}pl = 2^2 + \frac{1}{2}(8)(1.5) = 4 + 6 = 10$ cm^2.

15. A good estimate could be made by using the method in problem 3 (the napkin ring).

17. Using $\frac{\theta}{360}(\pi r^2)$ for the area of a sector, $270 = \frac{270}{360}(\pi r_s^2)$. r_s is the radius of the sector which, when rolled up, will become the slant height of the cone, l. Solving, we obtain $\frac{360}{\pi} = r_s^2 \Rightarrow r_s = \frac{60}{\sqrt{\pi}} = l$.

The arc length of the sector = $\frac{\theta}{360}(2\pi r) = \frac{270}{360}\left(2\pi \cdot \frac{60}{\sqrt{\pi}}\right) = \frac{90\pi}{\sqrt{\pi}}$. This will become the circumference of the base of the cone.
Using r_b as the radius of the base, $2\pi r_b = \frac{90\pi}{\sqrt{\pi}}$, or $r_b = \frac{45}{\sqrt{\pi}}$ cm.

(a)   Area = $\pi r_b^2 = \pi\left(\frac{45}{\sqrt{\pi}}\right)^2 = 202.5$ cm^2.

(b)   Form a right triangle with r_b, l, and h (cone height). Then $r_b^2 + h^2 = l^2$, or $\left(\frac{45}{\sqrt{\pi}}\right)^2 + h^2 = \left(\frac{60}{\sqrt{\pi}}\right)^2$.

Solving gives $h^2 = \frac{3600}{\pi} - \frac{2025}{\pi} = \frac{1575}{\pi}$, or $h = \sqrt{\frac{1575}{\pi}}$ cm.

19. 27 rounds represents the entire lawn; 27 rounds require 2(27) = 54 passes along the length and width, so the width is 54(3) = 162 feet. The rectangle left after the first 12 rounds has width $162 - 2 \cdot 12 \cdot 3 = 90$ feet and length $l - 2 \cdot 13 \cdot 3 = l - 72$. This rectangle has half the total area, or $90(l - 72) = \frac{1}{2}(162 \cdot l)$. Solving, we find $l = 720$ feet. The field is then 162 by 720 feet.

21. (a)   The figure will be a cone with base radius 10 cm and height 20 cm.

$$SA = \pi r^2 + \pi rl = \pi(10^2) + \pi(10)\left(\sqrt{20^2 + 10^2}\right) = 100\pi + 10\pi(10\sqrt{5}) = 100\pi(1 + \sqrt{5}) \text{ cm}^2.$$

(b)   The figure will be a right circular cylinder with base radius 15 cm and height 30 cm.
     SA = $2\pi r^2 + 2\pi rh = 2\pi(15^2) + 2\pi(15)(30) = 450\pi + 900\pi = 1350\pi$ cm^2.

21. (c) The figure will be a truncated cone, with large end radius 25 cm and small end radius 15 cm. If one considers the given area as part of a triangle, as shown, then using similar triangles:

$\frac{35}{10} = \frac{x}{25}$, where x is the hypotenuse of the large triangle. Solving, x = 87.5. The triangle, when rotated, will form a cone with slant height 87.5 and radius 25 cm, having
$SA = \pi r^2 + \pi r l = \pi(25^2) + \pi(25)(87.5) = 625\pi + 2187.5\pi = 2812.5\pi$ cm^2.
Cutting off the top eliminates the lateral surface area $\pi r l = \pi(15)(87.5 - 35) = 787.5$ cm^2 and adds the circular area $\pi r^2 = \pi(15^2) = 225\pi$ cm^2. The resulting SA is
$(2812.5 - 787.5 + 225)\pi = 2250\pi$ cm^2.

23. A regular tetrahedron is made of 4 equilateral triangles. The area of an equilateral triangle is $\frac{s^2\sqrt{3}}{4}$.

With total surface area = 400 cm^2, each triangle is 100 cm^2, or $\frac{s^2\sqrt{3}}{4} = 100$. Then $s = \sqrt{\frac{400}{\sqrt{3}}} \doteq 15.2$ cm.

25. The cross section is shown:

Then $\frac{10}{x} = \frac{40}{25} \Rightarrow$ x = 6.25. This is the radius of the cylinder.
Lateral surface area is $2\pi rh = 2\pi(6.25)(30) = 375\pi$ cm^2.

27. $d = \sqrt{10^2 + 20^2} = 10\sqrt{5}$ cm.

29. (a) Change 0.6 m to 60 cm. The hypotenuse is then $\sqrt{60^2 + 80^2} = 100$ cm. The perimeter is
60 + 80 + 100 = 240 cm, or 2.4 m.

Area is $\frac{1}{2}bh = \frac{1}{2}(60)(80) = 2400$ cm^2, or 0.24 m^2.

(b) Drawing an altitude to the end point of the top base forms a 45°-45°-90° isosceles triangle. The bottom base must be 5 cm longer on each side than the top; i.e., one leg of the isosceles triangle is 5 cm, so the height is also 5 cm. Using the Pythatorean theorem, the slanted segments on each side of the trapezoid are each $5\sqrt{2}$ cm. The perimeter is thus $20 + 10 + 2(5\sqrt{2}) = (30 + 10\sqrt{2})$ cm.

Area $= \frac{1}{2}(10 + 20)(5) = 75$ cm^2.

Problem Set 13-5

1. (a) 8000. 1 m^3 = 1000 dm^3 since $(1$ m$)^3 = (10$ dm$)^3$.

(b) 0.0005. 1 cm^3 = 0.000001 m^3, since $(1$ cm$)^3 = (0.01$ cm$)^3$.

(c) 0.000675. 1 m^3 = 0.000000001 km^3, since $(1$ m$)^3 = (0.001$ km$)^3$.

(d) 3,000,000. 1 m^3 = 1,000,000 cm^3.

(e) 7. 1 mm^3 = 0.001 cm^3.

(f) 2000.

1.   (g)   0.00857. $\frac{400 \text{ in}^3}{x \text{ yd}^3} = \frac{(36^3) \text{ in}^3}{1 \text{ yd}^3}$.

    (h)   675. $1 \text{ yd}^3 = 27 \text{ ft}^3$.

    (i)   345.6. $1 \text{ ft}^3 = 144 \text{ in}^3$.

    (j)   0.69.

3.   (a) $V = lwh = (4)(4)(4) = 64 \text{ cm}^3$.

    (b) $V = lwh = (8)(5)(3) = 120 \text{ cm}^3$.

    (c) $V = Bh$ (where B is the area of the triangle and h is its height).
         $B = \frac{1}{2}bh = \frac{1}{2}(6)(6) = 18 \text{ cm}^2$; h = 12. Thus $V = (18)(12) = 216 \text{ cm}^3$.

    (d) $V = \frac{1}{3}Bh$ (where B is the area of the base and h is the height) $= \frac{1}{3}(5^2)(6) = 50 \text{ cm}^3$.

    (e) $V = \frac{1}{3}\pi r^2 h = \frac{1}{3}\pi(3^2)(7) = 21\pi \text{ cm}^3$.

    (f) $V = \pi r^2 h = \pi(6^2)(12) = 432\pi \text{ cm}^3$.

    (g) $V = \frac{4}{3}\pi r^3 = \frac{4}{3}\pi(10^3) = \frac{4000}{3}\pi \text{ cm}^3$.

    (h)   V of triangular prism portion $= Bh = \frac{1}{2}(30(8)(40) = 4800 \text{ cm}^3$.
         V of rectangular prism portion $= lwh = (30)(40)(15) = 18,000 \text{ cm}^3$.

         Total volume $= 4800 + 18,000 = 22,800 \text{ ft}^3$.

    (i)   V of hemispherical portion $= \frac{1}{2}(\frac{4}{3}\pi r^3) = \frac{1}{2}(\frac{4}{3})\pi(10^3) = \frac{2000}{3}\pi \text{ ft}^3$.
         V of circular cylinder $= \pi r^2 h = \pi(10^2)(60) = 6000\pi \text{ ft}^3$.

         Total volume $= 6000\pi + \frac{2000}{3}\pi = \frac{20,000}{3}\pi \text{ ft}^3$.

    (j)   V of triangular prism portion $= \frac{1}{2}(10)(6)(60) = 1800 \text{ ft}^3$.
         V of trapezoidal prism portion $= \frac{1}{2}(8)(10 + 50)(60) = 14,400 \text{ ft}^3$.
         V of rectangular prism portion $= (50)(60)(20) = 60,000 \text{ ft}^3$.

         Total volume $= 1800 + 14,400 + 60,000 = 76,200 \text{ ft}^3$.

    (k)   V of hemispherical portion $= \frac{1}{2}(\frac{4}{3}\pi \cdot 4^3) = \frac{128}{3}\pi \text{ cm}^3$.

         V of conical portion $= \frac{1}{3}\pi(4^3)(8) = \frac{128}{3}\pi \text{ cm}^3$.

         Total volume $= \frac{256}{3}\pi \text{ cm}^3$.

5.   (a)   200.0 mL   (b)   0.320 L

    (c)   1.0 L   (d)   5.00 mL

7. $V_1 = 4^3 = 64$; $V_2 = 6^3 = 216$. $V_1:V_2 = 64:216 = 8:27$. If all lengths of the two objects have the ratio m:n, then their volumes will have the ratio $m^3:n^3$.

9. For each right rectangular prism, $V = lwh$. Then:

(a) 20 cm   10 cm   10 cm   2000   2   2

(b) 10 cm   2 dm   3 dm   6000   6   6

(c) 2 dm   1 dm   2 dm   4000   4   4 L

(d) 15 cm   2 dm   2.5   7500   7.5 dm³   7.5

11. Volume is proportional to the cube of the radius. Thus a sphere with 4 times the radius of another has $4^3 = 64$ times its volume.

13. $V = lwh = (50)(25)(2) = 2500 \text{ m}^3$. $1 \text{ m}^3 = 1000$ L, so $V = 2,500,000$ L.

15. The radius of the straw is 2 mm = 0.2 cm. $V = \pi r^2 h = \pi (0.2^2)(25) = \pi \text{ cm}^3 = \pi \text{ mL}$.

17. No. The volume of a pyramid is $\frac{1}{3}Bh$, compared to Bh for the box. Thus the pyramid provides only $\frac{1}{3}$ the popcorn for $\frac{1}{2}$ the price.

19. The circumference of a circle $= 2\pi r$, or $r = \frac{C}{2\pi}$. Thus the radius of the larger melon is $\frac{60}{2\pi} \doteq 9.55$ cm; similarly, the radius of the smaller melon is about 7.96 cm. The ratio of the radii is thus $\frac{9.55}{7.96} \doteq 1.2$. Since the volume of a sphere is proportional to the cube of the radius, the volume of the larger cantalope is 1.2^3, or about 1.7 times that of the smaller. The larger melon is the better buy; its volume is 1.7 times that of the smaller but its price is only 1.5 times as much.

21. $V_{prism} = AB \cdot BC \cdot AP$. $V_{pyramid} = \frac{1}{3}(AB \cdot BC \cdot AX) = \frac{1}{3}(AB \cdot BC \cdot 3AP) = AB \cdot BC \cdot AP$.
The volumes are the same.

23. Let r be the radius of each of the cans and h be the height of the box and the cans. The dimensions of the base of the box are 6r by 4r.
$V_{box} = (6r)(4r)(h) = 24r^2h$. $V_{6 \text{ cans}} = 6\pi r^2 h$. $V_{wasted} = 24r^2h - 6\pi r^2 h = 6r^2h(4 - \pi)$.

The portion wasted is $\frac{6r^2h(1 - \pi)}{24r^2h} = \frac{4 - \pi}{4} \doteq 21.5\%$.

25. Assume a regular pyramid. Then let s = length of a side = height. The slant height of the pyramid is the hypotenuse of the right triangle with height s and base $\frac{s}{2}$, or

$\sqrt{s^2 + \left(\frac{s}{2}\right)^2} = \sqrt{s^2 + \left(\frac{s^2}{4}\right)} = \sqrt{\frac{5s^2}{4}} = \frac{\sqrt{5}s}{2}$. The area of each of the four triangles in the lateral surface

of the pyramid is $\frac{1}{2}bh = \frac{1}{2} \cdot s \cdot \frac{\sqrt{5}s}{2} = \frac{\sqrt{5}s^2}{4}$. There are four sides, so the lateral surface area is $4 \cdot \frac{\sqrt{5}s^2}{4} = \sqrt{5}s^2$.

If lateral surface area is 2 m², then $\sqrt{5}s^2 = 2$ and $s = \sqrt{\frac{2}{\sqrt{5}}}$. $V = \frac{1}{3}Bh = \frac{1}{3}s^2s = \frac{1}{3}s^3 = \frac{1}{3}\left(\sqrt{\frac{2}{\sqrt{5}}}\right)^3$, or

$V \doteq 0.28 \text{ m}^3$.

27. Let two square pyramids have sides and heights of s, h, s_1, and s_2. If the pyramids are similar, then

$\frac{s}{s_1} = \frac{h}{h_1} = k$ (the common ratio). $\frac{V}{V_1} = \frac{\frac{1}{3}s^2h}{\frac{1}{3}s_1^2h_1} = \left(\frac{s}{s_1}\right)^2 \cdot \frac{h}{h_1} = k^2k = k^3$.

29. $h_{stack} = 20 \cdot \frac{1}{16}$ in = 1.25 inch; outer radius = 3.5 inch; and inner radius = 0.75 inch.
Volume of outer radius cylinder $= \pi r^2 h = \pi(3.5^2)(1.25) \doteq 15.3\pi \text{ in}^3$.
Volume of inner radius cylinder $= \pi(0.75^3)(1.25) \doteq 0.7\pi \text{ in}^3$.
Volume of record stack $= (15.3 - 0.7)\pi = 14.6\pi \doteq 45.9 \text{ in}^3$.

31. A cord is a box-shaped stack 4 by 4 by 8 feet. $V = (4)(4)(8) = 128 \text{ ft}^3$.

33. Volume is proportional to the cube of the radius; i.e., radius is proportional to the cube root of volume. If volume is halved, radius is decreased by a factor of $\sqrt[3]{0.5} \doteq 0.794$.

35. (a) Change 1.3 m to 130 cm. Then the other side of the rectangle is given by $w^2 = 130^2 - 120^2$, or $w = 50$ cm. $P = 2w + 2l = 2(120) + 2(50) = 340$ cm.

   (b) $A = lw = (120)(50) = 6000 \text{ cm}^2$.

37. The height of the printed material is $74 - (12 + 12) = 50$ cm.
   The width of the printed material is $w - (6 + 6) = w - 12$.
   The area of the printed material is $50(w - 12) = 2500$, or, solving, $w = 62$ cm.

Problem Set 13-6

1. (a) A car would weigh in thousands of pounds, so use kilograms or metric tons.

   (b) A woman could weigh 130 pounds, so use kilograms.

   (c) Juice would weigh in ounces, so use grams.

   (d) Metric tons.   (e) Grams.

   (f) Grams.   (g) Metric tons.

   (h) Grams or kilograms.   (i) Grams or kilograms.

3. (a) 15   (b) 8

   (c) 36   (d) 0.072

   (e) 4.23   (f) 3.007

   (g) 5750   (h) 5.75

   (i) 30   (j) $2.6 \cdot 16 = 41.6$

   (k) $25 \cdot \frac{1}{16} = 1\frac{9}{16}$ (l) $50 \cdot \frac{1}{16} = 3\frac{1}{8}$

   (m) $3.8 \cdot 16 = 60.8$

5. $V = lwh = (40)(20)(20) = 16{,}000 \text{ cm}^3$. $1 \text{ g} = 1 \text{ cm}^3$ of water; $16{,}000 \text{ cm}^3 = 16{,}000 \text{ g} = 16 \text{ kg}$.

7. $1 \text{ g} = 0.001 \text{ kg}$; cost is $(0.001)(20) = \$0.02 = 2\cancel{c}$ per g.

9. (a) $C = \frac{5}{9}(F - 32) = \frac{5}{9}(10 - 32) = \frac{5}{9}(^-22) \doteq ^-12° \text{ C}$.

   (b) $C = \frac{5}{9}(0 - 32) \doteq ^-18° \text{ C}$.

   (c) $C = \frac{5}{9}(30 - 32) \doteq ^-1° \text{ C}$.

9.   (d) $C = \frac{5}{9}(100 - 32) \doteq 38°$ C.

      (e) $C = \frac{5}{9}(212 - 32) = 100°$ C.

      (f) $C = \frac{5}{9}(^-40 - 32) = ^-40°$ C (this is the only temperature at which F and C have the same value).

11.   (a) $F = \frac{9}{5}C + 32 = \frac{9}{5}(10) + 32 = 50°$ F.

      (b) $F = \frac{9}{5}(0) + 32 = 32°$ F.

      (c) $F = \frac{9}{5}(30) + 32 = 86°$ F.

      (d) $F = \frac{9}{5}(100) + 32 = 212°$ F.

      (e) $F = \frac{9}{5}(212) + 32 \doteq 414°$ F.

      (f) $F = \frac{9}{5}(^-40) + 32 = ^-40°$ F.

13.   (a)   35   (b)   0.16

      (c)   400,000   (d)   5,200,000

      (e)   5200   (f)   0.0035

15.   The person has walked a total of 6km north and 5 km east, forming the legs of a right triangle.

      $d = \sqrt{6^2 + 5^2} = \sqrt{61}$ km.

Problem Set 13-7

1.   (a)   It draws a circle five times. The circumference is $\frac{1}{5}$ of the circumference of CIRCLE 1.

      (b)   It draws the same size circle as CIRCLE1 but draws it to the left.

3.   (a)   TO ARC :S :D
             REPEAT :D [FD :S RT 1]
             END

      (b)   TO ARCRAD :R :D
             REPEAT :D [FD 2*3.14159*R/360 RT 1]
             END

5.   (a)   TO CIRCS :RAD
             HT
             CIRCLE :RAD
             ARCRAD :RAD/2 180
             END

             TO CIRCLE :R
             VCIRCLE 2*3.14159*R/360
             END

5.   (a)

```
TO VCIRCLE :S
  REPEAT 360 [FD :S  RT 1]
END

TO ARCRAD :R :D
  REPEAT :D [FD 2*3.14159*R/360  RT 1]
END

TO LARCRAD :R :D
  REPEAT :D [FD 2*3.14159*R/360  LT 1]
END
```

(b)

```
TO EYES :RAD
  HT
  CIRCLE :RAD
  CIRCLE :RAD/2
  CIRCLE :RAD/4
  LCIRCLE :RAD
  LCIRCLE :RAD/2
  LCIRCLE :RAD/4
  ARCRAD (:RAD + 0.6*:RAD) 90
  LT 180
  LARCRAD (:RAD + 0.6*:RAD) 90
  RT 180
  LARCRAD (:RAD + 0.6*:RAD) 90
  HT
END

TO LCIRCLE :RAD
  LVCIRCLE 2*3.14159*:RAD/360
END

TO LVCIRCLE:S
  REPEAT 360 [FD :S  LT 1]
END
```

(c)

```
TO SEMIS :R
  ARCRAD :R 180
  RT 90 FD :R*2  RT 90
  ARCRAD :R/2 180
  RT 180
  ARCRAD :R/2 180
END

TO ARCRAD :R :D
  REPEAT :D [FD 2*3.14159*:R/360  RT 1]
END
```

(d)

```
TO CONCIRC :R
  HT CIRCLE :R
  PU LT 90 FD :R/2 RT 90 PD
  CIRCLE :R + :R/2
  PU LT 90 FD :R/2 RT 90 PD
  CIRCLE :R*2
END
```

```
5.  (d)   TO CIRCLE :R
            VCIRCLE  2*3.14159*:R/360
          END

          TO VCIRCLE :S
            REPEAT  360  [FD :S  RT 1]
          END

    (e)   TO FRAME SIZE
            SQUARE :SIZE
            FD :SIZE/2
            CIRCLE :SIZE/2
          END

          TO SQUARE :S
            REPEAT  4 [ FD :S  RT  90]
          END

7.  TO FLOWER :RAD
      REPEAT 6[PETAL :RAD 60 RT 60]
    END

    TO PETAL :RAD :DEG
      HT ARCRAD :RAD :DEG
      RT  180 — :DEG
      ARCRAD :RAD :DEG
      RT  180 — :DEG
      ST
    END

    TO ARCRAD :R :D
      REPEAT :D [FD 2*3.14159*:R/360  RT 1]
    END

9.  TO MASTERCARD :W
      CARD 3*: W  5*: W
      CARD 3*W/2 RD 90 FD :W LT 90 PD
      CIRCLES :W
    END

    TO CARD :W :L
      REPEAT 2 [FD :W  RT  90  FD :L  RT 90]
    END

    TO CIRCLES :R
      CIRCLE :R PU
      RT 90
      FD :R
      LT 90 PD
      CIRCLE :R
    END

    TO CIRCLE :R
      VCIRCLE 2*3.14159*:R/360
    END
```

9. ```
TO VCIRCLE :S
  REPEAT 360 [FD :S RT 1]
END
```
```

CHAPTER 14 - COORDINATE GEOMETRY

Problem Set 14-1

1.   (a)   The major perpendicular streets could be the zero lines represented by the axes. Other streets would use them as a reference in terms of north, south, east, and west.

     (b)
       S = School
       C = Church
       H = City Hall
       M = Museum
       U = College

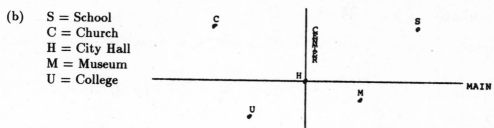

3.   (a)   I   (b)   III

     (c)   II   (d)   IV

     (e)   Between I and II

5.   D should be located at $(4, {}^-2)$. Its x-value must be the same as that of C and its y-value that of A.

7.   (a)   P(3, 4) and Q(6, 1)   (b) $M({}^-1, {}^-1)$ and $N({}^-1, 4)$

9.   (a)   A reflection in the x-axis causes the y-coordinates to change sign. Thus:
       $(0, 1) \rightarrow (0, {}^-1); (1, 0) \rightarrow (1, 0)$ (This point is on the x-axis and cannot reflect); $(2, 4) \rightarrow (2, {}^-4);$
       $({}^-2, 4) \rightarrow ({}^-2, {}^-4); ({}^-2, {}^-4) \rightarrow ({}^-2, 4); (2, {}^-4) \rightarrow (2, 4)$

     (b)   A reflection in the y-axis causes the x-coordinates to change sign. Thus:
       $(0, 1) \rightarrow (0, 1)$ (This point is on the y-axis and cannot reflect); $(1, 0) \rightarrow ({}^-1, 0); (2, 4) \rightarrow ({}^-2, 4);$
       $({}^-2, 4) \rightarrow (2, 4); ({}^-2, {}^-4) \rightarrow (2, {}^-4); (2, {}^-4) \rightarrow ({}^-2, {}^-4)$

     (c)   Under 90° counterclockwise rotation, the x- and y-coordinates are interchanged and the x'-coordinate changes sign. Thus:
       $(0, 1) \rightarrow ({}^-1, 0); (1, 0) \rightarrow (0, 1); (2, 4) \rightarrow ({}^-4, 2); ({}^-2, 4) \rightarrow ({}^-4, {}^-2); ({}^-2, {}^-4) \rightarrow (4, {}^-2);$
       $(2, {}^-4) \rightarrow (4, 2)$

     (d)   A half-turn causes the x- and y-coordinates to both change sign. Thus:
       $(0, 1) \rightarrow (0, {}^-1); (1, 0) \rightarrow ({}^-1, 0); (2, 4) \rightarrow ({}^-2, {}^-4); ({}^-2, 4) \rightarrow (2, {}^-4); ({}^-2, {}^-4) \rightarrow (2, 4);$
       $(2, {}^-4) \rightarrow ({}^-2, 4)$

     (e)   Each point will change its x- and y-coordinate by the same value that the coordinates of point A change from those of point O; i.e., we add 0 to the x-coordinate and ${}^-4$ to the y-coordinate of each point. Thus:
       $(0, 1) \rightarrow (0, {}^-3); (1, 0) \rightarrow (1, {}^-4); (2, 4) \rightarrow (2, 0); ({}^-2, 4) \rightarrow ({}^-2, 0); ({}^-2, {}^-4) \rightarrow ({}^-2, {}^-8;)$
       $(2, {}^-4) \rightarrow (2, {}^-8)$

11. (a) $P(2, 4) \rightarrow P'({}^-2, 4)$ after reflection in the y-axis; $P'({}^-2, 4) \rightarrow P''({}^-2, {}^-4)$ after reflection in the x-axis

     (b) $P(a, b) \rightarrow P''({}^-a, {}^-b)$

13. (a)   Since P and its center of rotation both have x-value *a*, the radius of rotation is *b*; i.e., P' will be *b* units away from the center, on the x-axis (with y-value 0). Thus $P(a, b) \rightarrow P'(a - b, 0)$.

     (b)   As in 9(c), $P(a, b) \rightarrow P'({}^-b, a)$.

15. $\overline{AB} = \sqrt{(^-4 - 0)^2 + (^-3 - 0)^2} = \sqrt{16 + 9} = \sqrt{25} = 5$

$\overline{AC} = \sqrt{(^-5 - 0)^2 + (0 - 0)^2} = \sqrt{25} = 5$

$\overline{BC} = \sqrt{(^-5 - {}^-4)^2 + (0 - {}^-3)^2} = \sqrt{(^-1)^2 + (3)^2} = \sqrt{10}$

So the perimeter of the triangle $= 5 + 5 + \sqrt{10} = 10 + \sqrt{10}$.

17. Using the distance formula, we find: $\overline{AB} = 5$, $\overline{AC} = 7\sqrt{2}$, and $\overline{BC} = 5$. Since $\overline{AB} = \overline{BC}$, the triangle is isosceles.

19. (a) $\left(\dfrac{^-3 + 3}{2}, \dfrac{1 + 9}{2}\right) = (0, 5)$ (b) $\left(\dfrac{4 + 5}{2}, \dfrac{^-3 + {}^-1}{2}\right) = (\tfrac{9}{2}, {}^-2)$

    (c) $\left(\dfrac{1.8 + 2.2}{2}, \dfrac{^-3.7 + 1.3}{2}\right) = (2, {}^-1.2)$

    (d) $\left[\dfrac{(1 + a) + (1 - a)}{2}, \dfrac{(a - b) + (b - a)}{2}\right] = (1, 0)$

21. Let point X be the midpoint of $\overline{AB}$, Y be the midpoint of $\overline{AC}$, and Z be the midpoint of $\overline{BC}$. Then:

    (a) $X = \left(\dfrac{0 + {}^-4}{2}, \dfrac{0 + 6}{2}\right) = (^-2, 3); Y = \left(\dfrac{0 + 4}{2}, \dfrac{0 + 2}{2}\right) = (2, 1); Z = \left(\dfrac{^-4 + 4}{2}, \dfrac{6 + 2}{2}\right) = (0, 4)$

    (b) The medians are $\overline{CX}$, $\overline{BY}$, and $\overline{AZ}$. The distance formula gives:

       $\overline{CX} = \sqrt{(^-2 - 4)^2 + (3 - 2)^2} = \sqrt{37}$

       $\overline{BY} = \sqrt{(^-4 - 2)^2 + (6 - 1)^2} = \sqrt{61}$

       $\overline{AZ} = \sqrt{(0 - 0)^2 + (4 - 0)^2} = 4$

23. Substitute the given coordinates in the equation $x^2 + y^2 = 9$. If the value $= 9$, the point is on the circle. If the value is less than 9, the point is inside the circle. If the value is greater than 9, the point is outside the circle.

    (a) $3^2 + (^-3)^2 > 9$; exterior.   (b) $2^2 + (^-2)^2 < 9$; interior.

    (c) $1^2 + 8^2 > 9$; exterior.   (d) $3^2 + 1982^2 > 9$; exterior.

    (e) $5.1234^2 + (^-3.7804)^2 > 9$; exterior.   (f) $\left(\dfrac{1}{387}\right)^2 + \left(\dfrac{1}{1983}\right)^2 < 9$; interior.

    (g) $\left(\dfrac{^-1}{2}\right)^2 + \left(\dfrac{35}{2}\right)^2 > 9$; exterior.   (h) $0^2 + 3^2 = 9$; on the circle.

25. The equations will be of the form $(x - 4)^2 + (y + 3)^2 = r^2$. Use the distance formula to find r.

    (a) $r = \sqrt{(4 - 0)^2 + (^-3 - 0)^2} = 5; (x - 4)^2 + (y + 3)^2 = 25$.

    (b) $r = \sqrt{(5 - 4)^2 + (^-2 - {}^-3)^2} = \sqrt{2}; (x - 4)^2 + (y + 3)^2 = 2$.

27. (a)   (b)

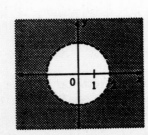
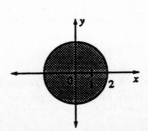

27. (c) 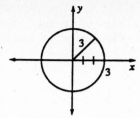   (d)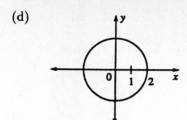

(e)   The graph is the empty set.   (f)   Same as (d).

29. Yes, Dividing both sides of the equation by 2 gives $x^2 + y^2 = \frac{1}{2}$. This is a circle with center (0, 0) and radius $\sqrt{\frac{1}{2}}$.

31. It is necessary to show that $AM = BM = OM$. $M = \left(\frac{0+a}{2}, \frac{b+0}{2}\right) = (\frac{a}{2}, \frac{b}{2})$. Thus:

$AM = \sqrt{(a - \frac{a}{2})^2 + (0 - \frac{b}{2})^2} = \sqrt{\frac{a^2}{4} + \frac{b^2}{4}}$. Similarly, $BM = OM = \sqrt{\frac{a^2}{4} + \frac{b^2}{4}}$.

Thus the midpoint of the hypotenuse is equidistant from the vertices of the triangle.

33. On a 5 by 5 grid, there are 25 coordinate pairs. Thus there is a $\frac{1}{25}$ chance of Professors Carlson and Lazzell choosing identical coordinates.

Problem Set 14-2

1.   Both graphs have slope $^{-}1$, so they are parallel. One has y-intercept $= 0$ and the other has y-intercept $= 3$.

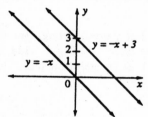

3.   One method of graphing is to plot the y-intercept and draw a line through that point with the given slope.

(a)   The y-intercept is at (0, 3). A line with slope $= \frac{rise}{run} = \frac{^{-}3}{4}$ goes down 3 units (negative rise) and to the right 4 units (positive run) from (0, 3), as shown:

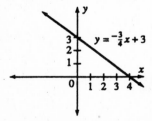

(b)   This line has zero slope (i.e., it is horizontal) and passes through all points where $y = {^{-}}3$.

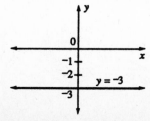

3.   (c)   The y-intercept is at $(0, {}^-30)$. The slope is 15 (i.e., a rise of a positive 15 for a run of a positive 1). Checking $(0, 0)$ in $y \geq 15x - 30$ gives $0 \geq 0 - 30$, which is a true statement; thus the half-plane containing $(0, 0)$ is the graph of the inequality. The line $y = 15x - 30$ is part of the solution, so it is a solid line.

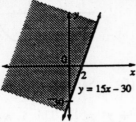

(d)   This line has an undetermined slope (i.e., is vertical) and passes through the point $x = {}^-2$.

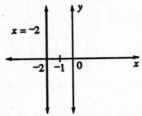

(e)   The y-intercept is at $(0, {}^-3)$; the slope is 3.

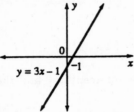

(f)   The y-intercept is at $(0, 0)$; the slope is $\frac{1}{20}$. Since the line passes through the origin, we cannot check the point $(0, 0)$; let us use $(0, 1)$ instead. Checking, we have $1 \leq 0 \cdot \frac{1}{20}$. This is not a true statement, so the half-plane on the other side of $y = \frac{1}{20}x$ from $(0, 1)$ is the solution set.

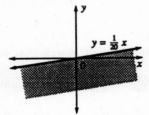

5.   (a)   The slope is $\frac{9}{5}$; the y-intercept is 32:

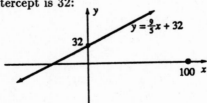

(b) $y = \frac{5}{9}x - 17\frac{7}{9}$; the slope is $\frac{5}{9}$ and the y-intercept is $^-17\frac{7}{9}$:

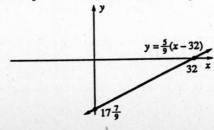

5. **(c)** The graphs intersect at ($^-$40, $^-$40). $^-$40° is the temperature at which both scales are numerically equal. To the right of the intersection, the Fahrenheit graph is higher; to the left the Celsius graph is higher.

7. Slope is given by: $m = \frac{y_2 - y_1}{x_2 - x_1}$.

(a) $m = \frac{0 - 3}{^-5 - 4} = \frac{^-3}{^-9} = \frac{1}{3}$

(b) $m = \frac{2 - ^-1}{5 - ^-4} = \frac{1}{9}$

(c) $m = \frac{2 - 2}{1 - \sqrt{5}} = 0$

(d) $m = \frac{198 - 81}{^-3 - ^-3} \Rightarrow$ no slope (vertical line)

(e) $m = \frac{12 - 10}{1.0001 - 1} = \frac{2}{0.0001} = 20{,}000$

(f) $m = \frac{b - a}{b - a} = 1$

9. Use the point-slope form of the line.

(a) $y - 0 = \frac{^-1}{2}(x - ^-3) \Rightarrow y = \frac{^-1}{2}(x + 3) \Rightarrow y = \frac{^-1}{2}x - \frac{3}{2}$

(b) $y - ^-3 = \frac{2}{3}(x - 1) \Rightarrow y + 3 = \frac{2}{3}x - \frac{2}{3} \Rightarrow y = \frac{2}{3}x - \frac{2}{3} - 3 \Rightarrow y = \frac{2}{3}x - \frac{11}{3}$

(c) $y + 3 = 0(x - 2) \Rightarrow y + 3 = 0 \Rightarrow y = ^-3$

(d) $y + 5 = \frac{^-5}{7}(x + 1) \Rightarrow y + 5 = \frac{^-5}{7}x - \frac{5}{7} \Rightarrow y = \frac{^-5}{7}x - \frac{5}{7} - 5 \Rightarrow y = \frac{^-5}{7}x - \frac{40}{7}$

11. Find the slope (m) of the given line and then use it in the point-slope form of the desired line.

(a) $y = ^-2x \Rightarrow m = ^-2$
$y - 3 = ^-2(x + 2) \Rightarrow y - 3 = ^-2x - 4 \Rightarrow y = ^-2x - 1$

(b) $3y + 2x + 1 = 0 \Rightarrow 3y = ^-2x - 1 \Rightarrow y = \frac{^-2}{3}x - \frac{1}{3} \Rightarrow m = \frac{^-2}{3}$

$y - 3 = \frac{^-2}{3}(x + 2) \Rightarrow y - 3 = \frac{^-2}{3}x - \frac{^-4}{3} \Rightarrow y = \frac{^-2}{3}x + \frac{5}{3}$

(c) $x = 0 \Rightarrow$ vertical line (slope undetermined)
A vertical line passing through ($^-2$, 3) has equation $x = ^-2$

(d) $y = ^-1 \Rightarrow$ horizontal line ($m = 0$)
A horizontal line passing through ($^-2$, 3) has equation $y = 3$

(e) $x = 3 \Rightarrow$ vertical line (slope undetermined)
A vertical line passing through ($^-2$, 3) has equation $x = ^-2$

(f) $y = ^-4 \Rightarrow$ horizontal line ($m = 0$)
A horizontal line passing through ($^-2$, 3) has equation $y = 3$

(g) $x + y = 2 \Rightarrow y = ^-x + 2 \Rightarrow m = ^-1$
$y - 3 = ^-1(x + 2) \Rightarrow y - 3 = ^-x - 2 \Rightarrow y = ^-x + 1$

(h) $\frac{x}{2} + \frac{y}{3} = 1 \Rightarrow 3x + 2y = 6 \Rightarrow y = \frac{^-3}{2}x + 3 \Rightarrow m = \frac{^-3}{2}$

$y - 3 = \frac{^-3}{2}(x + 2) \Rightarrow y - 3 = \frac{^-3}{2}x - 3 \Rightarrow y = \frac{^-3}{2}x$

13. Rise is 4 feet. $m = \frac{\text{rise}}{\text{run}} = \frac{1}{10}$. Thus $\frac{4}{x} = \frac{1}{10}$ and $x = 40$ feet. Length $= \sqrt{40^2 + 4^2} = \sqrt{1616} = 4\sqrt{101}$ ft.

15. Three points can be collinear only if the slopes of line segments joining them are the same. Label the given coordinates: A(0, $^-1$), B(1, 2), C($^-1$, $^-4$). Then:

$m_{\overline{AB}} = \frac{2 - ^-1}{1 - 0} = 3$ and $m_{\overline{BC}} = \frac{^-4 - 2}{^-1 - 1} = 3$. Since the slopes are the same, the points must be collinear.

17. (a) Since all points reflected in the x-axis have the signs of their y-coordinates changed, replace y by ⁻y in the equation:
$$⁻y = 3x + 1 \implies y = ⁻3x - 1$$

(b) Reflecting about the y-axis changes the signs of the x-coordinates. Thus replace x with ⁻x:
$$y = 3(⁻x) + 1 \implies y = ⁻3x + 1$$

(c) Reflecting about the line y = x reverses the coordinates. Thus replace x with y and y with x:
$$x = 3y + 1 \implies y = \tfrac{1}{3}x - \tfrac{1}{3}$$

19. A triangle is right if two of its sides (legs) are perpendicular.

(a) $m_{\overline{AB}} = \frac{5-3}{3-⁻2} = ⁻2$; $m_{\overline{AC}} = \frac{6-3}{4-⁻2} = \frac{1}{2}$. $\overline{AB}$ and $\overline{AC}$ are perpendicular; the triangle is right.

(b) $m_{\overline{AB}} = 1$; $m_{\overline{AC}} = 0$; $m_{\overline{BC}} = \frac{⁻1}{3}$. No sides are perpendicular; the triangle is not right.

21. Answers may vary.

(a) The points are on the line y = 2. Others are (⁻3, 2), (5, 2), ...

(b) The points are on the line x = ⁻1. Others are (⁻1, 7), (⁻1, ⁻5), ...

(c) The points are on the line y = 0 (i.e., the x-axis). Others are (2, 0), (4, 0), ...

(d) The points are on the line x = 0 (i.e., the y-axis). Others are (0, ⁻1), (0, 6), ...

(e) Same as (d)

(f) The points are on the line y = x [all points are of the form (a, a)]. Others are (3, 3), (1, 1), ...

23. The rectangle has dimensions 2 by 4. The area is thus 2·4 = 8; the perimeter is 2(2) + 2(4) = 12.

25. (a) This is a vertical line through (3, 0); its equation is x = 3.

(b) This is a horizontal line through (0, ⁻2); its equation is y = ⁻2.

(c) A horizontal line through (⁻4, 5); its equation is y = 5.

(d) A vertical line through (⁻4, 5); its equation is x = ⁻4.

27. The points to be graphed are:

(a) (0, 2), (1, 3), (2, 4), (3, 5), (4, 6).

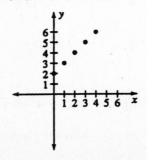

27.   (b)   ($^-$1, 0), (0, 1), (1, 2), (2, 3), (3, 4).

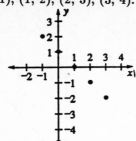

     (c)   Both x and y must be integers for a point to be classified as a lattice point. Points are (3, 0), ($^-$3, 0), (0, 3), (0, $^-$3).

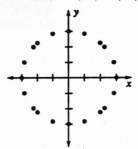

     (d)   ($^-$4, 16), ($^-$3, 9), ($^-$2, 4), ($^-$1, 1), (0, 0), (1, 1), (2, 4), (3, 9), (4, 16).

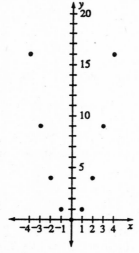

     (e)   (1, 5), ($^-$1, $^-$5)

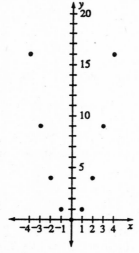

29.   (a)   The line reflects upon itself and is still x = 3.

     (b)   The line reflects to the left of the y-axis, becoming x = $^-$3.

29. (c)   The vertical line becomes horizontal, still 3 units from the origin; i.e., y = 3.

31.   Plot on the same graph the sets of inequalities as described in problem 3 of this section. The solution set is
       that which is common to all the graphs.

(a) 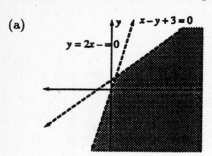   (b)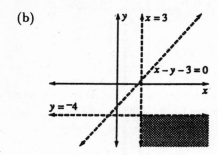

31. (c)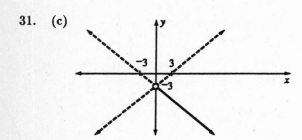

33. (a)   y-coordinates change signs; x − (⁻y) = 1 ⇒ y = ⁻x + 1.

    (b)   x-coordinates change signs; (⁻x) − y = 1 ⇒ y = ⁻x − 1.

    (c)   Coordinates are interchanged; y = x + 1.

    (d)   Both coordinates change signs; (⁻x) − (⁻y) = 1 ⇒ y = x + 1.

35.   The graph of an equation or inequality having no solutions is empty. Some examples are: |x − 3| = ⁻7;
       7 < x < 5, etc.

37. (a)   The points are on the line y = ⁻2; others include (3, ⁻2), (0, ⁻2), ...

    (b)   Move from P to Q right 10 units and up 12 (i.e., add 10 to x and 12 to y). To obtain other points,
           continue the pattern: (3 + 10, 4 + 12) = (13, 16), (13 + 10, 16 + 12) = (23, 28), ...

39. (a)   Base (along the x-axis) = 3; height = 1. A = $\frac{1}{2}$(3)(1) = $\frac{3}{2}$ units^2.

    (b)   Base (along the x-axis) = 10; height = 3. A = $\frac{1}{2}$(10)(3) = 15 units^2.

    (c)   Base (along the y-axis) = 5; height = 3. A = $\frac{1}{2}$(5)(3) = $\frac{15}{2}$ units^2.

    (d)   Base (along the line y = 2) = 5 − 1 = 4; height = 8 − 2 = 6. A = $\frac{1}{2}$(4)(6) = 12 units^2.

    (e)   Base (along the line y = 1) = 7 − 1 = 6; height = 1 − 0 = 1. A = $\frac{1}{2}$(6)(1) = 3 units^2.

1.   (a)   Solutions may be found by selecting any value of x or y and then solving algebraically for the other. E.g., if $y = 1$, then $2x - 3(1) = 5 \Rightarrow 2x = 8 \Rightarrow x = 4$; thus one solution is $(4, 1)$. It may be easier to first solve the equation for x or y; i.e., $^-3y = ^-2x + 5 \Rightarrow y = \frac{2}{3}x - \frac{5}{3}$. Now, for any value of x that is chosen, the corresponding value of y may be quickly found. E.g., for $x = 3$, $y = \frac{2}{3}(3) - \frac{5}{3} = \frac{1}{3}$. There are an infinite number of solutions, but some possibilities include $(4, 1)$, $(7, 3)$, or $(1, ^-1)$.

    (b) $2x - 3y = 5$ is a straight line. To graph the specified portion, find its endpoints $[(2, \frac{^-1}{3}), (^-2, ^-3)]$ by substituting $x = 2$ and $x = ^-2$ into the equation. Connecting these points gives the graph below.

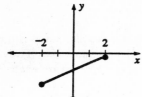

    (c)   Use $y = 0$ and $y = 2$ to obtain endpoints $(2.5, 0)$ and $(5.5, 2)$. See below.

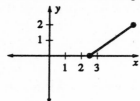

3.   (a)   Given: $y = x + 3$
                $3x - 4y + 1 = 0$
Then, by substitution, $3x - 4(x + 3) + 1 = 0 \Rightarrow 3x - 4x - 12 + 1 = 0 \Rightarrow x = ^-11$.
If $x = ^-11$, $y = (^-11) + 3 \Rightarrow y = ^-8$.
The solution set is $(^-11, ^-8)$.

    (b)   Given: $\frac{x}{3} - \frac{y}{4} = 1$

                   $\frac{x}{5} - \frac{y}{3} = 2$

Eliminating fractions gives the equivalent equations:
           $4x - 3y = 12$
           $3x - 5y = 30$

Multiplying the first equation by $^-5$ and the second by 3 yields:
           $^-20x + 15y = ^-60$
             $9x - 15y = 90$

Adding the equations to eliminate y gives:
           $^-11\,y = 30 \Rightarrow y = \frac{^-30}{11}$. Then substituting into one of the equivalent equations:

           $3x - 5\left(\frac{^-30}{11}\right) = 30 \Rightarrow x = \frac{^-84}{11}$. The solution set is $\left(\frac{^-84}{11}, \frac{^-30}{11}\right)$.

Using either substitution or elimination techniques, as demonstrated above, gives other solutions as follows:

    (c) $\left(\frac{13}{3}, \frac{43}{12}\right)$ (d) $(0, 0)$

    (e) $\left(^-1 + 3\sqrt{2}, 3 - \sqrt{2}\right)$ (f) $\left(\frac{^-6}{5}, \frac{^-4}{5}\right)$

5.   (a)   Solving each equation for y gives $y = \frac{3}{4}x - \frac{5}{4}$ and $y = \frac{5}{3}x - 5$. The slopes are different ($\frac{3}{4}$ and $\frac{5}{3}$), so there is a unique solution.

5. (b) The slope of both equations is $\frac{3}{4}$, while the y-intercepts ($^-1$ and $^-5$) are different. There are no solutions; the lines are parallel.

(c) Solving each equations for y yields $y = \frac{2}{3}x + 5$. The lines are the same, therefore, and there are an infinite number of solutions.

(d) These are the lines $x = 0$ and $y = 0$; i.e., the x- and y-axes. The slopes are therefore different and there is a unique solution.

7. Solve each of the equations for y.
   Equation 1: $^-3y = ^-x - 3 \Rightarrow y = \frac{1}{3}x + 1$. Equation 2: $2y = ^-x + 2 \Rightarrow y = \frac{^-1}{2}x - 4$.
   These equations represent two adjacent sides. Their parallels must have the same slopes and go through the point $(0, ^-4)$; i.e., since $(0, ^-4)$ is not a solution for either of the given equations. Thus we can use the point-slope form of the equation of a line, knowing the respective slopes and a point on each.

   Parallel line 1: $y - (^-4) = \frac{1}{3}(x - 0) \Rightarrow y = \frac{1}{3}x - 4$ is the equation of one side.

   Parallel line 2: $y - (^-4) = \frac{^-1}{2}(x - 0) \Rightarrow y = \frac{^-1}{2}x - 4$ is the equation of the other side.

9. (a) The slope of $\overline{AC} = \frac{1}{6}$; thus the slope of $\overline{BP}$ (its perpendicular) is $^-6$. The equation of $\overline{BP}$ [with $m = ^-6$ and passing through the point $(2, 5)$] is thus $y - 5 = ^-6(x - 2)$, or $y = ^-6x + 17$.

   The slope of $\overline{BC} = ^-1$; thus the slope of $\overline{AP} = 1$. The equation of $\overline{AP}$ is $y - 0 = 1(x - 0)$, or $y = x$.

   By substitution, $x = ^-6x + 17$, or $x = \frac{17}{7}$. Since $y = x$, then $y = \frac{17}{7}$. The point of intersection is $(\frac{17}{7}, \frac{17}{7})$.

(b) The slope of $\overline{AB} = \frac{5}{2}$; the line perpendicular to $\overline{AC}$ through C (the third altitude) thus has equation

   $y - 1 = \frac{^-2}{5}(x - 6)$, or $y = \frac{^-2}{5}x + \frac{17}{5}$. $(\frac{17}{7}, \frac{17}{7})$ is a solution of this equation; i.e., the line passes through P.

11. Write one equation for the contents of the truck (where G is the number of gallons of gasoline and K is the number of gallons of kerosene): $G + K = 5000$. Write another for the profit: $0.13G + 0.12K = 640$. Multiplying the first equation by $^-12$ and the second by 100 yields
   $$^-12G - 12K = ^-60,000$$
   $$13G + 12K = 64,000.$$
   Eliminating K and solving for G, we have $G = 4000$ gallons of gasoline. Substituting and solving for K finds $K = 1000$ gallons of kerosene.

13. Let A and B be the amounts of the two solutions. Write one equation for the amount of the solution and another for the amount of acid:
   $$A + B = 150$$
   $$0.6A + 0.9B = 0.8(150)$$
   Solving gives $A = 50$ liters of 60% solution and $B = 100$ liters of 90% solution.

15. (a) In eight months, $80 interest was earned. Since it is simple interest, this is $10 per month; thus in the first ten months (10 months)·($10 per month) = $100 was earned. The original balance was $2100 - 100 = 2000.

(b) Interest = (Principal)·(Rate)·(Time), or $100 = (2000) \cdot (\text{Rate}) \cdot (\frac{10}{12})$. Solving gives $R = 0.06 = 6\%$.

17. Write one equation for the number of coins and another for their value (where D is the number of dimes and Q is the number of quarters).

$$D + Q = 27$$
$$0.10D + 0.25Q = 5.25.$$

Solving gives $D = 10$ dimes and $Q = 17$ quarters.

19. The sides have slopes $\frac{c}{b}$, $\frac{c}{b-a}$, and 0. The slopes of the altitudes are thus $\frac{-b}{c}$, $\frac{a-b}{c}$, and undefined. The altitudes pass through $(a, 0)$, $(0, 0)$, and (b, c), respectively, and thus have equations:

$$y - 0 = \frac{-b}{c}(x - a), \text{ or } y = \frac{-b}{c}x + \frac{ab}{c},$$

$$y - 0 = \frac{a-b}{c}(x - 0), \text{ or } y = \frac{a-b}{c}x, \text{ and}$$

$$x = b.$$

Substituting for y with the first two gives $\frac{-b}{c}x + \frac{ab}{c} = \frac{a-b}{c}x$, or $\frac{ab}{c} = \frac{a}{c}x$, implying that $x = b$ and matching the third equation.

The three altitudes are then concurrent at the point $(b, \frac{ab-b^2}{c})$.

21. Write equations in the form $y = mx + b$ (i.e., solve for y) to most easily find the slope and y-intercept.

(a) $6y + 5x = y \Rightarrow y = \frac{-5}{6}x + \frac{7}{6}$. Thus $m = \frac{-5}{6}$ and $b = \frac{7}{6}$.

(b) $\frac{2}{3}x + \frac{1}{2}y = \frac{1}{5} \Rightarrow y = \frac{-4}{3}x + \frac{2}{5}$. $m = \frac{-4}{3}$ and $b = \frac{2}{5}$.

(c) $0.2y - 0.75x - 0.37 = 0 \Rightarrow y = 3.75x + 1.85$. $m = 3.75$ and $b = 1.85$.

(d) $y = 4$ is equivalent to $y = 0x + 4$; $m = 0$ and $b = 4$.

23. Graph by either determining intercepts (i.e., let x and then y equal 0 for y- and x-intercpts, respectively) or by following the slope from the y-intercepts. For inequalities, shade the half-plane containing the solution set. See below.

(a)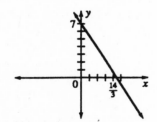

(b)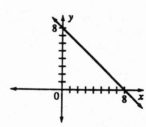

(c)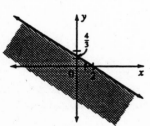

(d)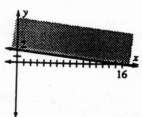

25. Solve the system of equations to locate the point of intersection:

$$3x + 5y = 7 \Rightarrow 3x + 5y = 7$$
$$2x - y = {}^-4 \Rightarrow 10x - 5y = {}^-20$$

Eliminating y and solving for x yields $x = {}^-1$; substituting, $y = 2$. The solution is $({}^-1, 2)$.

A line parallel to the x-axis has slope $m = 0$ and is of the form $y = a$; here, $y = 2$.

1.　The answer will vary depending upon the version of Logo used.

3.　TO AXES
　　　SETXY 0 120
　　　SETXY 0 (-120)]
　　　SETXY 0 0
　　　SETXY 130 0
　　　SETXY -130 0
　　　SETXY 0 0
　　END
　　(In LCSI, use SETPOS LIST instead of SETXY)

5.　TO FILL.RECT
　　　REPEAT 50 [SETY 30 SETY 0 RT 90 FD 1 LT 90]
　　END

7.　TO QUAD :X1 :Y1 :X2 :Y2 :X3 :Y3 :X4 :Y4
　　　PU SETXY :X1 :Y1 PD
　　　SETXY :X2 :Y2
　　　SETXY :X3 :Y3
　　　SETXY :X4 :Y4
　　　SETXY :X1 :Y1
　　END
　　(In LCSI, use SETPOS LIST instead of SETXY)

9.　Use the QUAD procedure from problem 7 and the following:

　　TO MEDIAL.QUADS :NUM :X1 :Y1 :X2 :Y2 :X3 :Y3 :X4 :Y4
　　　IF :NUM = 0 STOP
　　　QUAD :X1 :Y1 :X2 :Y2 :X3 :Y3 :X4 :Y4
　　　MEDIAL.QUADS :NUM − 1 (:X1 + :X2)/2 (:Y1 + :Y2)/2 (:X2 + :X3)/2 (:Y2 + :Y3)/2
　　　　　(:X3 + :X4)/2 (:Y3 + :Y4)/2 (:X4 + :X1)/2 (:Y4 + :Y1)/2
　　END
　　(In LCSI, use [STOP] instead of STOP and SETPOS LIST instead of SETXY)

11.　TO R.ISOS.TRI :LEN
　　　FD :LEN
　　　RT 90
　　　FD :LEN
　　　RT 135
　　　FD (SQRT 2)∗:LEN
　　END

13.　TO GENCIRC :X :Y :R
　　　PU
　　　SETXY :X :Y
　　　PD
　　　REPEAT 360 [FD 2∗3.14159∗:R/360 RT 1]
　　END
　　(In LCSI, use SETPOS LIST instead of SETXY)